Atlantic Ocean

WORLD BIBLIOGRAPHICAL SERIES

General Editors:
Robert L. Collison (Editor-in-chief)
Sheila R. Herstein
Louis J. Reith
Hans H. Wellisch

VOLUMES IN THE SERIES

VOLUME 61

Atlantic Ocean

H. G. R. King

Compiler

CLIO PRESS

OXFORD, ENGLAND · SANTA BARBARA, CALIFORNIA
DENVER, COLORADO

016.909
K 52

British Library Cataloguing in Publication Data

King, H. G. R.
Atlantic Ocean. – (World bibliographical series; 61)
1. Atlantic Ocean – Bibliography
I. Title   II. Series
016.909'0963   Z6005.A7/

ISBN 1-85109-004-5

Clio Press Ltd.,
55 St. Thomas' Street,
Oxford OX1 1JG, England.

ABC-Clio Information Services,
Riviera Campus, 2040 Alameda Padre Serra,
Santa Barbara, Ca. 93103, USA.

Designed by Bernard Crossland
Typeset by Berkshire Publishing Services
Printed and bound in Great Britain by
Billing and Sons Ltd., Worcester

THE WORLD BIBLIOGRAPHICAL SERIES

This series will eventually cover every country in the world, each in a separate volume comprising annotated entries on works dealing with its history, geography, economy and politics; and with its people, their culture, customs, religion and social organization. Attention will also be paid to current living conditions – housing, education, newspapers, clothing, etc. – that are all too often ignored in standard bibliographies; and to those particular aspects relevant to individual countries. Each volume seeks to achieve, by use of careful selectivity and critical assessment of the literature, an expression of the country and an appreciation of its nature and national aspirations, to guide the reader towards an understanding of its importance. The keynote of the series is to provide, in a uniform format, an interpretation of each country that will express its culture, its place in the world, and the qualities and background that make it unique.

SERIES EDITORS

Robert L. Collison (Editor-in-chief) is Professor Emeritus, Library and Information Studies, University of California, Los Angeles, and is currently the President of the Society of Indexers. Following the war, he served as Reference Librarian for the City of Westminster and later became Librarian to the BBC. During his fifty years as a professional librarian in England and the USA, he has written more than twenty works on bibliography, librarianship, indexing and related subjects.

Sheila R. Herstein is Reference Librarian and Library Instruction Coordinator at the City College of the City University of New York. She has extensive bibliographic experience and described her innovations in the field of bibliographic instruction in 'Team teaching and bibliographic instruction', *The Bookmark*, Autumn 1979. In addition, Doctor Herstein co-authored a basic annotated bibliography in history for Funk & Wagnalls *New encyclopedia*, and for several years reviewed books for *Library Journal*.

Louis J. Reith is librarian with the Franciscan Institute, St. Bonaventure University, New York. He received his PhD from Stanford University, California, and later studied at Eberhard-Karls-Universität, Tübingen. In addition to his activities as a librarian, Dr. Reith is a specialist on 16th-century German history and the Reformation and has published many articles and papers in both German and English. He was also editor of the *American Society for Reformation Research Newsletter*.

Hans H. Wellisch is a Professor at the College of Library and Information Services, University of Maryland, and a member of the American Society of Indexers and the International Federation for Documentation. He is the author of numerous articles and several books on indexing and abstracting, and has also published *Indexing and abstracting: an international bibliography*. He also contributes frequently to *Journal of the American Society for Information Science, Library Quarterly*, and *The Indexer*.

Contents

Contents

Contents

Contents

Introduction

The purpose of this bibliography is to meet what I believe to be a need for an up-to-date guide to the literature of the Atlantic Ocean in its broadest geographical and historical context. The closest approximation to such a listing appears to be the bibliography appended to Gerhard Schott's scholarly work *Geographie des Atlantischen Ozeans,* (Hamburg, 1943. 3rd ed.) (q.v.) now very dated and not readily accessible. No subsequent textbook or bibliography would seem to treat the region in the same thorough way, and the general reader with an interest in the Atlantic as a whole would require access to a large number of separate bibliographies. Naturally, a volume such as the present work which attempts to cover the field in under 1,000 publications can make no pretence to being definitive. My aim, therefore, has been to select from a large corpus of publications those which are most likely to stimulate interest in Atlantic studies and serve as pointers to further investigation. In making my selection I have borne in mind the interests of the following broad groups of users: the general non-specialist reader seeking expert information on a subject couched in plain English; the specialist requiring information on an adjacent or overlapping discipline; travellers and tourists looking for background and practical information; librarians, information specialists and members of the book trade needing to enlarge their collections; and students seeking an interdisciplinary approach to their chosen field of study.

In general I have attempted to cover commercially published books in print up to the end of the first quarter of 1985, including some government publications. I have also incorporated numerous out-of-print books where these are clearly essential reading. Articles in periodicals have been included where they provide useful information not available in book form. Newspaper articles and ephemera have been excluded. Since the bibliography is aimed on the whole at the general, rather than

Introduction

the specialist user, I have tended to avoid highly specialized monographs (though not invariably), and have concentrated rather on introductory works written by experts with the beginner in mind. The material selected is for the most part written in the English language, though here again there are a few exceptions. Over what is inevitably a very extensive range of subjects my selection must inevitably appear highly subjective. It is derived basically from a systematic searching of national and specialist bibliographies, but also as so often happens in research, from sheer serendipity. Inevitably there will be some omissions and I apologize for these in advance.

The annotations are intended to expand and shed further light on the titles, and in particular to draw the attention of the reader to aspects of the work related to the Atlantic. They are not necessarily to be regarded as full abstracts of the contents.

In general each section of the bibliography has been arranged alphabetically by author, editor or compiler, and in their absence by title. However, there are a few exceptions. For example, in the section entitled 'Spanish voyages' a chronological arrangement has been preferred.

Any definition of a region as broad as that encompassed by the Atlantic Ocean must necessarily be both arbitrary and subjective. The boundaries of the ocean itself can be debated. I have selected those adopted by the International Hydrographic Bureau in its publication *Limits of the ocean*, (Monte Carlo, 1953. 3rd ed. Special Publication no. 23). I have modified the Bureau's definition somewhat to terminate the southern boundary at latitude 60°, roughly corresponding to the northern limits of the Southern Ocean. A map showing these limits is reproduced at the end of the volume. The boundaries selected exclude the Arctic regions, as well as Greenland and Spitsbergen, and the Antarctic continent and adjacent islands. It should be pointed out at this point that it is hoped that the two polar regions will eventually be covered by subsequent volumes in the World Bibliographical Series. As the reader will discover I have followed the International Hydrographic Bureau's policy of omitting from this definition of the Atlantic Ocean all adjacent seas, straits, gulfs and bays. Although hydrologically speaking these form part of the ocean, they are more conveniently treated with the bordering countries. The islands covered by the bibliography are as follows: in the North Atlantic, the Faroe Islands, Rockall, the Azores, Cape Verde Islands, Madeira, the Canary Islands and St. Paul's Rocks; and in the South Atlantic Fernando de Noronha, South Trinidad (Ilha Trinidade), St. Helena, Ascension Island, Tristan da Cunha and Gough Island, the Falkland Islands and their dependencies (South Georgia and the South Sandwich Islands), and finally Bouvet

Introduction

Island (Bouvetøya). Among the islands which have been excluded are the following which have already been covered by the World Bibliographical Series: *Haiti* (vol. 39), *Iceland* (vol. 37), *Jamaica* (vol. 45) and *Puerto Rico* (vol. 52). For the literature of the Panama Canal the attention of readers is drawn to the volume on *Panama* (vol. 14). It should also be noted that the following islands will be among those covered by forthcoming volumes in the series: Bahamas; Barbados; Trinidad and Tobago; Cuba; the Dominican Republic; and Grenada.

Broadly speaking the bibliography is grouped under three sections; firstly the history of man's activities in the Atlantic region; secondly a review of Atlantic Ocean science, nature and wildlife; and thirdly aspects of selected Atlantic islands and island groups. Where possible I have tried to conform to the arrangement of topics and headings used in other volumes in the World Bibliographical Series. It is hoped that the full index to this volume will insure that the user misses nothing of significance.

Following a brief section dealing with the Atlantic region as a whole the bibliography reviews in outline the history of man's involvement with the Atlantic Ocean as explorer, trader, mariner and scientist. Here the reader's attention is particularly drawn to the sections entitled 'Scientific Exploration' and its subsection 'Selected expeditions' which includes the more important investigative British voyages in the Atlantic since the 17th century. Following this is a list of publications relating to the discoveries in the North Atlantic made by pre-Columbian seafarers, more especially the Vikings, leading to the great period of Western expansion into the ocean during the 15th and 16th centuries. Narratives of voyages as well as general accounts of the principal Portuguese, Spanish, English and Dutch voyages will be found under their respective headings.

Exploration and trade go hand-in-hand and under the broad heading of 'Economic history' are listed works dealing with the development of the European Atlantic coastal trade as well as transatlantic trade. Also covered is the slave trade, together with some references to pirates and privateers.

The 19th century witnessed a transatlantic phenomenon of great significance for the future when the trickle of European migrants to the Americas, which began in the 16th century, became a torrent. Under the heading of 'Social history and migration' are listed not only general accounts such as Basil Greenhill's *The great migration*, but also a few works dealing with economic cause and effect, and even one concerning that contemporary migratory phenomenon – the 'Brain Drain'.

Introduction

The logistic requirements of emigration in their turn influenced the development of shipping and helped to accelerate the gradual change from sail power to steam power during the middle years of the 19th century. A section on transport history lists a number of books describing this evolutionary process from the early paddle steamers of the 1830s to Edwardian floating palaces like the *Lusitania, Mauritania* and the ill-starred *Titanic*. This section also includes works dealing with the more modern luxury liners such as *Queen Elizabth 1* and *2*. The first non-stop aeroplane flight across the North Atlantic by Alcock and Brown in 1919 foreshadowed the inevitable close of the era of the 'grand saloon'. C. H. Gibbs-Smith's bibliography appended to his book *Aviation* provides a useful guide to this specialist field. My own selection includes a number of general histories including some relating to the airship, a powerful rival on the transatlantic run to the aeroplane until the disasters to the British *R.101* and the German *Hindenburg*. There are also references to balloon crossings and to the biographies of some of the Atlantic aviation pioneers including Charles Lindbergh and Amy Johnson. Finally, under transport history, I have included a related topic, telecommunications. Modern technology links the nations of the Atlantic together with its fibre-optic cables and messages beamed from space satellites to such a degree that it is now hard to conceive that Marconi's first transatlantic wireless message dates from only 1901. The selection here covers general developments from the transatlantic cable of 1854 to the present day, though technological aspects are deliberately omitted.

One corollary of expanding trade routes is their defence against rivals. Spain, Portugal, the Netherlands, Great Britain, France and finally the United States have in their turn sought to control, in their own economic interests, the vital transatlantic trade routes linking the Old World to the New. In his seminal work *The influence of sea power upon history* Alfred Thayer Mahan argued the importance of commercial and naval sea power in maintaining national supremacy. This thesis was never more forcibly demonstrated than by the battle of the Atlantic during the two World Wars when German submarines only narrowly failed in their efforts to cut the supply lines between Britain and North America. The literature on this subject of sea power is a considerable one as is evidenced by such bibliographies as those of Robert Albion and A. G. S. Enser. The present work only aims to draw attention to some of the classic works in the field and to the definitive general histories. The struggle for naval supremacy continues, though the scale has changed, and today the Atlantic Ocean is the haunt of atomic-powered submarines bearing the instruments of mutually assured

Introduction

destruction. Recent literature on international affairs and defence policy indicates that the North Atlantic Treaty Organization is now addressing itself not only to military and naval strategy but also to the changing political relationships between its member countries. The books and journal articles listed under 'The Atlantic as a Strategic Military Area and Contemporary Relations' only palely reflect the vast number to be found in specialist libraries and to which Colin Gordon's *The Atlantic alliance; a bibliography* (q.v.) is an essential guide. This latter work, incidentally, can readily be updated by writing for supplements published by the NATO Information Service in Brussels. The nations bordering the South Atlantic have not, to date, banded together in any system of mutual security akin to NATO. However, as Argentina's invasion of the Falkland Islands in 1982 has demonstrated there is an ever present danger that opposing interests in the South Atlantic may give rise to similar areas of conflict, and I have felt it appropriate to include a few publications from Argentina to reflect the Latin American viewpoint.

No consideration of sea power would be complete without reference to the international law of the sea. Increasing competition between nations in recent years for access to the resources of the ocean, both living and mineral, has led to the extension of national zones of jurisdiction and a need to redefine aspects of international law. The corpus of literature in this field is truly daunting, but the researcher's needs are well met by the Dag Hammarskjöld Library's select bibliography prepared for the various sessions of the United Nations Conference on the Law of the Sea, and by the bibliographies compiled by Nikos Papadakis. For a comprehensive treatise on the law of the sea as it relates to the Atlantic and other world oceans the late Professor D. P. O'Connell's textbook *The international law of the sea* (q.v.) is probably unsurpassed. The reader will find in this section a number of recent publications covering most aspects of the subject.

Consideration of resource jurisdiction leads logically to the resources themselves. For centuries the Northwest Atlantic has been the cradle of the Western world's staple fisheries, especially herring and cod, and also, before their eventual decline, whales and seals. The development of modern trawler technology and the search for new fishing grounds has enabled the industry to extend its activities to northwest Africa and as far south as the Falkland Islands and the continental shelf of South America. For this section I have selected material from a wide range of publications covering all aspects of these resources including consideration of their future conservation and management, along with some references to mineral deposits on the Atlantic sea bed. In particular the

Introduction

reader's attention is drawn to the publications issued by the United Nations Food and Agriculture Organization (FAO) in Rome, and the International Council for the Exploration of the Sea in Copenhagen, and the various Atlantic fisheries commissions. The Annual Report of the International Whaling Commission in Cambridge, England, is a prime source of information on the biology and conservation of whales and the current status of the whale fisheries.

From man's activities in the Atlantic we turn to a selection of the literature concerning ocean science and life science. For the countries bordering its shores the Atlantic Ocean has a significance which extends far beyond its function as an international waterway and a storehouse of economic resources. The world's second largest ocean, and an integral link in the global circulatory system whereby the cold waters of the Arctic Ocean interconnect with those of the circumpolar Southern Ocean, the Atlantic plays a key part in the functioning of an enormously complex world weather machine. The climates, and consequently the economies of Atlantic lands, are directly influenced by ocean air masses and marine currents whose energy is derived from what amounts to a vast heat exchange mechanism. The Gulf Stream provides the best known example of the phenomenon and has been the subject of so much research in its own right that it has been awarded a small section to itself in this bibliography. Moreover, the breeding and migration patterns of fish as well as marine birds and mammals are also directly linked to the physical properties of the ocean, its chemistry, currents and temperature. In addition the safety of North Atlantic shipping, along with the protection of vulnerable oil and gas rigs, requires extensive studies of occurrences such as the formation of sea ice and the movement of icebergs. Further removed from our immediate experience, though no less absorbing in interest, is the geological study of the Atlantic sea floor. With the help of modern technology research in recent years has produced not only charts of the ocean bottom but also, based on studies of the Mid-Atlantic Ridge, theories of sea floor spreading which, applied to the mass of available data, enable scientists to plot and date the movements of adjacent continents over millions of years. Accordingly, it is clear that no bibliography of the Atlantic Ocean could be taken seriously if it were not to pay due regard to the ocean sciences, and I make no excuse for devoting approximately one quarter of the volume to this field. The literature selected includes textbooks suitable for beginners and first-year students, including examples from the excellent Open University texts, as well as popular but informed articles from such sources as *Scientific American* and *National Geographic*. While concentrating on the more recent publications I have felt it appropriate to include a few of the basic classic works in the several fields covered such as Alfred Wegener's *The origin of continents* (q.v.) and Harald Sverdrup's *The Oceans* (q.v.).

Complementing the section on economic resources I have listed under the general heading of 'Ocean Fauna' a selection of publications likely to be of interest to students, teachers and the amateur naturalist. Once again I have chosen some popular books written by professionals ranging from Bernard Stonehouse on penguins to Nigel Bonner on whales, together with a sprinkling of such long established works as Robert Cushman Murphy's *Oceanic birds of South America* (q.v.) for the benefit of those wishing to probe more deeply into the subject. It should be noted that additional material relating to nature and wildlife will also be found under the various island headings. Pollution of the ocean, which equally affects not only the fish, birds, whales and seals but ourselves, is a topic of some concern to ecologists and politicians alike. Readers will find listed under this heading some references dealing with the practical and legal aspects, including the controversial dumping of nuclear waste in the Atlantic.

Accompanying this section on ocean science is a comprehensive listing of current atlases, Admiralty charts, pilots and handbooks covering the various sectors of the Atlantic Ocean. Hopefully, this will interest not only scientists but also navigators and small-boat enthusiasts. The interests of this last group are specifically catered for in the section concerned with small boat voyages and racing which contains the literature of transatlantic 'firsts' ranging from Erik the Red to Sir Francis Chichester. Other specialist interests considered include those of: the business man who, under the heading 'Trade and Communications', will find books on shipping, as well as practical handbooks, directories and nautical yearbooks; and the tourist, whose needs for practical information will be met under the heading of 'Tourism' as well as under the various island sections.

No bibliography of this kind would be complete without a passing glance at works of the imagination. The compiler's problem was again one of selection. If asked to name just one novel of the sea to list under the heading of 'The Atlantic in Fantasy and Fiction' it would, I think, have to be Herman Melville's classic *Moby Dick* (q.v.) which has so much to offer, not only concerning the ocean and its mysteries, and about the old whaling days, but about human nature itself. However, Smith and Weller's *Sea fiction guide* (q.v.) contains titles to suit most tastes. As for fantasy, much has appeared in print during recent years concerning that zone of ill-omen and disaster, the Bermuda Triangle, an

Introduction

area in which Charles Berlitz appears to be the principal investigator. Atlantis, the lost continent on which Plato speculated, and which in late mediaeval times was associated with such mythical islands as 'Brasil' and the 'Islands of the Blest', could claim a bibliography to itself; and only a small number of works can be included here.

The concluding section of the bibliography is devoted to the literature, again predominantly in the English language, of the islands of the Atlantic ranging from the Faroes in the northeast to the Falklands in the far southwest. The material available for the larger island groups justifies a number of sub-headings, including, for example, 'Islands and their peoples', 'Nature and wildlife', 'History', and 'Industry'. Naturally, the subjects covered vary substantially from one island group to another. In the case of the Faroes I have stressed language and literature which form the basis of Faroese nationalism. Listings for the Canaries, Madeira and the Azores are weighted more heavily towards the interests of the visitor. Not many travellers journey to the South Atlantic islands of St. Helena, Tristan da Cunha and Ascension Island, and my choice here tends to reflect both their history and wild life. One consequence of Argentina's invasion of the Falkland Islands in 1982, and the subsequent reoccupation of the islands by the British has been an eruption of books and articles covering not only the campaign itself but the economic and political future of the islands. In view of the tremendous importance of the Falklands War of 1982 and the world-wide interest in the conflict the section on the Falklands and their two dependencies, South Georgia and the South Sandwich Islands, deliberately occupies proportionately more space than that allocated to other island groups. Indeed the opportunity has been taken to provide a comprehensive listing of the British official and unofficial war publications, including those dealing with the prolonged debate on the *Belgrano* affair. In addition a number of items in Spanish stemming from Argentina have been included. Also covered in some detail is the literature dealing with: claims and counterclaims to sovereignty over the group; the economic prospects for the islands; and the Falkland islanders themselves, who are staunchly British in their lifestyle and in their form of local Government. Lastly, because philately is a major source of revenue not only for the Falkland Islands government but also for the governments of St. Helena and its dependency Tristan da Cunha, I have included a representative selection of recent literature detailing postal history, stamps and first-day covers.

This bibliography ends on the southernmost island of the Mid-Atlantic Ridge, Bouvet Island. Inhabited only by penguins, seabirds and seals and climatically more akin to Antarctica, it contrasts at latitude

Introduction

54° S quite dramatically with temperate Atlantic environments at corresponding northern latitudes. I have included works concerning the scientific interest in the island. In addition I have selected items to remind readers of the pioneer discoveries in the South Atlantic of De Lozier Bouvet, its French discoverer in the 18th century, and his great British contemporary, Captain James Cook. It was Cook, who while searching for evidence of this same island, delineated for the first time the boundary of the South Atlantic on our charts.

Acknowledgements

I would like to acknowledge my debt to the many libraries who have given me access to their collections. They include in Cambridge: the University Library; the Marshall Library of Economics; the Seeley Historical Library; the Squire Law Library; the libraries of the departments of Geography, Earth Sciences and Zoology; and the library of the Scott Polar Research Institute. Other libraries consulted in Cambridge included the Central Reference Library and the library of the Cambridgeshire College of Arts and Technology. In London the following libraries proved especially fruitful: the Royal Geographical Society; the Royal Commonwealth Society; and the British Museum (Natural History) Zoology Library. To the invariably courteous and helpful staffs of all these libraries my thanks are due. Lastly my thanks are due to Dr. Peter Speak, Head of the Department of Geography at the Cambridgeshire College of Arts and Technology for valued advice, and to Dr. Robert Neville of Clio Press for much editorial guidance and constructive criticism, all of which has helped to make the business of compilation a pleasure rather than a labour.

H. G. R. King
Cambridge.
June 1985

The Atlantic Region
in General

1 The Atlantic Ocean.
Charles H. Cotter. Glasgow: Brown, Son & Ferguson, 1974. 164p.

A broad study of all aspects of the Atlantic Ocean aimed at the general reader. Part I deals with the physical aspects, and part II with human aspects.

2 Oceans: an atlas-history of man's exploration of the deep.
Edited by G. E. R. Deacon. London: Hamlyn, 1968. 2nd ed. 295p. bibliog.

A popular, profusely illustrated general introduction to all aspects of the oceans. Sir George Deacon was, until his death in 1984, the doyen of British oceanographers.

3 An introduction to the world's oceans.
Alyn C. Duxbury, Alison Duxbury. Reading, Massachusetts: Addison-Wesley, 1984. 549p. maps. bibliog.

Primarily intended for teaching at first-year university level, the emphasis of this text-book is on the physical and geological aspects of the seas, though biological relationships are introduced.

4 The encyclopedia of oceanography.
Edited by Rhodes W. Fairbridge. Stroudsberg, Pennsylvania: Dowden, Hutchinson & Ross, 1966. 1,021p. (Encyclopedia of Earth Sciences, vol. 1).

This work includes a useful introductory article on the Atlantic Ocean with a bibliography.

5 The commanding sea.
Clare Francis, Warren Tute. London: British Broadcasting Corporation and Pelham Books, 1981. 280p. maps.

This work includes accounts by Clare Francis of her two transatlantic voyages together with contributions by specialists on all aspects of the world's oceans.

The Atlantic Region in General

6 **The Atlantic.**
Edited by Pat Hargreaves. Hove, East Sussex, England: Wayland
Publishers, 1980. 72p. maps. bibliog.
This book is essentially an introduction to the ocean for younger readers with
well-illustrated contributions by experts.

7 **The Atlantic Ocean: bridge between two worlds.**
F. George Kay. London: Museum Press, 1954. 208p. maps. bibliog.
The opening chapters dealing with the geology and natural resources of the
Atlantic are now somewhat outdated, but the historical chapters, which cover the
discovery and commercial exploitation of the ocean, are useful as a summary
introduction to the subject. The penultimate chapter covers 'Atlantis' and the
oceanic islands.

8 **The Oxford companion to ships and the sea.**
Edited by Peter Kemp. London: Oxford University Press, 1976.
972p.
An indispensable compendium of all manner of information embracing the
world's oceans, with contributions by named experts.

9 **Ocean Yearbook.**
Chicago: University of Chicago Press, 1978- . annual.
An authoritative, impartial and up-to-date review of major ocean issues, and
each volume contains an overview of the principal events of the year, including significant incidents, legislative acts, negotiations, treaties and scientific
discoveries. There are also articles on specialized subjects, such as ocean resources,
communications and treaties.

10 **Geographie des Atlantischen Ozeans.** (The geography of the
Atlantic Ocean.)
Gerhard Schott. Hamburg: Verlag von C. Boysen, 1942. 3rd ed.
438p. maps. bibliog.
A general survey of the Atlantic Ocean in all its aspects. Although dated, in many
respects, this volume is probably the most scholarly work of its kind.

The Mitchell Beazley atlas of the oceans.
See item no. 484.

The Times atlas of the oceans.
See item no. 485.

World atlas vol. 2. Atlantic and Indian oceans.
See item no. 486.

History

Exploration and discovery

11 **The quest for America.**
Geoffrey Ashe. London: Pall Mall Press, 1971. 298p. maps. bibliog.

This work includes chapters by experts dealing with early myths and legends, the Viking voyages and other aspects of New World exploration including the 'historic' discovery of America by Christopher Columbus. A well-illustrated account intended for the general reader.

12 **History of cartography.**
Leo Bagrow, revised and enlarged by R. A. Skelton. London: C. A. Watts, 1964. 312p. maps. bibliog.

A revision of the original German edition *Geschichte der Kartographie* (Berlin: Safari Verlag. 1951). Over 200 notable maps are reproduced in black-and-white and colour. Chapters 10 and 11 cover the cartography of the great discoveries and nautical cartography in the 16th century. They include numerous references to, and reproductions of, early Atlantic charts ranging from a woodcut of Ptolemy's *Oceanus occidentalis* (1513) to the more sophisticated charts of the Atlantic in the late 16th century associated with the sailing directions in seabooks.

13 **A history of geographical discovery and exploration.**
J. N. L. Baker. London: Harrap, 1932. 544p. map. bibliog.

Written as an undergraduate text book, this work has retained its value as an introduction to the whole field of geographical discovery.

14 **A reference guide to the literature of travel including voyages,**
    descriptions, adventures, shipwrecks and expeditions. Vol. 1 The
    old world. Vol. 2 The new world. Vol. 3 Great Britain.
    Edward Godfrey Cox. Seattle, Washington: University of
    Washington, 1948-49. 3 vols. (University of Washington publi-
    cations in language and literature vol. 9).
    This reprint of the 1935 edition provides 'a listing in chronological order from the
    earliest date ascertainable to 1800 of all books on foreign travel, voyages and
    descriptions printed in Great Britain together with translations from foreign
    tongues and continental renderings of English works'.

15 **The discovery of America.**
    G. R. Crone. London: Hamish Hamilton, 1969. 224p. maps.
    bibliog.
    A history of transatlantic exploration and its motivation with an appendix on
    navigation and cartography. The author is a leading map historian.

16 **The principall navigations voiages and discoveries of the English**
    nation . . . imprinted at London, 1589 . . . Vols. 1, 2.
    Richard Hakluyt, introduction by D. B. Quinn, R. A. Skelton.
    Cambridge, England: Hakluyt Society, 1965. 2 vols. map. bibliog.
    (Hakluyt Society extra series, no. 39).
    This epic history of exploration was chiefly designed by its compiler to stimulate
    English voyages of trade and overseas settlement. This is a facsimile reprint of the
    first edition of 1589. A much fuller second edition of 1598-1600 was also
    reprinted by the Hakluyt Society in 12 volumes, 1903-05. The principal maritime
    voyages described by Hakluyt are to Africa (including the Canaries, Cape Verde
    Islands and Madeira), America (north and south), Asia and the Arctic, as well as
    the circumnavigations of Sir Francis Drake and others.

17 **The blind Horn's hate.**
    Richard Hough. London: Hutchinson, 1971. 336p. maps. bibliog.
    A popular history of the discovery of the southernmost part of South America
    where the Atlantic and Pacific oceans meet.

18 **Non-Mediterranean influences that shaped the Atlantic in the early**
    portolan charts.
    J. E. Kelly, Jr. *Imago Mundi; Journal of the International Society*
    for the History of Cartography, 31 (second series, vol. 4), (1979)
    p. 18-35, maps. bibliog.
    The author discusses 14th and 15th-century charts of the Atlantic and their place-
    names.

19 **Atlas of maritime history.**
Christopher Lloyd. London: Hamlyn Publishing Group for
Country Life, 1975. 144p. maps.

A useful summary in map format with an adjacent text concerning the main
episodes in maritime history. Of particular relevance are the sections covering the
Norse voyages, the discovery of America, the search for the Northwest Passage,
the voyages of Captain James Cook, North Atlantic trade routes and the slave
trade, and the Second World War and the Battle of the Atlantic.

20 **The European discovery of America: the northern voyages A.D.**
500-1600.
Samuel Eliot Morison. New York: Oxford University Press, 1971.
712p. maps. bibliog.

A history of exploration in the North Atlantic Ocean from St. Brendan and the
Irish monks in 400-600 to the founding of the first and second Virginia colonies
in 1585.

21 **The European discovery of America: the southern voyages**
A.D. 1492-1616.
Samuel Eliot Morison. New York: Oxford University Press, 1974.
758p. maps. bibliog.

This history complements the author's previous volume dealing with the European discovery of America. The work deals with voyages in the central and south
Atlantic from the time of Columbus to the discoverers of Cape Horn, the Dutch
navigators Willem Cornelius Schouten (1567?-1625) and Jakob Le Maire (1585-
1616).

22 **The great explorers: the European discovery of America.**
Samuel Eliot Morison. New York: Oxford University Press,
1978. 752p. maps.

A new edition of material selected from the author's two volume work *The European discovery of America* (q.v.).

23 **The Atlantic; a history of an ocean.**
Leonard Outhwaite. New York: Coward-McCann; London:
Constable, 1957. 479p. maps. bibliog.

An attempt to gather together the main facts about the Atlantic Ocean namely:
its discovery by early explorers; the development of trade; and the societies
bordering its shores. The book concludes with a critical bibliography. The author
is himself a seasoned Atlantic navigator.

5

24 The age of reconnaissance; discovery, exploration and settlement 1450-1650.

John Horace Parry. London: Sphere Books, 1973. 428p. maps. bibliog.

An outline narrative of European geographical exploration, trade and settlement outside the bounds of Europe during the 15th, 16th and 17th centuries. The author defines the factors which stimulated expansion and made it possible. Chapter 9 'The Atlantic and the South Sea' outlines geographical discoveries from the 15th-century Portuguese voyages to the Canaries, the Madeira group, the Azores and Cape Verde islands, and the counterclaims of Castile to these islands, to Magellan's voyage of 1519-22 leading to the discovery of the Magellan Straits, gateway from the Atlantic to the Pacific Ocean. Chapter 11 'Atlantic trade and piracy' is concerned with the growth of the seapower of the Netherlands and England and their attacks on the prosperous Spanish transatlantic commerce. The work concludes with a brief account of the attempts of the French and English to find an alternative North Atlantic route to the Orient via the fabled Northwest Passage.

25 The discovery of the sea.

John Horace Parry. London: Weidenfeld & Nicolson, 1975. 319p. bibliog.

A history of the great age of discovery by a leading scholar in the field. The author traces the course of European maritime exploration down to the first circumnavigation of the globe and investigates the extent to which success depended on utilizing the skill and knowledge of the seafaring peoples in the regions explored. Two chapters, 'The Atlantic crossing' (p. 217-70) and its sequel 'A new world' (p. 244-70) discuss Columbus' voyages across the western Atlantic, and a further chapter 'West Africa and the islands' outlines the history of the discovery of the Canary Islands, Madeira, the Azores and the Cape Verde Islands.

26 Hakluytus posthumus or Purchas his pilgrimes; contayning a history of the world in sea voyages and lande travells by Englishmen and others.

Samuel Purchas. Glasgow: James MacLehose, 1905-07. 20 vols. maps. (Hakluyt Society extra series 14-33).

This is an exact reprint of the folio edition of 1625 in four volumes including the original maps and plates. It is one of the fullest and most important collections of English voyages in the English language, being an enlargement of Hakluyt's collection. On Hakluyt's death in 1616 Purchas acquired a large quantity of his unpublished manuscript material.

27 **North American world; a documentary history of North America to 1612. Vols. I-V.**
Edited with a commentary by David B. Quinn with Alison M.
Quinn, Susan Hillier. New York: Arno Press and Hector Bye,
1979. 5 vols. maps.

A magnificent collection of transcribed documentary source material relating to
the discovery of America. The history follows the chronological sequence of
exploration in the Atlantic leading to Columbus's landfall of 1492-93; and there-
after it is concerned with the further discovery and exploration of the territory
that about 1507 became defined as 'North America'. The contents of the volumes
are as follows: 1, 'America from concept to discovery. Early exploration of North
America'; 2, 'Major Spanish searches in eastern North America. The Franco-
Spanish clash in Florida'; 3, 'English plans for North America. The Roanoke
voyages. New England ventures'; 4, 'Newfoundland from fishery to colony.
Northwest Passage searches'; and 5, 'The extension of settlement in Virginia and
the Spanish southwest'.

28 **Sixteenth century North America; the land and the people as seen by Europeans.**
Carl Ortwin Sauer. Los Angeles: University of California Press,
1971. 319p. maps. bibliog.

The 16th century witnessed the major discoveries along the Atlantic coast of
North America from Baffin Bay to the Gulf of Mexico. This monograph attempts,
with the aid of contemporary reports, both official and private, to reconstruct
conditions in these regions both before and immediately after the arrival of the
Europeans.

29 **Explorers maps; chapters in the cartographic record of geographical discovery.**
R. A. Skelton. London: Routledge & Kegan Paul, 1958. 337p.
maps. bibliog.

A revised reprinting of 14 articles written for *The Geographical Magazine* July
1953-August 1956. The chapters are grouped in rough regional order and present
episodes and phases in the history of geographical discovery for which the
evidence of contemporary maps is especially interesting and accessible. The book
is lavishly illustrated with reproductions of maps and charts for which annotations
are provided at the end of each chapter. Chapter 2 'The Portuguese sea-way'
considers the Canary Islands and Cape Verde Islands in the 15th century. Chapter
3 'Cathay or a new world' discusses Columbus's Atlantic voyages, and Chapter 4
'New World in the sixteenth century' reviews Atlantic discoveries in North and
South America during the 16th century by Spanish, French and English adventurers.

30 The western ocean; the story of the North Atlantic.
Alan Villiers. London: Museum Press, 1957. 288p. map.

A history of Atlantic exploration and navigation by one of its most experienced navigators. The author sees the North Atlantic ocean as having 'greater importance to man than all the others rolled together' and his opening chapter 'Wild ocean' constitutes an excellent introduction to the Atlantic in general. Subsequent chapters deal with the Gulf Stream, the history of Atlantic exploration, the privateers, pirates and slavers who infested its waters, and the whalers and fishermen who farmed them. In conclusion the conquest of the Atlantic firstly by sail and steam ship and finally by aircraft is outlined and the Atlantic battles of the two World Wars are reviewed.

Scientific exploration

General

31 Scientists and the sea 1650-1900; a study of marine science.
Margaret Deacon. London: Academic Press, 1971. 445p. bibliog.

This is a valuable introduction to the gradual development of the study of the hydrography of the oceans with special reference to circulation currents, temperature and tides. The author is primarily concerned with British science and there is much information relative to the history of Atlantic investigations including: Edmond Halley's work on tides in the 17th century; research on Atlantic currents in the early 19th century; and the pioneer studies carried out on *Challenger* in the North Atlantic during her oceanographic cruise of 1872-75.

32 Some aspects of Anglo-American co-operation in marine science, 1660-1914.
Margaret Deacon. In: *Oceanography: the past.* Edited by Mary Sears and D. Merriman. New York: Springer-Verlag, 1980, p. 101-13. bibliog.

The author provides examples of how the interchange of information concerning navigation and scientific study of the Atlantic Ocean was fostered between the two countries over the centuries. There is a valuable historical bibliography with over 40 references.

33 A union list of oceanographic expeditions including results of some major cruise reports.
Compiled by Rita Estok, Rosemary E. Boykin. College, Texas: Texas A. & M. University Libraries, 1976. 138p.

This work provides a list of published reports of the classic oceanographic expeditions and hydrographic cruises held by thirteen major oceanographic institutions in the USA.

34 **Selected references to literature on marine expeditions 1700-1960.**
Fisheries-oceanography library, University of Washington. Compiled
by Mary C. Grier, Laurence Murphy, Gerald J. Oppenheimer, Helen
Strickland, Helen Remsberg. Boston, Massachusetts: G. K. Hall,
1972. 517p.

An unedited working file of citations to oceanographic research located in the
Fisheries-Oceanography Library at the University Library, Seattle, Washington,
USA. Consisting of about 9,000 cards it is an index to ships and expeditions
involved in research from the 18th to the mid 20th centuries.

35 **On the importance of an international exploration of the Atlantic**
Ocean.
Geographical Journal, vol. 33, no. 1 (1909), p. 65-71.

Sets out a recommended programme of scientific investigation following on a
resolution of the Ninth International Geographical Congress at Geneva that 'the
physical and biological investigaton of the Atlantic is one of the most pressing
problems in oceanography'.

36 **A history of oceanography; the edge of an unfamiliar world.**
Susan Schlee. London: Robert Hale, 1975. 398p. bibliog.

The study of oceanography from the mid 19th century through World War II
is reviewed in this study, which also contains a concluding chapter on contemporary geophysical studies.

37 **The major deep-sea expeditions and research vessels 1873-1960;**
a contribution to the history of oceanography.
George Wüst. *Progress in Oceanography*, vol. 2 (1964), p. 3-52.
maps. bibliog.

A valuable summary of the major oceanographic expeditions of this period and
the progress of oceanographic research. A chronological list of expeditions is
provided which includes the oceans visited and the main studies carried out. The
bibliography lists the major deep-sea expedition reports and selected monographs.

Selected expeditions

38 **The three voyages of Edmond Halley in the *Paramore* 1698-1701.**
Edited by J. W. Thrower. London: Hakluyt Society, 1981. 392p.
maps. bibliog. (Hakluyt Society second series, no. 156).

An introduction to, and an account of, the voyages is followed by an edited transcription of Halley's journals, now in the British Museum, London. Edmond Halley (1656-1742) was the first to commission and command a naval vessel for the purposes of scientific investigation, and was the initiator and commander of the three voyages of the pink *Paramore* in 1698-1701. He had previously visited St. Helena in 1676-78 to determine the position of southern hemisphere stars and observe the transit of Mercury across the Sun. The Atlantic voyage of 1698-99 included observations on latitude and longitude and an attempt to discover 'Terra incognita' – the supposed southern continent. The second voyage of 1699-1701 was more extensive including visits to the Cape Verde Islands, St. Helena and Ilhas Trinidade (South Trinidad). The farthest south reached in the Atlantic was lat. 52° 24' S. where *Paramore* was halted by icebergs. A third voyage was confined to the English Channel. As a result of observations made on the first two voyages, Halley was able to produce the first chart of the Atlantic Ocean showing magnetic variations (reproduced here in facsimile). The published chart (1702) became very influential and was widely used at sea.

39 **The journals of Captain James Cook on his voyages of discovery.
The voyage of the *Resolution* and *Adventure* 1772-1775.**
Edited from the original manuscripts by J. C. Beaglehole.
Cambridge, England: Cambridge University Press for the Hakluyt
Society, 1961. 1,021p. maps. bibliog. (Hakluyt Society extra
series, no. 35).

This volume which is devoted to Cook's journal of his second circumnavigation of the world between 1772 and 1775 is a magnificent work of scholarship, taking into account all available sources both published and manuscript. It includes Cook's letters and reports on the voyage, and extracts from officers' records. The object of the voyage was to explore the southern Pacific and Atlantic oceans in the highest achievable latitudes seeking to prove or disprove the existence of a supposed Southern Continent. Cook, an astute observer of natural phenomena, has much to say in his journal on the hydrology of the Atlantic Ocean from the viewpoint of the practical seaman. An historic event of the voyage was the discovery of the island of South Georgia on 16th January 1775, followed shortly after by the first sighting of 'Sandwich Land', now known as the South Sandwich Islands. Other Atlantic ports of call included Ascension Island, St. Helena, the Azores, the Canary Islands and Madeira.

40 **A narrative of a voyage to the Southern Atlantic Ocean, in the years 1828, 29, 30, performed in H.M. Sloop *Chanticleer*, under the command of the late Captain Henry Forster, F.R.S. From the private journal of W. H. B. Webster.**
W. H. B. Webster. Folkestone, England: Dawsons of Pall Mall, 1970. 2 vols. maps.
This expedition despatched by the British Admiralty was the first to carry out scientific investigations on Deception Island in the South Atlantic. It included visits to St. Helena, Ascension Island and Fernando Noronha. This is a reprint of the original edition (London: R. Bentley, 1834.)

41 **Journal of researches into the natural history and geology of the countries visited during the voyage round the world of H.M.S. *Beagle* under the command of Captain Fitz Roy R.N.**
Charles Darwin. London: John Murray, 1890. 538p. maps.
The author's preface indicates that 'this journal contains, in the form of a journal, a history of our voyage and a sketch of those observations in natural history and geology which I think will possess some interest for the general reader'. Darwin visited, *inter alia*, St. Paul's Rocks, Fernando Noronha, Tristan da Cunha, the Falkland Islands, the Straits of Magellan, St. Helena and Ascension Island.

42 **Charles Darwin and the voyage of the *Beagle*.**
Edited with an introduction by Nora Barlow. London: Pilot Press, 1945. 279p. map. bibliog.
An edited edition, by a granddaughter of Darwin, of his twenty-four pocket-books and thirty-nine letters written to his father and sisters. The notes are mainly geological, but tell of inland expeditions and are of special interest as a record of his immediate impressions. The letters home constitute an intimate personal narrative.

43 **Darwin and the *Beagle*.**
Alan Moorehead. London: Hamish Hamilton, 1969. 280p. maps. bibliog.
A popular narrative of the historic voyage of the *Beagle* in 1831-36 which included visits to such Atlantic islands as the Cape Verdes, Falklands, St. Helena and Ascension. The book's illustrations include colour reproductions of original sketches by Augustus Earle and Conrad Martens.

44 **The Atlantic; a preliminary account of the general results of the exploring voyage of H. M. S. *Challenger* during the year 1873 and the early part of the year 1876. Vol. 1, 2.**
Sir Charles Wyville Thomson. London: Macmillan, 1877. 2 vols.
This is the story of the classic British oceanographic expedition under the command of Captain George Nares written by the head of the civilian staff. It relates how *Challenger* traversed both the North and South Atlantic between latitudes 40°N and 40°S bringing back a vast amount of scientific data.

45 **Log letters from 'The Challenger'.**
Lord George Campbell. London: Macmillan, 1877. 3rd ed. rev.
504p. maps.

Lord George Campbell, youngest son of the 8th Duke of Argyll, was a sub-lieutenant on the *Challenger* oceanographic expedition of 1872-76. These letters, written home during the cruise, have the charm of immediacy and include descriptions of such Atlantic islands as the Canaries, Azores, St. Paul's Rocks, Tristan da Cunha and the Falkland Islands.

46 **The cruise of Her Majesty's Ship 'Challenger'.**
W. J. J. Spry. London: Sampson Low, Marston, Searle & Rivington,
1876. 388p. map.

Under the command of Captain George Nares with Sir Charles Wyville Thomson as chief scientific officer, this important oceanographic expedition carried out a comprehensive programme of deep sounding, ocean temperatures and currents and ocean bed charting between 1872 and 1876 in the Atlantic and Pacific. This is a summary narrative written by one of *Challenger's* officers.

47 **The voyage of the *Challenger*.**
Eric Linklater. London: John Murray, 1972. 288p. bibliog.

A popular and well-illustrated account of this significant British oceanographic expedition to the Atlantic and Pacific in 1873-76 under the leadership of Captain George Nares.

48 **The depths of the ocean; a general account of the modern science of oceanography based largely on the scientific researches of the Norwegian steamer *Michael Sars* in the North Atlantic.**
Sir John Murray, Johan Hjort. London: Macmillan, 1912. 821p.
maps.

This work provides an account of the cruise of the Norwegian research vessel *Michael Sars*, which lasted from April to August 1910 under the scientific direction of Dr. Johan Hjort. The route taken was Plymouth, Gibraltar, Canary Islands, Azores, Newfoundland, Glasgow and Bergen, Norway. This volume, which constitutes a major textbook in the field of oceanography, contains chapters on the depths and deposits of the North Atlantic, its pelagic life, sea-bottom fauna and general biology. The introductory chapter on the history of oceanography is by Sir John Murray, organizer of the *Challenger* expedition and one of the founders of the discipline.

49 The *Meteor* expedition, an ocean survey.
J. Emery. In: *Oceanography: the past.* Edited by Mary Spears,
D. Merriman. New York: Springer-Verlag, 1980, p. 690-702. map.
bibliog.

The German expedition to the South Atlantic in 1925 under the leadership of Dr. Alfred Merz is the subject of this essay. Its object was to carry out a systematic survey focussing on a description of the ocean's circulation, both surface and subsurface. It was the first major oceanographic expedition to concentrate on physical oceanography and the results it obtained still have relevance to studies of the South Atlantic.

50 **Die Deutsche Atlantische Expedition auf dem Vermessungs – und Forschungschiff 'Meteor'; Vorbericht.** (The German Atlantic Expedition on the survey and expedition vessel *Meteor*; preliminary account.)
Alfred Merz. *Sitzungsberichte der Physikalisch-Mathematischen Preussischen Akademie der Wissenschaften,* Bd.XXX (1925), p. 1-28. maps. bibliog.

A general review of the work of this important expedition which forms an introduction to the collected scientific reports published in issues of *Zeitschrift der Gesellschaft für Erdkunde zu Berlin* (Jahrg. 1926 nos. 1 and 5-6; Jahrg. 1927, nos. 5-8).

51 **Discovery Reports.**
London: Cambridge University Press, 1929-76.

The thirty-six published volumes of Discovery Reports constitute the principal results of investigations in the South Atlantic and Antarctic waters organized by the Discovery Committee on behalf of the Government of the Dependencies of the Falkland Islands. The name originates with the research ship *Discovery* which took Captain Scott to the Antarctic for the 1901 to 1904 voyage.

52 **On almost any wind; the saga of the oceanographic research vessel *Atlantis*.**
Susan Schlee. Ithaca, New York: Cornell University Press, 1978. 301p.

Based on logs, letters and the memories of the ship's company this is an account of the first deep-water research vessel built for the Woods Hole Oceanographic Institution in Massachusetts. Her career spanned the years 1931 to 1966 and is especially associated with the series of cruises to the Mid-Atlantic Ridge under Professor Maurice Ewing.

53 **Atlantide-report. Nos. 1-12. Scientific results of the Danish expedition to the coasts of tropical west Africa 1945-1946.**
University of Copenhagen, British Museum (Natural History). London, Copenhagen: Danish Science Press/Scandinavia Science Press, 1950-77. 12 vols. maps. bibliog.

The scientific reports of a joint Danish-British marine biological survey undertaken in the motor yacht *Atlantide*. The itinerary included the Canary Islands and the Azores.

54 **The Galathea deep sea expedition 1950-1952 described by members of the expedition.**
Edited by Anton F. Bruun, Sv. Greve, Hakon Mielche, Ragnar Spärck, and translated from the Danish by Reginald Spink.
London: Allen & Unwin, 1956. 296p. map.

This Danish expedition carried out important research into fisheries biology off the west coast of Africa, in the Indian and Pacific Oceans, and in the Atlantic off the Azores.

55 **Assault on the unknown; the International Geophysical Year.**
Walter Sullivan. New York: McGraw-Hill, 1961. 460p. maps. bibliog.

This is probably the best popular account of the world-wide programme in scientific cooperation known as the International Geophysical Year (IGY), 1957-58 which led to a number of expeditions. The author of this work was the science correspondent of *The New York Times*. Described as 'the single most significant peaceful activity of mankind since the Renaissance and the Copernican revolution' the IGY covered many disciplines including intensive studies of the Atlantic Ocean, in particular the movement of submerged currents.

56 **H. M. S. "Owen" oceanographic cruise (North and South Atlantic) 1960-1961.**
Great Britain. Hydrographic Department. London: Hydrographic Department, 1963. 17p. maps. (Admiralty Marine science publications, no. 1).

Records the scientific results from stations on the line of the Mid Atlantic Ridge occupied by H. M. S. *Owen* in 1960-61 including seabed cores, water samples, plankton hauls, magnetic observations, and biological collections. The stations included the Azores, and St. Paul's Rocks, a small group of isolated islets 64 feet high, and the precipitous and volcanic Ilhas Martin Vaz and the first recorded landing there (4 December 1960). Other islands visited included Tristan da Cunha, Gough Island, South Georgia, the Falkland Islands, Ascension Island and Tenerife in the Canaries.

Logbook for Grace; whaling brig *Daisy* 1912-1913.
See item no. 351.

Physical oceanography. Vols. 1 and 2.
See item no. 370.

Oceanographic institutions; science studies the sea.
See item no. 629.

Pre-Columbian voyages

57 **The Viking saga.**
Peter Brent. London: Weidenfeld & Nicolson, 1975. 264p. maps. bibliog.
A well-illustrated history of the Vikings including the Iceland and Vinland settlements and their Atlantic voyages.

58 **The sea around them; the Atlantic Ocean A.D. 1250.**
Vincent H. Cassidy. Baton Rouge, Louisiana: Louisiana State University Press, 1968. 202p. map. bibliog.
This book is primarily concerned with the extent of knowledge of the North Atlantic available to Western Europeans around the year AD 1250. All known sources likely to be available at this time are reviewed and there is a comprehensive non-selective bibliography. A valuable handbook for pre-Columbian studies.

59 **European expansion in the later Middle Ages.**
Pierre Chaunu. Amsterdam: North-Holland Publishing, 1979. 326p. maps. bibliog.
A translation of the French original, this is an analysis of the 'spatial revolution' which began between northern Italy and the Spanish Atlantic coast states under the stimulus of the Aristotelian intellectual revolution in the 13th century. A detailed source bibliography is included.

60 Prince Madoc and the discovery of America in 1477.
Arthur Davies. *Geographical Journal,* vol. 150, no. 3 (Nov. 1984), p. 363-72.

Columbus is still credited with being the first European to discover America, apart from the early visits of the Vikings. The author suggests that this was because he received a royal charter which gave him possession of all lands which he might discover in the west; hence he had no need for secrecy. Archaeological and carto-graphic evidence is then used to suggest that Welsh traders, led by the bastard Prince Madoc, were actively trading, illicitly, with the Greenlanders in the 12th century, and that the trade was banned by Norway in the 13th century. Finally the author attempts to show that there was Welsh trading activity in Hudson Strait in the 1470s under the leadership of one 'John Scolvus', probably the Welsh ship master John Lloyd (or Llwyd).

61 The Norse discoveries of America; the Wineland sagas.
G. M. Gathorne-Hardy. Oxford, England: Clarendon Press, 1970. 304p. bibliog.

This is a reprint of the 1921 edition. The first part of the book is a translation of the Icelandic sagas relating to Eric the Red and his son Leif, and the coloniza-tion of Greenland together with early voyages to Wineland (Vinland). Part 2 discusses the historical significance of the sagas.

62 The Vikings.
James Graham-Campbell, Dafydd King. London: British Museum Publications, 1980. 200p. maps.

A reappraisal of the contribution to European civilization made by the Vikings and published on the occasion of *The Vikings,* an exhibition shown consecutively at the British Museum and Metropolitan Museum of Art, New York. Many of the items displayed served to illustrate this book and a catalogue of the exhibits and their provenance is appended.

63 Early man and the ocean.
Thor Heyerdahl. London: Allen & Unwin, 1978. 392p. maps. bibliog.

This book sums up at a popular level the author's highly idiosyncratic thinking on ocean migration routes. In part 2 'The Atlantic problem' Heyerdahl contrasts the position of the 'isolationists', who see the Americas as being sealed off from the Old World by the Atlantic until 1492, with that of the 'diffusionists' who believe in a common cradle of civilization and postulate various hypothetical pre-Columbian voyages. Here the author explores the role of ocean-going reed ships as a 'culture element' in drawing transatlantic parallels.

64 **Westward to Vinland; the discovery of pre Columbian Norse house-sites in North America.**
Helge Ingstad. London: Cape, 1969. 250p. maps. bibliog.
A translation from the Norwegian of the author's account of excavations of a group of pre-Columbian house-sites of Norse origin at L'Anse aux Meadows, Newfoundland, between 1960 and 1968.

65 **A history of the Vikings.**
Gwyn Jones. London: Oxford University Press, 1968. 504p. maps. bibliog.
A scholarly and well-documented account of the emergence, development, civilization and culture of the Vikings and their achievements at home and overseas, with special reference to the period 780-1070 AD. The work includes an excellent select bibliography.

66 **The Norse-Atlantic saga; being the Norse voyages of discovery and settlement to Iceland, Greenland, America.**
Gwyn Jones. London: Oxford University Press, 1964. 246p. maps.
This work deals with the Norsemen's search for new land westward across the Atlantic Ocean and their discoveries in Iceland, Greenland and the east coast of North America.

67 **A history of the Vikings.**
T. D. Kendrick. London: Cass, 1968. 412p. maps. bibliog.
Viking settlements in the Faroes, Iceland, Greenland and North America are covered in this scholarly history.

68 **Viking Expansion westwards.**
Magnus Magnusson. London: Bodley Head, 1973. 152p. map. bibliog.
A popular and well-illustrated account of Viking activity in Britain, Ireland, the Faroes, Iceland, Greenland and North America (Vinland).

69 **The Vinland sagas; the Norse discovery of America. Graelendinga saga and Erik's saga.**
Translated by Magnus Magnusson, Hermann Palsson. Harmondsworth, England: Penguin Books, 1968. 124p. maps.
An annotated translation of two mediaeval Icelandic sagas telling of the founding of a colony on the west coast of Greenland by Eric the Red and of subsequent voyages to the shores of the New World.

70 The conquest of the North Atlantic.

G. J. Marcus. Woodbridge, England: Boydell Press, 1980. 224p. maps. bibliog.

This scholarly work assesses the voyages of the Irish monks to Iceland followed by the journeys of the Norsemen to Greenland and America. New light is also cast on the earliest phases of English maritime expansion and the rediscovery of the New World in the 15th century.

71 Westviking; the ancient Norse in Greenland and North America.

Farley Mowat. Boston, Massachusetts: Little, Brown; London: Secker & Warburg, 1966. 494p. maps.

A reconstruction of the Norse voyages from 960 to 1010 AD. The author commences with a straight chronological account based on the original saga. An epilogue shows the unbroken continuity of westward voyaging from the cessation of the Norse voyages to the beginning of modern times. In a series of analytical appendixes the author deals with the technicalities of his research, e.g. sources, past climate and former sea levels, Norse geographical concepts, Norse ships and navigation. The book concludes with a chronology of western voyages.

72 In northern mists; Arctic exploration in early times. Vols. 1 and 2.

Fridtjof Nansen. London: Heinemann, 1911. 2 vols.

These two volumes by the famous Norwegian oceanographer and polar explorer represent a seminal work in this field. They cover the Norse voyages and settlements, and the discoveries by the Portuguese and John Cabot in Newfoundland and southern Labrador.

73 Early voyages and northern approaches 1000-1632.

Tryggvi J. Oleson. Toronto: McClelland & Stewart; London: Oxford University Press, 1964. 211p. map. bibliog.

A history of pre-Columbian voyages to North America which submits evidence of some cultural intermixing of peoples from Iceland with the peoples of Dorset in what is now the Canadian Arctic.

74 Atlantic crossings before Columbus.

Frederick J. Pohl. New York: W. W. Norton, 1961. 315p. bibliog.

An investigation of: the early Irish and Viking voyages to North America; the highly speculative voyage made by the Venetian brothers Nicolò and Antonio Zeno to Iceland and Greenland in 1380-87; and the Kensington runestone, the supposed relic of a 14th-century Scandinavian expedition to North America.

75 Prince Henry Sinclair; his expedition to the New World in 1398.

Frederick J. Pohl. London: David-Poynter, 1974. 230p. maps. bibliog.

An attempt to demonstrate that an expedition from the Orkney Islands led by this local chieftain, made a landfall in Newfoundland and Nova Scotia in 1398-99, nearly a century before the discoveries of Columbus. The Nicolò Zeno papers with which this story originated are viewed with suspicion by many historians.

76 **North America from earliest discovery to first settlement; the Norse voyages to 1612.**
David B. Quinn. New York: Harper & Row, 1977. 621p. maps. bibliog.

A scholarly and balanced account of the discovery, early exploration, economic exploitation and settlement of North America by Europeans. An extensive critical bibliography is appended.

77 **Northern mists.**
Carl O. Sauer. Berkeley, California: University of California; Cambridge, England: Cambridge University Press, 1968. 204p. maps. bibliog.

The early voyages into the North Atlantic extending as far as North America, before the time of Columbus, form the subject-matter of this work.

78 **The Vinland map and the Tartar relation.**
R. A. Skelton, Thomas E. Marston, George D. Painter. New Haven, Connecticut; London: Yale University Press, 1965. 291p. maps. bibliog.

Part of this book is devoted to a discussion of a mediaeval world map, supposedly the earliest known cartographic representation of the North American mainland. Though the map itself was subsequently shown to be a forgery the expert discussion makes a valuable contribution to the study of pre-Columbian discoveries in the North Atlantic.

79 **Norsemen before Colombus [*sic*]; early American history.**
J. Kr. Tornöe. London: Allen & Unwin, 1965. 127p. maps. bibliog. (North Atlantic Library, no. 2).

An interpretation of the Norse sagas relating to the North American discoveries of Bjarne Herjulfsson, Leiv Eiriksson, Thorvald Eiriksson and Thorfinn Karlsefne, with a chapter devoted to the construction and speed of Viking ships.

80 **The Vikings and their origins.**
David M. Wilson. London: Thames & Hudson, 1980. 96p. maps. bibliog.

Based on archaeological evidence, this is a well-illustrated introduction to the subject. Chapter 3 contains an account of the Viking discoveries in the Atlantic – Iceland, Greenland and finally America itself – between 870 and 985 AD.

Vinland voyage.
See item no. 581.

High latitude crossing; the Viking route to America.
See item no. 588.

The Brendan voyage.
See item no. 603.

Portuguese voyages

81 **Four centuries of Portuguese expansion, 1415-1825: a succinct survey.**
C. R. Boxer. Johannesburg: Witwatersrand University Press, 1961. 102p. map. bibliog.
Reproduces four public lectures delivered by the author as visiting professor to the Ernest Oppenheimer Institute of Portuguese Studies in 1960 to commemorate the 500th anniversary of the death of the Infante Dom Henrique (Henry the Navigator) and the overseas expansion of Europe which began in his day. Chapter 4 is devoted to Portuguese colonization of Brazil which dates from the 1530s and whose 'golden age' was the 18th century.

82 **The Portuguese seaborne empire 1415-1825.**
C. R. Boxer. London: Hutchinson, 1969. 426p. maps. bibliog.
An authoritative history to which is added an account of Portugal's South Atlantic trade with Brazil.

83 **The discovery of the Atlantic.**
Costa Brochado. Lisbon: Commissão Executiva dos Comemorações do Quinto Centenario da Morte do Infante D. Henrique, 1960. 127p. map.
The part played by Portuguese navigators in the opening up of the Atlantic in the 15th century is discussed, and the work ends with a chapter on Portuguese participation in the crossing of the Atlantic by aircraft in the present century.

84 **Le Portugal et l'Atlantique au XVIIe siècle (1570-1670); étude économique.** (Portugal and the Atlantic in the 17th century (1570-1670); an economic study.)
Frédéric Mauro. Paris: École Pratique des Hautes Etudes, SEVPEN, 1960. 550p. maps. bibliog.
An economic analysis of the development of the Portuguese Atlantic empire.

85 **Portuguese voyages to America in the fifteenth century.**
Samuel Eliot Morison. Cambridge, Massachusetts: Harvard University Press, 1940. 151p. maps.
A useful appendix to this history is the chronological list of Portuguese and other voyages to, or towards, America between 1447 and 1500.

86   **A history of the Portuguese discoveries.**
Damião Peres. Lisbon: Comissão Executiva das Comemorações
do Quinto Centenário da Morte do Infante D. Henrique, 1960.
129p.
An outline history of Atlantic discoveries from the time of Henry the Navigator in
the 15th century, and including the central and south Atlantic islands.

87   **Prince Henry the Navigator.**
John Ure. London: Constable, 1977. 207p. maps. bibliog.
This well-research biography casts new light on some aspects of the character of
this 15th-century promoter of exploratory voyages.

Spanish voyages

88   **The explorers of South America.**
Edward J. Goodman. New York: Macmillan; London: Collier-
Macmillan, 1972. 408p. bibliog.
Part 1 of this book which deals with discovery and conquest, serves as a useful
introduction to the early discoveries.

89   **The Spanish conquistadores.**
F. A. Kirkpatrick. London: Adam & Charles Black, 1946. 2nd ed.
367p. maps.
A useful introduction to the history of the Spanish conquests in the Americas
based on the works of Spanish-American historians.

90   **The Spanish seaborne empire.**
John Horace Parry. Harmondsworth, England: Penguin Books,
1973. 438p. maps. bibliog. (Pelican Books).
An authoritative summary of the growth of the Spanish kingdoms in the Americas
and the interaction between these kingdoms and metropolitan Spain from the late
15th century to the early 19th century.

91   **Enterprise and adventure; the Genoese in Seville and the opening
of the New World.**
Ruth Pike. Ithaca, New York: Cornell University Press, 1966.
243p. bibliog.
An account of the commercial and financial role played by the Genoese merchant
colony of Seville in Spanish overseas expansion during the 16th century.

92 **The battle of the Atlantic, 1500-1700.**
Geoffrey W. Symcox. In: *First images of America; the impact of the New World on the old.* Edited by Fredi Chiappelli. Berkeley, California: University of California Press, 1976. vol. 1, p. 265-84.

This paper traces the manner in which the Iberian monopoly of sea power in the Atlantic was broken by the French, Dutch and British and how the New World, by the end of the 17th century, had come to be integrated with the Old World both politically and commercially.

93 **Amerigo and the New World; the life and times of Amerigo Vespucci.**
Germán Arciniegas. New York: Farrar, Straus & Giroux, 1978. 329p. maps. bibliog. (Octagon Books)

A life of the Florentine explorer and navigator whose name is given to the American continents. He led several expeditions across the Atlantic on one of which, sponsored by Portugal, he voyaged along the coast of South America and discovered the Rio de la Plata (1501-02). The author is one of Colombia's most distinguished historians and elder statesmen. This is a reprint of a translation of the Spanish language original published in 1955.

94 **The letters of Amerigo Vespucci and other documents illustrative of his career.**
Translated with notes and an introduction by Clement R. Markham. London: Hakluyt Society, 1894. 121p. (Hakluyt Society first series, no. 90).

Amerigo Vespucci took part in several early voyages to the New World, in 1497, 1499, 1501 and 1503. He claimed to have accompanied Alonso de Ojeda's (1465?-1515) expedition of 1499-1500 which first discovered the northeastern coast of South America. In his last two voyages, 1505-07 he explored Darien.

95 **Amerigo Vespucci, pilot major.**
Frederick J. Pohl. New York: Columbia University Press, 1944. 249p. maps. bibliog.

A reappraisal of Vespucci's achievements based on a repudiation of the so-called 'Soderini letter' (1504) a prime source for a relation of his voyages.

96 **Christopher Columbus.**
Ernle Bradford. London: Michael Joseph, 1973. 286p. maps. bibliog.

A well-illustrated popular life of the explorer whose three transatlantic voyages in 1492-93, 1493-94 and 1498-1500 changed the course of European history.

97 **Columbus divides the world.**
Arthur Davies. *Geographical Journal*, vol. 133, part 3 (Sept. 1967), p. 337-44.

The author considers some of the consequences, both for Colombus and for geography, of the Treaty of Tordesillas of June 1494 between Spain and Portugal. By this treaty the two nations divided the non-Christian world into two zones of influence, giving the entire New World and Africa to Spain and India to Portugal.

98 **The journal of Christopher Columbus.**
Translated by Cecil Jane, revised and annotated by L. A. Vigneras with an appendix by R. A. Skelton. London: Blond & Orion Press, 1960. 227p. maps. bibliog.

This finely illustrated and carefully edited edition contains the only surviving text of Columbus' log-book of his first voyage, edited originally by Bartolomé de las Casas, possibly from a copy of the original (both of which have disappeared). Also included is the letter from Columbus dated 15 February 1493 giving a condensed account of the voyage. R. A. Skelton contributes an appendix entitled 'The cartography of Columbus' first voyage'.

99 **Admiral of the ocean sea; a life of Christopher Columbus. Vols. 1 and 2.**
Samuel Eliot Morison. Boston, Massachusetts: Little, Brown, 1942. 2 vols. map.

A vivid account of Columbus's four voyages written in the light of the author's expedition in a chartered yawl along the line of the Windward and Leeward Islands, 1939-40.

100 **Christopher Columbus: the journal of his first voyage to America.**
Introduction by Van Wyck Brooks. London: Jarrolds, [1925?]. 215p.

An annotated translation of the journal account of Columbus' first voyage of 1492-93.

English voyages

General

101 **Drake's voyages; a re-assessment of their place in Elizabethan maritime expansion.**
Kenneth R. Andrews. London: Weidenfeld & Nicolson, 1967. 190p.

The author offers a new interpretation of Drake's voyages. He sees Drake, in the context of the Elizabethan age, as a great corsair rather than a great admiral, for the characteristic of English sea power then was privateering, the royal navy being not yet distinct from the general sea forces of the nation.

102 **Trade, plunder and settlement; maritime enterprise and the genesis of the British empire 1480-1630.**
Kenneth R. Andrews. Cambridge, England: Cambridge University Press, 1984. 394p. maps. bibliog. (Cambridge Paperback Library).

This early period of English overseas enterprise is reappraised in the light of modern research. In his introduction and epilogue the author reflects on the motives for English expansion and its results. By and large, English activity overseas was patchy and seemed more concerned with large-scale privateering or piracy under the cover of war, than with colonization. The latter became important only after the Civil War.

103 **The westward enterprise; English activities in Ireland, the Atlantic and America 1480-1650.**
Edited by K. R. Andrews, N. P. Canny, P. E. H. Hair. Liverpool, England: Liverpool University Press, 1978. 326p. maps. bibliog.

A collection of essays written in honour of the historian David Quinn reflecting his interest in the history of early English exploration and settlement in the New World. Most of the essays are concerned with North America, and with English ideas or endeavours. The volume concludes with a bibliography of the works of David Quinn.

104 **Britain and the western seaways.**
E. G. Bowen. London: Thames & Hudson, 1972. 196p. maps. bibliog. (Ancient Peoples and Places, vol. 80).

A cultural history of the peoples of the 'Atlantic ends of Europe' from Iceland to Spain linked by the natural highway of the sea.

105 **The Mayflower.**
Kate Caffrey. London: Andre Deutsch, 1975. 392p. maps.
bibliog.
An account of the historic vessel and the events leading up to her voyage across
the Atlantic and the foundation of Plymouth plantation in December 1620.
Appendixes include the ship's passenger list and other documents. This is a well-
researched and readable account based principally on Governor William Bradford's
journal *Of Plymouth plantation.*

106 **England and the discovery of America 1481-1620. From the
Bristol voyages of the fifteenth century to the Pilgrim settlement
at Plymouth: the exploitation, and trial-and-error colonization of
North America by the English.**
David Beers Quinn. London: Allen & Unwin, 1974. 516p. maps.
bibliog.
The author seeks to demonstrate that England had a more active and positive role
in the exploration, discovery and exploitation of the Atlantic in the 15th century
than is usually recognized.

107 **The age of Drake.**
James A. Williamson. London: Adam & Charles Black, 1965.
5th ed. 400p. maps.
An introductory textbook by a scholar in this field describing the course of
British overseas expansion during the reign of Elizabeth I.

108 **The Cabot voyages and Bristol discovery under Henry VII.**
James A. Williamson. Cambridge, England: Cambridge
University Press for the Hakluyt Society, 1962. 332p. maps.
bibliog. (Hakluyt Society Second Series, no. 120).
The introductory essay in this collection 'Knowledge of the Atlantic in the
fifteenth century' and the supplementary chapter by R. A. Skelton 'The cartography of the voyages' are of special relevance. The book also includes several
reproductions of early maps depicting the North Atlantic Ocean.

Contemporary accounts

109 **The world encompassed by Sir Francis Drake, being his next voyage to that to Nombre de Dios collated with an unpublished manuscript of Francis Fletcher, chaplain to the expedition.**
Francis Fletcher, introduction by W. S. W. Vaux. London: Hakluyt Society, 1854. 295p. (Hakluyt Society first series, no. 16).

An account of Sir Francis Drake's circumnavigation of 1577-80 compiled by his nephew fifty years later, chiefly from notes and recollections of the expedition's chaplain Francis Fletcher, and other contemporaries. Drake was not only the first captain ever to sail his own ship round the world, he was the first Englishman to sail the Pacific, the Indian Ocean and the South Atlantic.

110 **The voyages and colonising enterprises of Sir Humphrey Gilbert. Vols. I and II.**
Introduction and notes by D. B. Quinn. London: Hakluyt Society, 1940. 2 vols. maps. (Hakluyt Society second series, no. 83-84).

Gilbert led two colonising expeditions to the New World; that of 1577-79 failed and got no further than the Cape Verde Islands; but the second in 1583 succeeded in establishing the first British colony in North America at St. John's, Newfoundland.

111 **Virginia voyages from Hakluyt.**
Edited by David Beers Quinn, Alison M. Quinn. London: Oxford University Press, 1973. 175p. map. bibliog.

Fifteen extracts from Richard Hakluyt's *The principal navigations . . . of the English nation* (1st ed. 1589) relating to the voyages to Virginia in 1584-90, with annotations. Hakluyt regarded these narratives not only as historical documents but also as guides and an inspiration to future transatlantic explorers and planters.

112 **Richard Hakluyt and the English voyages.**
George Bruner Parks. New York: American Geographical Society, 1928. 290p. maps. bibliog. (American Geographical Society Special Publication, no. 10).

A biography of Richard Hakluyt and his connexion with the Elizabethan voyagers evoking the intellectual atmosphere in which ideas of colonization developed.

113 **The discovery of the large, rich and beautiful empire of Guiana
with a relation of the great and golden city of Manoa (which the
Spaniards call El Dorado) etc., performed in the year 1595 by
Sir W. Raleigh, knt.**
Edited by Sir Robert H. Schoonburk. London: Hakluyt Society,
1848. 240p. map. (Hakluyt Society first series, no. 3).
A reprint of the edition of 1596. An expedition in search of gold in the fabled
mines of El Dorado this remains one of the finest narratives of Elizabethan
adventure.

114 **Narratives of voyages towards the north-west in search of a
passage to Cathay and India 1496 to 1631.**
Thomas Rundall. London: Hakluyt Society, 1849. 259p. maps.
This compilation includes documented accounts of the voyages of: Sebastian
Cabot (1496); Sir Martin Frobisher (1576-81); John Davis (1585-87); Henry
Hudson (1610); Robert Bylot and William Baffin (1615-16); and others.

Dutch voyages

115 **The Dutch seaborne empire 1600-1800.**
C. R. Boxer. London: Hutchinson, 1972. 326p. maps. bibliog.
A thematic history of the rise of Dutch sea power to its final decay in the last
quarter of the 18th century.

116 **The Netherlands in the seventeenth century: part I 1609-1648;
part 2 1648-1715.**
Pieter Geyl. London: Ernest Benn; New York: Barnes & Noble,
1961, 1964. 2 vols. maps. bibliog.
A revised and enlarged edition of the author's *The Netherlands divided*. London:
Williams & Norgate, 1936. This authoritative history is a basic starting point for
an understanding of the motivation of Dutch transatlantic enterprise in the 17th
century in Brazil, the West Indies and in North America.

117 **The Dutch Republic and the Hispanic world 1606-1661.**
Jonathan I. Israel. Oxford: Clarendon Press, 1982. 478p. maps.
bibliog.
A scholarly analysis of the struggle between the Dutch Republic and the Spanish
Empire during the years 1621-48 both in Europe and across the Atlantic in the
New World. This struggle, the author maintains, was a basic factor in Europe's
commercial, industrial and agricultural development. The book is based on
research carried out on national archives in the Netherlands, Belgium and Spain.

Economic history

General

118 **The rise of the Atlantic economies.**
Ralph Davis. London: Weidenfeld & Nicolson, 1973. 353p.
maps.
An economic history of Portugal, Spain, France, England and the Netherlands in
North and South America from the Portuguese discoveries in the 15th century to
the American declaration of independence. There is a very full and critical bibliography.

Migration and economic growth.
See item no. 151.

Migration and urban development.
See item no. 152.

Trade

119 **Sea lanes in wartime; the American experience 1775-1945.**
Robert Greenhalgh Albion, Jennie Barnes Pope. Archon Books
(W. W. Norton), 1968. 2nd ed. 386p. bibliog.
The first part of this work investigates shipping and trade between Europe and the
USA between 1775 and 1865, the period of the 'old wars', and the second part
deals with the two world wars concluding with shipping conditions in the North
Atlantic in 1942.

120 **European economic institutions and the New World; the
chartered companies.**
E. L. J. Courtenaert. In: *The Cambridge economic history of
Europe vol. IV. The economy of expanding Europe in the
sixteenth and seventeenth centuries.* Edited by E. E. Rich,
C. H. Wilson. Cambridge, England: Cambridge University Press,
1967, p. 220-74. bibliog.
A review of Spanish, Portuguese, English and French mercantile expansion from
the 15th to the 18th century.

121 **The North Atlantic world in the seventeenth century.**
K. G. Davies. Minneapolis, Minnesota: University of Minnesota
Press; London: Oxford University Press, 1974. 366p. maps.
bibliog.
An account of how the Atlantic Ocean became transformed into a European
trading lake during the 17th century. A critical bibliography is appended.

122 **The trade makers; Elder Dempster in West Africa.**
P. N. Davies. London: Allen & Unwin, 1973. 526p. maps.
bibliog.
A carefully researched and well-documented history of the Elder Dempster
Shipping Company from its origins in 1852. The account is set against the background of the development of British West Africa which the company did much
to stimulate and expand. A full bibliography of published and unpublished
sources is appended.

123 **The northern seas; shipping and commerce in northern Europe
A.D. 300-1100.**
Archibald R. Lewis. Princeton, New Jersey: Princeton
University Press, 1958. 498p. maps. bibliog.
This work studies the development of trade in the countries bordering on the
Bay of Biscay, the Irish Sea, the English Channel, the North Sea and the Baltic.

124 **Crops and livestock.**
G. B. Masefield. In: *The Cambridge economic history of Europe
vol. IV. The economy of expanding Europe in the sixteenth and
seventeenth centuries.* Edited by E. E. Rich, C. H. Wilson.
Cambridge, England: Cambridge University Press, 1967,
p. 275-301. bibliog.
The first transferences of European crops and livestock overseas were to the
Atlantic islands such as Madeira and the Canaries. This chapter reviews the
development of the movement of crops and livestock between the Americas,
Europe and Africa in the 16th and 17th centuries.

125 **The European fisheries in early modern history.**
A. R. Michell. In: *The Cambridge economic history of Europe.*
Vol. V. The economic organization of early modern Europe.
Edited by E. E. Rich, C. H. Wilson. Cambridge, England:
Cambridge University Press, 1977, p. 133-84. maps. bibliog.
(p. 644-45).
A review of the European fishing industry and fish trade, and the general fortunes
of the cod, herring and whaling industries in the 16th-18th centuries. The author
emphasizes the long-distance trade in fish, pointing out that the fisheries were an
important part of the international economy during this period providing outlying
parts of Europe and America with produce to exchange for manufactures and
imported food and drink.

126 **Transport and trade routes.**
John Horace Parry. In: *The Cambridge economic history of*
Europe. Vol. IV. The economy of expanding Europe in the
sixteenth and seventeenth centuries. Edited by E. E. Rich,
C. H. Wilson. Cambridge, England: Cambridge University Press,
1967, p. 155-219. bibliog. (p. 595-97).
Two sections in this chapter relate to the Atlantic trade. The first, 'The trades of
the Atlantic coasts', shows that 16th-century European trade was by no means
polarised between the Mediterranean and the Baltic but included an active and
prosperous trade along the whole stretch of coastline from Seville to Rotterdam.
At first dominated by Spain and Portugal, by the end of the 17th century the
English had begun to overhaul these countries, especially in the Mediterranean.
A section entitled 'The ocean trades' reviews, *inter alia*, the expansion of transatlantic trade during the 16th and 17th centuries and compares the performances
of Spain, Portugal, England, Holland and France.

127 **English overseas trade in the centuries of emergence; studies in**
some modern origins of the English-speaking world.
G. D. Ramsay. London: Macmillan, 1957. 279p. bibliog.
Chapter 7 'The British Atlantic community' provides a useful synthesis of the
history of trade between Britain and colonial North America.

128 **Studies in British overseas trade 1870-1914.**
S. B. Saul. Liverpool, England: Liverpool University Press,
1960. 246p. bibliog.
A series of studies of particular aspects of the British external economy between
1870 and 1914. Chapter 7 'British trade with the Empire' deals specifically with
Canada, trade with whom has always been closely linked with the USA, three
economies which naturally integrated as an 'Atlantic Partnership'.

129 **Seville and the Atlantic: cycles in Spanish colonial trade.**
Robert S. Smith. *Journal of Economic History*, vol. 22 (1962),
p. 253-59.
This article provides a critical review of Huguette and Pierre Chaum's *Seville et
l'Atlantique (1504-1650)* (Paris: Armand Colin, 1955-60), a definitive history of
Spanish Atlantic trade based on material in the Archives of the Indies, Seville.

130 **Great maritime routes; an illustrated history.**
Bruno Tavernier, translated by Nicholas Fry. London:
Macdonald, 1972. 285p. maps.
A well-illustrated popular history of trade routes from antiquity to the age of the
container ship. Themes of special relevance to the economic history of the
Atlantic Ocean include the Viking routes, the Spanish gold and silver routes, the
slave trade routes and the emigration routes from Europe to the Americas from
the 16th century to the present time.

131 **The ocean in English history; being the Ford Lectures.**
James A. Williamson. Oxford, England: Clarendon Press, 1941.
208p.
In a series of seven lectures, the author explores English enterprise in the Atlantic
up to the threshold of the 19th century, with reference also to the Far East and
the Pacific. The final chapter, 'The oceanic factor in the shaping of modern
England', shows how after the Restoration of 1660 'national thought had
accepted the promotion of oceanic trade as one of the prime objects of English
policy'.

Convoy; the defence of sea trade 1890-1990.
See item no. 226.

Atlantic Quarterly.
See item no. 253.

**Securing the seas; the Soviet naval challenge and Western Alliance
options. An Atlantic Council policy study.**
See item no. 285.

Hints to exporters: Portugal, Madeira and the Azores.
See item no. 665.

**Atlantic islands; Madeira, the Azores and the Cape Verdes in
seventeenth-century commerce and navigation.**
See item no. 666.

Slave trade

132 **The Atlantic slave trade and British abolition.**
Roger Anstey. London: Macmillan, 1975. 456p. maps. bibliog.
A study of the slave trade as an economic phenomenon and an analysis of the philosophical, theological and political concepts that brought about its abolition in Britain.

133 **The Atlantic slave trade; a census.**
Philip D. Curtin. Madison, Wisconsin: University of Wisconsin Press, 1969. 338p. map. bibliog.
A thorough investigation of the numbers of slaves brought across the Atlantic over the centuries, the parts of Africa from which they came and the destinations in the New World to which they were consigned.

134 **Black mother; Africa and the Atlantic slave trade.**
Basil Davidson. Harmondsworth, England: Penguin Books, 1980. rev. ed. 304p. maps. bibliog.
In this book the author takes a fresh look at the 500 year-old slave trade whereby African labour was exported by Europeans to the West Indies and the Americas. The author pays particular attention to the consequence of the trade for Africa itself. The book begins with a consideration of affairs in Africa before the slave trade got into its stride and how far leading states in Africa differed from contemporary states in Europe. Subsequent sections deal with the course, growth and ending of the trade.

135 **Slave ships and slaving.**
George Francis Dow. New York: Dover Publications, 1970. 349p.
A new edition of this history first published in 1927. Sir John Hawkins was the first Englishman to involve himself in the Atlantic slave trade in the year 1562, transporting slaves from the Guinea coast of West Africa to America. His voyage brought great profit and led to a long succession of similar ventures. The chapters in this book constitute a vivid history of the trade mainly in the form of excerpts from contemporary personal accounts.

136 **The United States and Africa; a history.**
Peter Duignan, L. H. Gann. Cambridge, England: Cambridge University Press and Hoover Institution, 1984. 450p. maps. bibliog.
A broad picture, by two senior fellows of the Hoover Institution, of US activity in the African continent concentrating on the essentially American aspect of African affairs. Part 1 of the book deals with aspects of the transatlantic slave trade, the US Navy and the antislavery campaign, and the effects of the trade in Africa and the USA. Subsequent chapters cover the United States' political, social, economic and scientific interests in the continent up till the present time.

137 **The abolition of the Atlantic slave trade.**
Edited by David Eltis, James Walvin. Madison, Wisconsin:
University of Wisconsin Press, 1981. 314p. maps. bibliog.

A collection of fifteen essays focussing on the world impact of the abolition of
the slave trade. Their concern is mainly with the British slave trade and its
abolition, with some attention being given to the Danish, Dutch and French
experiences. The third section of this book is perhaps the most relevant to the
Atlantic trade examining as it does the operations of the illegal slave trade with
America in the early 19th century. A map on p. 178 shows the regions involved in
the period after 1820.

138 **The British trans-Atlantic slave trade after 1807.**
David Eltis. *Maritime History*, vol. 4, no. 1 (1974), p. 1-11.
bibliog.

The author examines the problems of curtailing the illicit British slave trade after
its official abolition.

139 **The Atlantic slave trade and black Africa.**
P. E. H. Hair. London: Historical Association, 1978. 36p. map.
bibliog. (Historical Association Pamphlet General Series, no. 93).

A brief investigation of the economic and social rationale of the African Atlantic
slave trade from the 15th to the 19th centuries. A critical selective bibliography is
appended.

140 **Colonial settlement and its labour problems.**
E. E. Rich. In: *The Cambridge economic history of Europe
vol. IV. The economy of expanding Europe in the sixteenth and
seventeenth centuries.* Edited by E. E. Rich, C. H. Wilson.
Cambridge, England: Cambridge University Press, 1967,
p. 302-73. bibliog.

This chapter deals with the origins of the Atlantic slave trade which had its roots
in Portugal 'a slave-owning country before she became a colonial power'. This
system is contrasted with the solution to the labour shortage problems in the
North American colonies where immigration was encouraged through the
provision of land grants.

St. Helena 1502-1938.
See item no. 733.

Piracy

141 **Pirates of the western seas.**
A. G. Course. London: Frederick Muller, 1969. 213p. map. bibliog.

An account of pirates and privateers in the North Atlantic, the Caribbean and the Gulf of Mexico. Fairly typical of these pirates were the Welshman, Henry Morgan, operating from Cuba and the West Indies in the 1660s, and the notorious Edward Teach, known as 'Bluebeard', who plundered shipping off the Carolinas in the reign of Queen Anne. The West coast of Africa concealed numerous nests of pirates during this period. Piracy in the Atlantic finally petered out in the middle of the 19th century.

142 **The history of piracy.**
Philip Gosse. London: Cassell, 1954. 349p. bibliog.

A broad outline history but with chapters relating to piracy in the Caribbean as well as off the coasts of North America and West Africa. The first serious threat to Atlantic commerce came in the early 17th century from the notorious pirates of the Barbary coast of North Africa who, having learned the art of constructing square-rigged sailing vessels, were enabled to menace shipping and ports as far away as the British Isles.

Trade, plunder and settlement; maritime enterprise and the genesis of the British empire 1480-1630.
See item no. 102.

Social history & migration

143 **The brain drain.**
Edited by Walter Adams. New York: Macmillan; London: Collier-Macmillan, 1968. 273p.

Reproduces papers presented at an international conference on the 'brain drain' at Lausanne, Switzerland, in August 1967. Though there is nothing new about the migration of talent there have been accusations of a transatlantic drain from Europe to North America. The object of the conference was to analyse the problem in an effort to arrive at a balanced interpretation of the phenomenon.

144 **North Atlantic maritime cultures; anthropological essays on changing adaptations.**
Edited by Raoul Anderson. The Hague: Mouton, 1979. 365p.

The proceedings of the 9th International Congress of Anthropological and Ethno-logical Science, a symposium of social scientists active in the study of maritime societies bordering the North Atlantic. The contributions cover the historical, contemporary and cultural adaptations of fishing people in eastern Canada, Sweden, Portugal.

145 **Passage to America; a history of emigrants from Great Britain and Ireland to America in the mid-nineteenth century.**
Terry Coleman. London: Hutchinson, 1972. 317p. bibliog.

The story of the transatlantic emigrants between 1846 and 1855, who they were, why and how they left home, and what happened to them.

146 **The great migration; crossing the Atlantic under sail.**
Basil Greenhill. London: HM Stationery Office, 1968. 31p.
maps. (National Maritime Museum).

A popular, largely pictorial, account by a former Director of the National Maritime Museum, Greenwich, of the 'Great Migration'; the populating of North America from Britain and Europe during the 19th century which is one of the most important human migrations in history. This booklet conveys an impression of what happened and of what it was like to be an emigrant travelling by sailing ship from Britain to North America at that time. References are given to some other published accounts.

147 **The great migration; the Atlantic crossing by sailing ship since 1770.**
Edwin C. Guillet. Toronto: Thomas Nelson, 1937. 284p. bibliog.

The story of emigration from the British Isles to North America between 1770 and 1890 based on published and archival sources.

148 **The Atlantic migration 1607-1860; a history of the continuing settlement of the United States.**
Marcus Lee Hansen. Edited by Arthur M. Schlesinger.
Cambridge, Massachusetts: Harvard University Press, 1945. 391p.
map. bibliog.

An account of the great transatlantic migration of white people first to the thirteen colonies and then to the early Republic, down to the eve of the Civil War. It is the latter movement to which emphasis is given. The author describes the economic and social conditions in Europe which precipitated the migration rather than the story of the settlement of immigrants in the USA.

149 **Economics of migration.**
Julius Isaac. London: Kegan Paul, Trench, Trubner, 1947.
285p. bibliog.

An examination of the causes and effects of the great international migrations, which have taken place during the period 1814 to 1914. As the statistics make clear in Chapter 3, Section 4 entitled 'Volume of migration', 87% of the total volume of European emigrants crossed the Atlantic to the USA, Canada, Brazil and Argentina during this period.

150 **The distant magnet: European emigration to the U.S.A.**
Philip Taylor. London: Eyre & Spottiswoode, 1971. 326p.
bibliog.

Between 1830 and 1930 some 35 million Europeans emigrated to the United States. This volume examines the socioeconomic and political conditions which these people experienced in their home countries and explains the lure of the United States, a powerful magnet which continued to possess advantages that no other overseas land could rival. The work also considers the rigours of the voyage across the Atlantic and two chapters are particularly relevant: chapter 7 'The Journey Under Sail' and chapter 8 'The Journey by Steam'. This well-illustrated book contains a valuable bibliography.

151 **Migration and economic growth; a study of Great Britain and the Atlantic economy.**
Brinley Thomas. Cambridge, England: Cambridge University
Press, 1973. 2nd ed. 498p. bibliog.

In this highly sophisticated analysis of emigration cycles the author begins with the idea of an 'Atlantic Economy' which presupposes that British and American development was complementary and characterized by alternating decades of investment and migration. Thus, when British investment in the USA was rising so was emigration; when it fell migration fell. British capital exports to America went into railroads and indirectly into urban development. When the capital stayed in Britain it went into house building. This thesis is much disputed but this book is a valuable source for information and includes a bibliography on trans-atlantic migration.

152 **Migration and urban development; a reappraisal of British and American long cycles.**
Brinley Thomas. London: Methuen, 1972. 259p. bibliog.

The central issue of this book is the significance of the inverse relation between British and American long cycles in capital formation and the mechanism by which migration and capital movements influenced the course of urban development in the USA and Great Britain.

Transport history

Ships and shipping

153 The hey-day of the great Atlantic liners.
Rex Barratt. Redruth, England: Truran Publication, 1983. 69p.

A short history of the great liners which traversed the Atlantic before 1914. This half-century saw the emigration of thousands of Cornish men and women to the USA where mining and quarrying skills were in demand. This episode is dealt with in a chapter entitled 'The perilous sea' which also contains information on Atlantic liners which came to grief – many on Cornwall's rock-bound coasts.

154 North Atlantic seaway; an illustrated history of the passenger services linking the old world with the new. Vol. 1-3.
N. R. P. Bonsor. Newton Abbot, England: David & Charles, 1975, vol. 1, 867p.; Jersey, Channel Islands: Brookside Publications, 1978-79, vols. 2-3.

This revised and enlarged edition of the 1955 publication encompasses virtually the entire story of passenger travel by sea across the North Atlantic. In addition to the dates, dimensions and backgrounds of a vast number of ships, the work includes launching dates, steamship losses, and 270 scale drawings. The publication of vols. 4 and 5 is also planned.

155 A century of Atlantic travel 1830-1930.
Frank C. Bowen. London: Sampson Low, Marston: [n.d.] 374p.

An historical review of a century of transatlantic passenger liners and the shipping business, with illustrations of the star liners.

156 Fifty famous liners.
Frank O. Braynard, William H. Miller. Bar Hill, Cambridge, England: Patrick Stephens, 1982. 233p.

Provides brief illustrated histories of ocean liners from the *Great Eastern* to the *Queen Elizabeth II*. The arrangement is chronological with an account of the history of each ship, vital statistics, illustrations and some deck plans.

157 The sway of the grand saloon; a social history of the North Atlantic.
John Malcolm Brinnin. London: Macmillan, 1971. 599p. bibliog.

A comprehensive history of transatlantic passenger ships taking as a starting date the year 1818 marking the departure of the first scheduled Atlantic carrier, the *James Monroe*, from Boston, Massachusetts to Liverpool, England. The bias of the book is towards the human involvement and the day-to-day experiences of those who crossed the Atlantic rather than with economic and engineering aspects.

History. Transport history. Ships and shipping

158   Voyage of the iceberg; the story of the iceberg that sank the
       Titanic.
       Richard Brown.   Toronto: James Lorimer, 1983. 152p.

Recounts the story of the iceberg that sank the *Titanic* from the day it was calved
into Baffin Bay until 15 months later when it sank the liner in the North Atlantic.
The author, a marine biologist, is an experienced traveller both in the Arctic and
in North Atlantic waters.

159   The liners; a history of the North Atlantic crossing.
       Terry Coleman.   London: Allen Lane, Penguin Books, 1976.
       232p. bibliog.

A well-illustrated social history which begins with the maiden voyages of the
Cunard sister ships *Mauretania* and *Lusitania* in 1907, 'the first Atlantic liners in
which it was the invariable rule to dress for dinner in first class'. It ends with the
Queen Mary, now a floating museum at Long Beach, California, and the *Queen
Elizabeth II*, now essentially a cruise ship.

160   The geography of sea transport.
       A. D. Couper.   London: Hutchinson University Library, 1972.
       208p. bibliog.

The main theme of this book is the effect of technological change in sea transport
and its impact on the character and distribution of economic activities.

161   The rise of the English shipping industry in the seventeenth and
       eighteenth centuries.
       Ralph Davis.   Newton Abbot, England: David & Charles, 1972.
       427p. bibliog.

A history of the English shipping industry as a service industry carrying goods
and people by sea. Chapter 13 contains a discussion of the transatlantic freight
trade between England and the plantation colonies in North America during the
18th century, with some reference to the trade with the more self-sufficient
northerly settlements and to the English-operated slave trade. A chapter on
sources is appended together with notes on shipping statistics.

162   British transport; an economic survey from the seventeenth
       century to the twentieth.
       H. J. Dyos, D. H. Aldcroft.   Leicester, England: Leicester
       University Press, 1969. 473p. maps. bibliog.

A comprehensive account which covers aspects of the North Atlantic trade.

38

163 **The greatest iron ship *S. S. Great Eastern.***
George S. Emmerson. Newton Abbot, England: David & Charles, [n.d.]. 182p.

This work tells the story of Isambard Kingdom Brunel's (1769-1849) historic steamship and the part it played in the laying of the first Atlantic telegraph cable in 1865.

164 **Samuel Cunard; pioneer of the Atlantic steamship.**
Kay Grant. London: Abelard-Schuman, 1967. 192p. bibliog.

A life of Sir Samuel Cunard (1787-1865) who founded the first regular Atlantic steamship line. In 1839 he established the British and North America Royal Mail Steam Packet Company, better known as the Cunard Line.

165 ***Mary Celeste*; a centenary record.**
Macdonald Hastings. London: Michael Joseph, 1972. 174p. bibliog.

In 1867 the *Mary Celeste* left New York for Genoa and was discovered deserted off Gibraltar, her sails set, a half-eaten meal on the cabin table and obviously abandoned in a hurry. This is a history of that most famous and most baffling of Atlantic derelicts and her fateful last voyage.

166 **The book of shipwrecks.**
Kenneth Hudson, Ann Nicholls. London: Macmillan, 1979. 170p. maps. bibliog.

A well-illustrated record of wrecks selected from the period 2,500 BC to the present day. The arrangement is chronological with brief factual accounts of each wreck. Maps are appended showing coastal and off-shore wreck locations, each identified by a code number.

167 **The Blue Riband of the Atlantic.**
Tom Hughes. Cambridge, England: Patrick Stephens, 1973. 192p.

The story of the transatlantic steamship passenger services from the Cunard paddle steamer *Britannia* (1840) to the *United States* (1973). Appended is a list of record breaking passages and Blue Riband ships.

168 **Cunard and the North Atlantic; a history of shipping and financial management.**
Francis Edwin Hyde. London: Macmillan, 1975. 382p. bibliog.

Based on the Cunard company archives held by the University of Liverpool, this work provides a definitive full-scale history of the subject.

169 **A night to remember.**
Walter Lord. Harmondsworth, England: Penguin Books, 1981.
186p.
An account of the sinking of the *Titanic* in 1912. Reproduced is the White Star
Line's list of lost and saved. A hardback edition of this book was published by
Allen Lane (London) in 1976.

170 **The maiden voyage.**
Geoffrey Marcus. London: Allen & Unwin, 1969. 319p. map.
An account of the sinking of the *Titanic* and a critical inquiry into the causes of
the disaster.

171 **The North Atlantic run; 'The only way to cross'.**
John Maxtone-Graham. London: Cassell, 1972. 434p. bibliog.
A history of transatlantic liners from the *Mauretania* to the *Queen Elizabeth II*
which dominated the Atlantic from the turn of the century until after World
War II. This is very much a personal account rather than an attempt at a definitive
history. The author has selected his favourite ships which are principally those
which he feels have some historical significance. Much material has been
assembled from contemporary records and company archives as well as from
interviews with crew, passengers and shore staff.

172 **Transatlantic liners 1945-1980.**
William H. Miller. Newton Abbot, England: David & Charles;
New York: Arco, 1981. 222p.
The author provides details, histories and illustrations of liners arranged alpha-
betically by steamship lines.

173 **North Atlantic panorama 1900-1976.**
P. Ransome-Wallis. London: Ian Allan, 1977. 192p. bibliog.
This book describes and illustrates the development, during the 20th century, of
the North Atlantic passenger liner serving Europe and the eastern seabord of the
USA. The more important express lines are also detailed in chronological order.

174 **Transatlantic paddle steamers.**
H. Philip Spratt. Glasgow: Brown, Son & Ferguson, 1980.
2nd ed. 92p. bibliog.
A general and technical account of these vessels arranged chronologically with
illustrations. Appendixes give tabulated details of construction and dimensions,
machinery and service.

175 **The transatlantic mail.**
Frank Staff. London: Adlard Coles, 1956. 191p. bibliog.
Directed at postal historians and those interested in the development of sea
transport, this a comprehensive history of the mail services.

176 **The coracle guide to old ships, boats & maritime museums.**
Dick Sullivan. London: Coracle Books, 1978. 132p.

A list of maritime museums and old ships in the British Isles arranged by county, with notes on the principal objects of interest and their histories.

177 **Steam conquers the Atlantic.**
David Budlong Tyler. New York: Appleton-Century, 1939.
425p. bibliog.

The story of the substitution of steam for sail and of the consequent speeding-up of communications across the Atlantic. The book is based on contemporary sources.

178 **The Titanic; end of a dream.**
Wyn Craig Wade. London: Weidenfeld & Nicolson, 1979. 338p.
bibliog.

This account of the *Titanic* disaster on 14-15 April 1912 focuses on the American inquiry held immediately after the shipwreck and is based on published, archival and private sources, including survivors' accounts.

179 **Ocean ships.**
London: Ian Allan, 1982. 225p.

An illustrated listing of the fleets of numerous companies and covering passenger liners and cruise ships, cargo ships and tankers. The name of the compiler is not provided.

180 **The White Star triple-screw Atlantic liners *Olympic* and *Titanic*.**
London: Patrick Stephens, 1970. 164p. (Ocean liners of the past, no. 1).

A facsimile edition of the souvenir number of *The Shipbuilder* (1911) plus later extracts from this periodical dealing with the sinking of the *Titanic*. Sectional plans of the ships are included.

181 **The Cunard express liners *Lusitania* and *Mauretania*.**
London: Patrick Stephens, 1970. 208p. (Ocean liners of the past, no. 2).

A facsimile reprint from the special number of *The Shipbuilder* (1907). *Lusitania* was torpedoed by a German U-boat with great loss of life in the Irish Sea in May 1915 and her sinking was one of the factors responsible for America's participation in World War I. *Mauretania* gave years of valuable service on the North Atlantic route before being scrapped in 1935. Sectional plans are appended.

History. Transport history. Ships and shipping

182   The Cunard quadruple-screw Atlantic liner *Aquitania.*
      London: Patrick Stephens, 1971. 176p. (Ocean liners of the
      past, no. 3).
A facsimile reprint from *The Shipbuilder* (June 1914). Sectional plans of the ship
are included.

183   The Cunard White Star quadruple-screw North Atlantic liner
      Queen Mary.
      London: Patrick Stephens, 1972. 90p. (Ocean liners of the past,
      no. 6).
A facsimile of a special souvenir number of *The Shipbuilder and Marine Engine-
Builder* (June 1936). The liner *Queen Mary* 'has evoked more British and
American sentiment [than any other vessel] since the *Mayflower* of 1620'.
Sectional plans of the ship are appended.

Norsemen before Colombus [*sic.*]: early American history.
See item no. 79.

Sea lanes in wartime; the American experience 1775-1945.
See item no. 119.

Sea power.
See item no. 209.

The International Ice Patrol.
See item no. 463.

Trans-ocean rowing boats and Portuguese working craft; major
collections at Exeter Maritime Museum.
See item no. 628.

Canary Islands shipping handbook 1983/84.
See item no. 709.

The Great Britain.
See item no. 793.

The postal service of the Falkland Islands including South Shetlands
(1906-1931) and South Georgia.
See item no. 800.

Aircraft and aviation

184 **Airship; the story of R.34 and the first east-west crossing
of the Atlantic by air.**
Patrick Abbott. Bath, England: Adams & Dart, 1975. 163p.
map. bibliog. (Juniper Books)

The journey from East Fortune in Scotland to New York was accomplished in
108 hours and 12 minutes, from 2nd to 13th of July 1919, thus creating a world
record for endurance.

185 **Our transatlantic flight.**
Sir John Alcock, Sir Arthur Whitten Brown. London: William
Kimber, 1969. 195p.

An account of the first non-stop flight across the Atlantic 14-15 June 1919 by a
British crew in a Vickers Vimy aircraft. Appended is an account of an unsuccessful
attempt a few weeks earlier by Harry Hawker and K. M. Grieve.

186 **Amy Johnson.**
Constance Babington Smith. London: White Lion Publishers,
1967. 384p. map.

A well-researched biography of this pioneer British woman aviator, the first to fly
solo from England to Australia. As pilot to her husband Jim Mollison she crossed
the Atlantic in 1933.

187 **The history of airships.**
Basil Clarke. London: Herbert Jenkins, 1961. 194p. bibliog.

A broad treatment of this rather sparsely recorded aspect of aviation history
from the 18th-century experiments with balloons by the Montgolfier brothers
onwards. Chapter 11 is devoted to an account of the first transatlantic airship
flight, that of the British dirigible *R.34* in July 1919, and subsequent chapters
recall the commercially successful Atlantic crossings of the German airship *Graf
Zeppelin* and *Hindenburg.* The disastrous flight of the latter in May 1937 put
paid to any future developments in this direction.

188 **Atlantic adventure; a complete history of transatlantic flight.**
Basil Clarke. London: Allan Wingate, 1958. 236p.

This history of transatlantic aviation includes good summaries of all the famous
North Atlantic 'firsts' between the two world wars from Alcock and Brown to
Amelia Earhart and Charles Lindbergh. A short chapter is devoted to airship flights
ending with the *Hindenburg* disaster of 1937. A chapter outlining early South
Atlantic flights is followed by an account of the development of commercial
aviation, with a later chapter on postwar commercial services. The book is
rounded off with chapters covering World War II and flying the Atlantic from the
passengers' viewpoint.

189 *Zanussi*: **transatlantic balloon.**
Christopher Davey, Don Cameron. Jersey, Channel Islands:
Sponsorship Promotions, 1982. 180p. map.

An account of a British transatlantic balloon flight from Newfoundland to within
110 miles of the French coast at Brest in July 1978. A list of previous major
Atlantic balloon attempts since 1958 is included.

190 **Atlantic air conquest; the complete story of all North Atlantic
flights and attempts during the pioneer years from 1910 to 1940.**
F. H. Ellis, E. M. Ellis. London: William Kimber, 1963. 223p.

A history of transatlantic flight from Walter Wellman's unsuccessful attempt in
the airship *America* in 1910 to the advent of scheduled flights by national
airlines such as Pan-American Airways and Imperial Airways in the 1930s.

191 **Aviation; an historical survey from its origins to the end of
World War II.**
Charles Harvard Gibbs-Smith. London: HM Stationery Office,
1970. 316p. bibliog. (Science Museum Publication).

A useful introductory textbook with a chronological list of events and a full
bibliography. Chapters 16 and 17 are those most relevant to the history of transatlantic flight. They cover the first completed crossing in stages by US Lieutenant-
Commander A. C. Reid in May 1919, followed shortly after by the first non-stop
crossing by the Britishers Alcock and Brown in June, and leading on to the development of commercial passenger and freight services in the 1920s and 1930s.

192 **Britain's imperial air-routes 1918 to 1939; the story of Britain's
overseas airlines.**
Robin Higham. London: G. T. Foulis, 1960. 407p. bibliog.

Chapter 9 entitled 'Conquering the North Atlantic 1919-1939' deals with the
tardy development of this route by Great Britain.

193 **The long, lonely flight.**
Joe W. Kittinger, Jr. *National Geographic*, vol. 167, no. 2
(Feb. 1985), p. 270-76. map.

Colonel Kittinger's account of his flight in the balloon *Rosie O'Grady* from
Caribou, Maine, USA, to Cairo Montenotte, Italy, in September 1984. This was
the first solo transatlantic balloon flight and the longest ever made by a single
balloonist – 3,543 miles. The total time taken was 83 hours and 40 minutes.

194 **Double Eagle.**
Charles McCarry. London: W. H. Allen, 1980. 278p. map.

An account of the first successful crossing of the North Atlantic by the American
balloon *Double Eagle II* in August 1978. A previous attempt in 1977 by the same
crew, Ben Abruzzo, Maxie Anderson and Larry Newman, ended when their
balloon *Double Eagle* was forced into the sea off Iceland.

195 **Charles Lindbergh, a biography.**
Leonard Mosley. London: Hodder & Stoughton, 1976. 352p.
bibliog.
A very well documented biography of this controversial American pioneer aviator,
who in 1927 became the first person to fly the Atlantic solo.

196 **Ocean flying.**
Louise Sacchi. New York: McGraw-Hill, 1979. 230p.
An account of the author's practical flying experience gained after 333 crossings
of the Atlantic and Pacific oceans. Chapter 10 is entitled 'Route characteristics
of the North Atlantic'.

197 **The geography of air transport.**
Kenneth R. Sealy. London: Hutchinson University Library,
1966. 198p. bibliog.
A discussion of the technical and economic possibilities of commercial aviation,
and a consideration of actual or potential operations on many world air routes,
including those across the Atlantic.

198 **Annals of British and Commonwealth air transport 1919-1960.**
John Stroud. London: Putnam, 1962. 675p.
A full record of the main events of the first pioneering services across the Atlantic.

199 **Air Atlantic; a history of civil and military transatlantic flying.**
Alan Wykes. London: Hamish Hamilton, 1967. 210p. bibliog.
An account of transatlantic flights from Walter Wellman's (1858-1934) attempt
by airship in 1910 to the age of the jet aircraft.

**Aircraft versus submarine; the evolution of the anti-submarine aircraft
1912 to 1980.**
See item no. 243.

System

Communications

200 Telecommunications; a technology for change.
Eryl Davies. London: HM Stationery Office, 1983. 60p. map.
(Science Museum publication).

A history of telephone technology from the attempted laying of an Atlantic cable
in 1857 (unsuccessful) to the present-day fibre optic cables with a capacity of
4,000 channels each. Telecommunications via space satellites such as *Telstar*,
which passes over the Atlantic every 2½ hours, are also considered. Today there
are several *Intelsat* satellites in orbit giving coverage for television, high-capacity
speech and data channels thus greatly enhancing the quality and speed of transatlantic communications. This introductory booklet was published in connexion
with a telecommunications exhibition at the Science Museum, London.

201 The story of the Atlantic telegraph.
Henry M. Field. New York: Charles Scribner's 1893. 415p.

A full history of this remarkable achievement executed through the inspiration of
the US financier Cyrus W. Field and the British scientist Lord Kelvin. The first
Atlantic telegraph cable laid in 1857 was a failure; the first successful working
cable was laid in 1866.

202 Marconi.
W. P. Jolly. London: Constable, 1972. 292p.

A biography of Guglielmo Marconi, the world-famous pioneer of communications,
who first successfully transmitted wireless signals across the Atlantic on 12
December 1901. The transmitting station was sited at Poldhu, Cornwall, England,
the receiving station being at St. John's, Newfoundland. On 15 December 1902, a
commercial service was attempted and a regular service began in September 1907.

203 From semaphore to satellite.
Anthony R. Michaelis. Geneva: International Telecommunication
Union, 1965. 343p. maps. bibliog.

This popular illustrated volume was published on the occasion of the centenary of
the International Telecommunication Union. Essentially the theme of the book is
a century of successful progress in international cooperation in the field of telecommunications, but there is much concerning the history of transatlantic
communications including the historic wireless message which led to the arrest
of the murderer Dr. Crippen and his secretary after their flight from justice across
the Atlantic aboard the Canadian Pacific liner *Montrose* in July 1910.

204   **The North Atlantic telegraph via the Faeroe Isles, Iceland, and
      Greenland. Proceedings of the Royal Geographical Society of
      Great Britain, January 28th and February 11th, 1861 . . .**
      Royal Geographical Society. London: Edward Stanford, 1861.
      94p. maps.

The reports of an official survey expedition, under the command of Sir Leopold
McClintock, to ascertain the practicability of a northern route for a proposed
transatlantic telegraph.

205   **The Atlantic telegraph (1865).**
      W. H. Russell. Newton Abbot, England: David & Charles, 1972.
      117p.

A reprint of the first edition (1865) of this account of the laying of the Atlantic
telegraph cable in 1865 by the *Great Eastern*. The cable snapped on this occasion
but was completed the following year when the first successful transatlantic
telegraph cable was laid.

206   **Marconi and wireless.**
      R. N. Vyvyan. Wakefield, England: EP Publishing, 1974. 256p.

A reprint of the first edition published in 1933 by Routledge & Kegan Paul,
London, under the title *Wireless over thirty years*. The emphasis is placed on the
technological developments which made transatlantic wireless transmission,
pioneered by Marconi, a competitive rival to the cable companies.

**The physical geography of the sea and its meteorology, being a
reconstruction and enlargement of the eighth edition of 'The physical
geography of the sea'.**
See item no. 382.

Naval history

General

207   **Naval & maritime history; an annotated bibliography.**
      Robert Greenhalgh Albion. Newton Abbot, England: David &
      Charles, 1973. 4th ed. 370p.

Some 5,000 items are covered in this revised and expanded edition of a work first
issued in 1951. A most comprehensive work in its field, it ranges over the whole
of the relevant English language material, including dissertations as well as
published works.

208 **Empire of the North Atlantic; the maritime struggle for North America.**
Gerald S. Graham. Toronto: University of Toronto Press; London: Oxford University Press, 1958. 2nd ed. 338p. maps. bibliog.

This book is concerned chiefly with three centuries of European rivalry and overseas expansion whereby England, in competition first with Spain, then with Holland and finally with France, achieved command of North Atlantic sea power and commerce. This marks the completion of what Professor Graham regards as her 'first empire'. This supremacy, rudely shaken by the revolt of the North American colonies, led in the years after Trafalgar (1805) to the building of an even greater 'second empire' and to the period of relative peace and prosperity known as 'Pax Britannica'. This was ended by Britain's loss of absolute control over the seas, in particular the vital transatlantic trade routes, in the course of the two world wars.

209 **Sea power.**
Lord Hill-Norton, John Decker. London: Faber & Faber, 1982. 192p.

Based on a series of television documentary films this book explores concepts of British sea power as demonstrated by the instruments of that power – warships. These include battleships, aircraft carriers, gunboats, commando units, cruisers, destroyers and, perhaps most pertinent in the context of Atlantic warfare, the submarine.

210 **Naval warfare; an illustrated history.**
Edited by Richard Humble. London: Orbis Publishing, 1983. 304p. bibliog.

A lavishly illustrated account of the history of naval warfare covering the significant campaigns in naval history, the decisive battles in these campaigns and biographical sketches of the principal naval leaders involved. These accounts of battles are linked with introductions to each new era of naval evolution explaining the changes wrought in strategy and tactics by the development of new naval technology. The coverage is world-wide ranging from Salamis to the Falklands.

211 **Submarine command; a pictorial history.**
Reginald Longstaff. London: Robert Hale, 1984. 264p. bibliog.

An illustrated history of the submarines that dominated the North Atlantic in two world wars and continue to do so. Propelled by nuclear power and armed with atomic warheads they are now perceived in some respects as the ultimate weapon. This book traces the evolution of the submarine from the tiny Holland submersible in 1902 to the 'Hunter Killer' and *Polaris* submarines of the present day. The author describes their deployment in the two world wars and provides accounts of many of their engagements. Their weaponry and highly technical equipment are also discussed along with reference to the growth of the Soviet submarine fleet and the role of *Trident* in modern defence.

212 **The influence of sea power upon history 1660-1805.**
Alfred Thayer Mahan. London: Hamlyn, 1980. 255p. (Bison Books).

A lavishly illustrated reprint of this seminal work on naval strategy. The author's specific objective is to examine the effect of sea power on the histories of Europe and America. Mahan's thesis, which concludes with Britain's great sea victory over Napoleon at Trafalgar in 1805 has influenced strategists up to the present day and, as his editor points out, we still have much to learn from his writing. The remarkable Armada despatched across the Atlantic at the shortest notice to counter Argentina's invasion of the Falkland Islands in 1982 is a contemporary case in point.

213 **Seapower and politics from the Norman conquest to the present day.**
John Moore. London: Weidenfeld & Nicolson, 1979. 184p. bibliog.

'The aim of this book is to point out to the average citizen how the activities of politicians have affected the balance of seapower over the years and how some, realizing the value of the instrument which they have controlled have successfully utilized seapower for the benefit of their country's policies [author's introduction]'. In his concluding chapter Captain Moore questions whether Western politicians will have the wit to appreciate the role of seapower as it is taught by history, and the will and determination to re-erect this bulwark against an expanding USSR who will otherwise most certainly overwhelm them.

214 **Tide of empires; decisive naval campaigns in the rise of the West. Vol. 1, 1481-1654. Vol. 2, 1654-1763.**
Peter Padfield. London: Routledge & Kegan Paul, 1982. 2 vols. maps. bibliog.

An economic interpretation of naval history which is seen as part of the struggle for trade and markets.

215 **Sea power; a naval history.**
Edited by E. B. Potter, Chester W. Nimitz. London: Prentice-Hall International, 1960. 932p. maps. bibliog.

A history of the US Navy, of American naval power and of the world's navies. The authors also study the evolution of naval warfare and the part that sea power has played in the exercise of national power. *Sea power*, though a multi-author work, is much influenced by the professional analyses of Admiral Nimitz and by the writings of Alfred Thayer Mahan. Readers will find this volume valuable for its summary, from the American viewpoint, of the Battle of the Atlantic during World War II.

216 **Convoy; the defence of sea trade 1890-1990.**
John Winton. London: Michael Joseph, 1983. 378p. bibliog.
This well-researched book, by a retired naval officer, traces the history of the concept of the convoy and the part played by the convoy system in the Atlantic and other oceans during the two world wars. The theory has its opponents who advance the notion of 'defended sea lanes' as being more practicable in these times of limited naval resources. In his final chapter the author argues that a third world war is likely once more to centre on convoys and that we should plan for these.

Sea lanes in wartime; the American experience 1775-1945.
See item no. 119.

Naval lessons from the South Atlantic.
See item no. 829.

Malvinas: clave geopolítica. (Malvinas: geopolitical key.).
See item no. 872.

World War I

217 **Coronel and the Falklands.**
Geoffrey Bennett. London: Batsford, 1962. 191p. map. bibliog.
In November 1914 a British cruiser squadron was decisively beaten by the new-born German navy off the coast of Chile. The disaster was avenged six weeks later off the Falkland Islands with reinforcements from Scapa Flow. In this account the author has attempted the first comprehensive study of these battles since the official histories of World War 1.

218 **The enemy fought splendidly, being the 1914-1915 diary of the Battle of the Falklands & its aftermath.**
Thomas Benjamin Dixon. Poole, England: Blandford Press, 1983. 96p. maps. bibliog.
An eye-witness account of this famous battle in the South Atlantic, seen through the eyes of a young naval surgeon, during which his ship, HMS *Kent*, chased and sank the German battleship *Nürnberg* after a running battle lasting two and a half hours.

219 **A subject bibliography of the First World War: books in English 1914-1978.**
A. G. S. Enser. London: André Deutsch, 1979. 485p.
(A Grafton book).

This bibliography is aimed at the general reader and researcher. It omits pamphlet material, poetry, fiction, juvenilia, humour and the publications of the War Graves Commission. Information on Atlantic naval operations needs to be searched under a number of subject headings including, for example, the Falkland Islands, the Merchant Navy and submarines.

220 **The last voyage of the Lusitania.**
A. A. Hoehling, Mary Hoehling. London: Longmans, Green, 1957. 184p. bibliog.

The story of the fateful voyage of the Cunard liner *Lusitania* which sailed from New York on 1 May 1915 and was torpedoed off the Irish coast on 7 May by the German submarine *U 20* with the loss of some 1,200 lives, among them many Americans. Within two years the USA was herself projected into the European war and a new position of world leadership.

221 **The Great War at sea 1914-1918.**
Richard Hough. New York: Oxford University Press, 1983. 353p. maps. bibliog.

An up-to-date history of the part played by the Royal Navy in World War I. Chapter 8 is partly devoted to the battle of the South Atlantic and the British victory of the Falkland Islands. It is the author's contention that the Royal Navy not only beat the Kriegsmarine without resort to 'a bloody Trafalgar' but was the prime factor leading to the defeat of the continental armies in 1918.

222 **Coronel and the Falklands.**
John Irving. London: A. M. Philpot, 1927. 247p. maps. bibliog.

An account of these decisive battles in the South Pacific and the South Atlantic, November-December 1914, which took place to counteract the German menace to British Atlantic-Pacific trade routes.

223 **From the Dreadnought to Scapa Flow; the Royal Navy in the
Fisher era, 1904-1919. 5 vols.**
Arthur J. Marder. London: Oxford University Press, 1961-70.
5 vols. maps. bibliog.

This magnificent work, based on Admiralty records and other official records and
personal archives as well as German naval records, provides a definitive history of
the British Navy in World War I. An account of the Battle of the Falklands and
the first years of the German U-boat menace in the Atlantic will be found in
vol. 2. The fourth volume covers Admiral John Rushworth Jellicoe's (1859-1935)
arrival at the Admiralty in December 1916 to cope with the U-boat menace until
his dismissal a year later. It also deals with such anti-submarine measures as the
convoy system and its development. The final phases of the U-boat campaign are
detailed in the fifth volume which also contains an extensive and annotated
bibliography.

224 **Command the far seas; a naval campaign of the First World War.**
Keith Middlemas. London: Hutchinson, 1961. 255p. maps.
bibliog.

A balanced account of the Coronel and Falklands naval battles of November-
December 1914, and a critical appraisal of British and German strategy.

225 **Before Jutland; Admiral von Spee's last voyage. Coronel & the
battle of the Falklands.**
Hans Pochhammer. London: Jarrolds, 1931. 255p.

An account of the battle of the Falkland Islands by the first officer of the
German armoured cruiser *Gneisenau* which, along with the *Scharnhorst*, was
sunk by the Royal Navy on the 8th December 1914.

226 **The battle of the Falkland Islands before and after.**
H. Spencer-Cooper. London: Cassell, 1919. 224p.

An account of the battle of 8 December 1914 and the events leading up to it.
Part 1 examines the movements of the British and German warships including the
duel fought by the *Germania* and the action off Coronel; part 2 considers the
Falklands battle itself and the fate of the German cruiser *Dresden*; and part 3
deals with official despatches bearing on these exploits.

The Cunard express liners *Lusitania* and *Mauretania*.
See item no. 181.

The 1933 centenary issue of the Falkland Islands.
See item no. 806.

World War II

227 The battle of the Atlantic.
John Costello, Terry Hughes. Glasgow: Fontana/Collins, 1980.
352p. maps. bibliog.

A re-assessment of the battle of the Atlantic during the Second World War, the crucial sea campaign whose concern was the defence of the Atlantic shipping lanes against the depredations of German U-boats. The authors' aim is to set out the main political and military developments based on information taken from recently released official records, authoritative publications, and personal memoirs and contemporary sources, both Allied and German.

228 ATFERO; the Atlantic Ferry Organization.
Jeffrey Davis. *Journal of Contemporary History*, vol. 20, no. 1
(Jan. 1985), p. 71-93. bibliog.

An account of the work of the Atlantic Ferry Organization from its origins under the auspices of the Canadian Pacific Railway in August 1940 until its take-over by Royal Air Force Ferry Command in August 1941. The scheme was initiated by Lord Beaverbrook as Minister of Aircraft Production in May 1940 and organized by Morris Wilson, President of the Royal Bank of Canada. By August 1941 AFTERO had delivered 315 aircraft to Britain. The organization made a significant, and largely unrecognized, contribution to the Battle of the Atlantic and the final destruction of the Axis powers in World War II.

229 Memoirs: ten years and twenty days.
Karl Doenitz, translated by R. H. Stevens in collaboration with
David Woodward. London: Weidenfeld & Nicolson, 1959. 500p.

First published in German in 1958 under the title *Zehn Jahre und zwanzig Tage*, Grand Admiral Doenitz's memoirs contain a detailed account of German U-boat operations against Allied shipping in the North Atlantic from 1940 to 1943. Doenitz was chief of the U-boat arm in 1939 and later became commander-in-chief, and Hitler's successor as head of state.

230 A subject bibliography of the Second World War: books in English 1939-1974.
A. G. S. Enser. London: André Deutsch, 1977. 592p.
(A Grafton book).

This bibliography is intended as a guide to the general reader and researcher. Omitted are pamphlets, poetry, fiction juvenilia, humour, cartoons, and the literature of the War Graves Commission. Information on warfare in the Atlantic needs to be searched for under a number of subject headings, including, for example, convoys, submarines and merchant navy.

History. Naval history. World War II

231 **Victory at sea 1939-1945.**
P. K. Kemp. London: White Lion, 1976. 383. maps.
First published in 1957, this is a single volume account of the war at sea during the Second World War written by the official Admiralty Archivist. It is a broad and comprehensive account of events and strategy, with emphasis on those actions and episodes of outstanding importance which illustrate the central strategic theme. Chapters 4, 6 and 11 deal specifically with the Battle of the Atlantic.

232 **Menace; the life and death of the *Tirpitz*.**
Ludovic Kennedy. London: Sphere Books, 1981. 157p. bibliog.
This Second World War German battleship together with her sister ship *Bismarck*, dominated the Baltic and was a constant preoccupation of the British Admiralty. The account is partly based on decoded signals from German naval units and bases.

233 **The naval war against Hitler.**
Donald Macintyre. London: Batsford, 1971. 376p. maps. bibliog.
A general history of British naval operations in the Second World War with chapters devoted to the U-boat campaign in the North Atlantic between 1940-43.

234 **The battle of the Atlantic.**
Donald Macintyre. London: Severn House Publishers, 1975. 208p.
A concise account of the Allied campaign against German U-boats carried out on the North Atlantic convoy routes between 1939 and 1943.

235 **U-boat killer.**
Donald Macintyre. London: Seeley Service, 1976. 176p.
Captain Donald Macintyre DSO and two bars, DSC, RN, an Escort Force Commander during the Battle of the Atlantic, who served for three and a half years in Western Approaches Command, here relates the more exciting moments in the anti U-boat campaign. This book was first published in 1956 by Weidenfeld & Nicolson, London.

236 **The battle of the Atlantic September 1939-May 1943.**
Samuel Eliot Morison. Boston, Massachusetts: Little, Brown, 1947. 434p. maps. (History of the United States Naval Operations in World War II, Vol. 1).
A full record of the activities of the US Navy in the North and South Atlantic during the Second World War. Appendixes include those concerning: losses of merchant shipping; sinkings of German and Italian submarines; and mine fields laid by U-boats in the western Atlantic in 1942. Details are also given of the US Atlantic fleet 1941-42.

237 **History of United States naval operations in World War II. Vols. I-XV.**
Samuel Eliot Morison. Boston, Massachusetts: Little, Brown, 1947-62. 15 vols. maps. bibliog.

A definitive history of the work of the United States Navy in World War II, two volumes of which are especially relevant to Atlantic studies. Vol. I *The battle of the Atlantic, September 1939-May 1943* gives a detailed account of the trans-atlantic convoys, the North Russia run, the German U-boat offensive and, in the form of appendixes, a statistical analysis of merchant shipping losses, minefields laid by U-boats in the western Atlantic and the Atlantic fleet of the US Navy. Vol. X *The Atlantic battle won, May 1943-May 1945* includes an account of the sinking of the German battleship *Scharnhorst* and continues the story of the war on German submarines in the north, central and south Atlantic. Vol. XV *Supplement and general index* includes additional related material, for example, ships and aircraft of the US Navy, including many illustrations, as well as indexes and errata. A condensation of this work by the author was published as *The two-ocean war; a short history of the United States Navy in the Second World War* (Boston, Massachusetts: Little, Brown, 1963. 611p. maps.)

238 **Atlantic meeting; an account of Mr. Churchill's voyage in H.M.S. *Prince of Wales* in August, 1941, and the conference with President Roosevelt which resulted in the Atlantic Charter.**
H. V. Morton. London: Methuen, 1943. 160p. map.

The author accompanied Winston Churchill on the voyage to the historic meeting with President Roosevelt in the role of official journalist (along with author Howard Spring). The meeting itself took place off Placentia, Newfoundland, and the conversations with the President were on board his cruiser *Augusta*. The text of the Atlantic Charter is appended. It was in fact not 'signed and sealed' but merely 'approved' by the President and the British Prime Minister.

239 **Atlantic rendez vous.**
William Murray. Lymington, England: Nautical Publishing, London: Harrap, 1970. 317p. maps. bibliog.

The author, a merchant navy wireless operator in the Second World War, was taken prisoner on board the German supply ship *Nordmark* when his own ship, SS *Tribesman*, was sunk by the *Admiral Scheer* on 1 December 1940. This is his account of his experiences on the *Nordmark* during her voyage to the South Atlantic to resupply the German raiders. Eventually he was sent to a camp in occupied France from which he finally escaped. Details of German ships and their movements are listed in an appendix.

240 **Focke-Wulf Condor; scourge of the Atlantic.**
Kenneth Poolman. London: Macdonald & Jane's, 1978. 191p. bibliog.

A specialist history of these German long-range bombers whose ability to destroy Allied shipping and liaise with U-boats caused Winston Churchill to describe them as 'the scourge of the Atlantic'.

241 The sea hunters; escort carriers v. U-boats.
Kenneth Poolman. London: Arms & Armour Press, 1982. 196p.

The first detailed account of the battle in the North Atlantic between converted merchant ships, known as CVEs (Convoy Escort Carriers), fitted with catapult bombers, and the German U-boats.

242 The battle of the River Plate.
Dudley Pope. London: Kimber, 1956. 259p.

An account of the Royal Navy's action against the German pocket battleship *Graf Spee* in the South Atlantic and her eventual scuttling off Montevideo, Uruguay, on 17 December 1939.

243 Aircraft versus submarine; the evolution of the anti-submarine aircraft 1912 to 1980.
Alfred Price. London: Jane's, 1980. 2nd ed. 272p. maps. bibliog.

Presents a history of the evolution of the aircraft as an anti-submarine weapon, based on British, German, Japanese and US sources. This book is a valuable adjunct to a study of the part played by submarines in the Battle of the Atlantic in World War II to which subject the work is largely devoted. The final chapter considers submarine methods in the nuclear age.

244 Escort; the Battle of the Atlantic.
D. A. Rayner, edited by S. W. Roskill. London: Kimber, 1955. 250p.

A Royal Navy captain, who served continuously for more than five years in command of escort vessels, provides a first-hand account of the Battle of the Atlantic.

245 Night raider of the Atlantic (formerly The Golden Horseshoe).
Terence Robertson. London: Evans Brothers, 1981. 210p.

An account of the exploits of U-boat commander Captain Otto Kretschmer, who is said to have inflicted heavier losses on Allied shipping in the Atlantic during the Second World War than did any other man.

246 The critical convoy battles of March 1943; the battle for HX 229/SC 122.
Jurgen Rohwer. London: Ian Allan, 1977. 256p.

German and Allied archival sources form the basis of this account of Atlantic convoy and U-boat operations.

247 The war at sea 1939-1945. Vols. I-III (parts I and II).
S. W. Roskill. London: HM Stationery Office, 1954-61. 4 vols. bibliog. (History of the Second World War United Kingdom Military Series, edited by J. R. M. Butler).

This is the official British history of Second World War naval operations, including the battle of the Atlantic. Based on both British and German official records.

248 **The Russian convoys.**
B. B. Schofield. London: B. T. Batsford, 1964. 224p. bibliog.
The history of the Allied convoys carrying war material to the Russian port of
Murmansk during the Second World War.

249 **The defeat of the U-boats during World War II.**
B. B. Schofield. *Journal of Contemporary History*, vol. 16, no. 1
(Jan. 1981). p. 119-29.
The availability of shipping was the key factor to all military operation in the
Second World War but the British Admiralty initially underestimated the threat
from German U-boats. American lease-lend, the deciphering of German coded
messages, and techniques of refuelling at sea made transatlantic convoys feasible.
There were further set-backs, however, after the USA entered the war, but by
1943 the campaign against the U-boats was virtually won.

250 **The far distant ships; an official account of Canadian naval
operations in the Second World War.**
Joseph Scull. Ottawa: Queen's Printer, 1952. 527p. bibliog.
This summary is based on navy and admiralty records and includes an account of
the Battle of the Atlantic.

251 **War in the southern oceans.**
L. C. F. Turner, H. R. Gordon-Cumming, J. E. Betzler. Cape
Town: Oxford University Press, 1961. 268p. maps. bibliog.
An account of South African naval operations during the Second World War.
German raiders disguised as merchant ships were active in the South Atlantic from
1940-43. There are detailed accounts of operations against the auxiliary cruisers
Atlantis and *Pinguin* and the subsequent U-boat menace in the Atlantic narrows
and the waters between South Africa and Brazil.

252 **The German navy in World War II.**
Edward P. Von der Porten. London: Arthur Barker, 1969. 274p.
The book includes an account of the North and South Atlantic campaigns.
A statistical appendix lists information relating to German submarines and Allied
merchant vessels.

The cruel sea.
See item no. 623.

Atlantic convoy.
See item no. 625.

The Atlantic as a Strategic Military Area and Contemporary Foreign Relations

253 **Atlantic Quarterly.**
Harlow, England: Longmans, 1983- . quarterly.
The purpose of this journal is to provide a platform for the expression of European and American points of view in an explicitly European forum. The topics covered, or to be covered, include security issues, cultural affairs, and world trade and Atlantic community affairs in general.

254 **New strategic factors in the North Atlantic.**
Edited by Christoph Bertram, Johan Jørgen Holst. Oslo: Universitetsforlaget; Guildford, England: IPC Science and Technology Press, 1977. 193p. (Norwegian Foreign Policy Studies, no. 21).
Conceived at a conference held in Iceland in October 1975 and organized by the International Institute for Strategic Studies and the Norwegian Institute for International Affairs, this book examines the range of new and traditional factors of strategic significance in the North Atlantic. The work consists of contributions by scholars, analysts and policy makers from all the littoral states of the North Atlantic.

255 **New strategic factors in the North Atlantic.**
Christoph Bertram. *Maritime Policy*, vol. 1, no. 1 (Jan. 1977), p. 37-44.
The author, who is Director of the International Institute for Strategic Studies in London, discusses the build-up of Soviet naval forces, the growth of new naval technologies and the implications of paying greater attention to ocean resources and the emerging Law of the Sea. These outstanding current developments are of profound significance for the sea area of the North Atlantic and for the security of Europe.

256   **The future of the Atlantic community; toward European-American partnership.**
Kurt Birrenbach.   New York: Praeger, 1963. 94p.

A comprehensive survey of the problems involved in the building up of the community and the necessity for doing so.

257   **The Atlantic fantasy; the US, NATO and Europe.**
David Calleo.   Baltimore, Maryland: Johns Hopkins Press, 1970.
182p. bibliog. (Studies in International Affairs, no. 13).

The author argues a case for the renunciation by the USA of 'imperial pretensions' in Europe whilst at the same time avoiding a return to isolationism.

258   **The United States and six Atlantic outposts; the military and economic considerations.**
Edward W. Chester.   Port Washington, New York: Kennikat Press, 1980. 260p.

A review of United States' commercial and military interest in the North Atlantic islands of the Bahamas, Jamaica, Bermuda, Iceland, the Azores and Greenland.

259   **El mar y los intereses Argentinos.** (The sea and Argentine interests.)
Mario Raul Chingotto.   Buenos Aires: Ediciones Renglon, 1982.
197p. maps. bibliog.

This is essentially a textbook for university students which draws attention to the strategic, geopolitical, commercial and resource value of the South Atlantic to Argentina.

260   **The future of the Atlantic alliance.**
Christopher Coker.   London: Macmillan, 1984. 241p. (Royal United Services Institute Defence Studies Series).

Part 1 of this book is an examination by the author of the North Atlantic Treaty Organization (NATO) as an alliance, and in particular the erosion of the traditional bipartisan consensus on defence. This is followed by a discussion of alternatives to NATO put forward in recent years. Much of this study is devoted to restating the reasons why there can be no alternative to NATO. Part 2 contains varying perceptions of NATO by professionals, both military and civilian.

261   **The North Atlantic Alliance and the Soviet Union in the 1980s.**
Julian Critchley.   London: Macmillan, 1982. 210p.

The author traces the probable course, during the present decade, of the trial of strength between the Soviet Union and the USA and its allies.

The Atlantic as a Strategic Military Area and Contemporary Foreign Relations

262 **Political problems of Atlantic partnership; national perspectives.**
Edited by William C. Cromwell. Bruges, Belgium: College of
Europe, 1969. 458p. (College of Europe studies in contemporary
European issues, no. 3).

Examines the role of the Atlantic community in the context of the foreign
policies of the United States, Great Britain and the German Federal Republic. The
volume consists of three studies derived from a course seminar at the College of
Europe, 1965-66.

263 **El mar y la Antártida en la geopolítica argentina.** (The sea and
Antarctica in Argentine politics.)
Jorge Alberto Fraga. Buenos Aires: Instituto de Publicaciones
Navales, 1980. 300p. maps.

A collection of Admiral Fraga's newspaper and journal articles dealing with
Argentina's geopolitical interests in the South Atlantic, and more especially the
Falkland Islands (Malvinas), South Georgia and the South Sandwich Islands.
Relations with Chile concerning the islands disputed in the Beagle Channel are
also discussed.

264 **Challenge to the Western Alliance; a symposium organised by
The Times, London, and the Center for Strategic and Inter-
national Studies, Washington.**
Edited by Joseph Godson. London: Times Books, 1984. 208p.

This book reproduces, with later additions and substantial enlargements, the texts
of a series of essays published in *The Times* between January and June, 1984,
together with papers from a conference held in Brussels in January 1984, in
connection with the 35th anniversary of the Atlantic Alliance. Major military,
political and economic issues are analysed by leading European and American
politicians and academics. Appendixes include the text of the North Atlantic
treaty and a chronology of thirty-five years of NATO.

265 **The Atlantic alliance; a bibliography.**
Colin Gordon. London: Frances Pinter; New York: Nichols,
1978. 216p.

This bibliography, compiled by a former North Atlantic Treaty Organization
(NATO) research fellow, lists some 3,000 English language references drawn from
British, Canadian, US, Scandinavian and Soviet sources. The material is arranged
under four chronological periods: the late 1940s to the accession of the Federal
Republic of Germany to NATO in 1955; 1955 to the Cuban missile crisis of
October 1962; 1962 to the advent of the era of negotiation in 1970; and 1970 to
the review of the Helsinki accord on European security and cooperation in 1977.
Each period is prefaced by a brief historical outline and materials listed are books,
reports, pamphlets, occasional papers, and articles. A general bibliographical
introduction lists background reading.

266 **The Western Alliance; European-American relations since 1945.**
Alfred Grosser. New York: Continuum, 1980. 375p. bibliog.
A translation by Michael Shaw of the original German edition (Munich, 1978).
This work represents the first detailed analysis of the transatlantic relationship
during the period 1949-80.

267 **NATO arms co-operation. A study in economics and politics.**
Keith Hartley. London: Allen & Unwin, 1983. 228p. bibliog.
An examination of the economic arguments for the standardisation of weapons
by the members of the North Atlantic Treaty Organization.

268 **American opinion and European defence.**
Dennis Hartshorne. London: British Atlantic Publications, 1982.
16p. bibliog.
A review of American attitudes towards the role and effectiveness of NATO with
an analysis of the various factors determining the effectiveness of pressure groups.
An analysis of news coverage of NATO in newspapers and the major news
magazines is given in tabulated form. The author concludes that though opinion
in the USA is now firmly committed to NATO the problem remains of how to
improve understanding of the alliance's purpose.

269 **The birth of NATO.**
Sir Nicholas Henderson. London: Weidenfeld & Nicolson, 1982.
130p.
A history of the North Atlantic Treaty Organization (NATO) with the text of the
treaty signed in Washington on 4 April 1949 'to promote stability and well being
in the north Atlantic area'.

270 **No soft options; the politico-military realities of NATO.**
Sir Peter Hill-Norton. London: Christopher Hurst, 1978. 172p.
The author of this book, Admiral Hill-Norton, has had long experience of NATO
and held high office as chairman of the NATO military committee. He attempts
to describe how the idea of NATO originated, how the organization came into
being and has developed to the present day, and why its future strength and
influence must be of overriding importance to all its members.

271 **The Atlantic future; the record of a conference held at Ditchley
Park from 6 to 8 May 1963.**
Edited by H. V. Hodson. London: Longmans, Green, 1964.
129p.
The proceedings of a conference concerning the future of the Atlantic community
and the problem of nuclear arms. The conference was attended by distinguished
speakers from Great Britain and the USA.

The Atlantic as a Strategic Military Area and Contemporary
Foreign Relations

272 **The politics of South Atlantic security: a survey of proposals for a South Atlantic treaty organization.**
Andrew Hurrell. *International Affairs*, vol. 59, no. 2 (spring 1981), p. 179-93. bibliog.

The author points out that, in the aftermath of the Falklands War, relatively little attention has been paid to the task of relating Western concern for South Atlantic security to the interests and perceptions of the major Latin American powers, especially Argentina and Brazil. In this paper he examines those interests and focuses on the various proposals that have been made for the formation of a South Atlantic treaty organization. His conclusion is that such an organization offers no constructive basis for improving relations between the countries involved.

273 **International Affairs.**
Guildford, England: Butterworth Scientific for the Royal Institute of International Affairs. 1922- . quarterly.

This periodical publishes articles covering a broad range of topics of international interest in the fields of politics, economics, trade, defence, sociology and law. New books in these fields are critically reviewed or listed.

274 **Creating the entangling alliance; the origins of the North Atlantic Treaty Organization.**
Timothy P. Ireland. London; Westport, Connecticut: Aldwych Press, 1981. 245p. bibliog. (European Studies, no. 6).

A critical re-examination of the process whereby the USA came to abandon its traditional isolationist policy after signing the North Atlantic Treaty in 1949, and became 'entangled' in its first extra-hemispheric alliance since 1800.

275 **The Atlantic alliance; Jackson subcommittee hearings and findings.**
Edited by Henry M. Jackson. New York: Praeger, 1967. 309p.

A US Senate study of the Atlantic Alliance in 1965, the first general review since the Senate's first consideration of the Treaty in 1949. Staff reports and basic statements of witnesses are reproduced virtually intact. The North Atlantic Treaty document is appended.

276 **NATO after thirty years.**
Edited by Lawrence S. Kaplan, Robert W. Clawson. Wilmington, Delaware: Scholarly Resources, 1981. 262p.

Reproduces papers read at a conference in Kent, Ohio, 1980, which was sponsored by the Center for NATO Studies, Kent University. The authors, representing historians and political scientists, examine the origins of NATO and consider how and why the alliance has reached the place it has in the course of its first generation.

277   Can NATO survive?
      Stanley Kober. *International Affairs*, vol. 59, no. 3 (summer
      1983), p. 341-49.
The author detects a new crisis in the NATO alliance brought about by a change
in public opinon in Europe regarding the plausibility of a Soviet threat to the
West. If the NATO leadership fails to agree on the real nature of this threat then
there is a risk that the organization could disintegrate. There is therefore a real
need to redefine the nature of the threat and the purpose of the alliance.

278   The new nationalism; implications for transatlantic relations.
      Edited by Werner Link, Werner J. Feld. New York: Pergamon,
      1978. 165p.
A collection of papers presented to the annual conference of the Committee on
Atlantic Studies held in Luxembourg, 23-24 September 1977. The committee
fosters collaboration and contacts between North America and European
academics.

279   Dilemmas of the Atlantic Alliance; two Germanys, Scandinavia,
      Canada, NATO and the EEC.
      Peter Christian Ludz (et al.).   New York: Praeger Publishers for
      the Atlantic Institute for International Affairs, 1975. 253p.
      (Atlantic Institute Studies, no. 1).
A collection of four papers concerned with predominantly political developments
related to the Atlantic Alliance: 'Two Germanys in one world' by P. C. Ludz;
'Scandinavia faces Europe' by H. Peter Dreyer; 'The Canadian dilemma' by
Charles Pentland; and 'The Nine and NATO' by Lothar Ruhe.

280   The Kremlin and the peace offensive.
      Terry McNeill.   London: British Atlantic Publications, 1983.
      16p. bibliog.
The author argues that over the years the Soviet Union has invariably and consis-
tently followed Lenin's directive to explore the weaknesses of one's enemies and
drive a wedge between them. Thus Soviet strategy today has two priorities: to
mobilise opinion against NATO's defence policy; and to drive a wedge between
Europe and the USA. By infiltrating the various peace movements and whipping
up fear and war hysteria the Kremlin hopes that the democracies can be panicked
into disarmament. An appendix lists NATO and Warsaw Pact force comparisons.

281   La Atlantártida; un espacio geopolítico. (The Atlantarctic;
      a geopolitical region.)
      F. A. Milia. Buenos Aires: Ediciones Pleamar, 1978. 255p. maps.
A collection of articles on the geopolitics of the South Atlantic, emphasizing
Latin American interests and Argentina's economic concern with Antarctica.

The Atlantic as a Strategic Military Area and Contemporary Foreign Relations

282 **North Atlantic security; the forgotten flank?**
Kenneth A. Myers. Beverly Hills, California: Sage Publications, for the Center for Strategic and International Studies, Georgetown University, 1979. 72p. bibliog. (Washington Papers, Vol. VI, 62).

The author discusses the problems of maintaining a constructive politico-military balance in the North Atlantic. Long-term threats to regional stability can result not only from Soviet politics but also from economic pressures facing the littoral states and from a weakening of NATO's stance.

283 **NATO the next thirty years; the changing political, economic and military setting.**
Edited by Kenneth A. Myers. Boulder, Colorado: Westview Press; London: Croom Helm, 1980. 469p.

Presents twenty-six papers prepared as background material for a major international conference on the future of NATO convened in Brussels in 1979.

284 **NATO facts and figures.**
NATO Information Service. Brussels: NATO Information Service, 1981. 10th ed. 376p. maps.

An invaluable work of reference covering all aspects of the Atlantic Alliance including, for example, its origin and evolution, structure, defence policy, infrastructure and logistics, scientific affairs, non-governmental activities, treaty documentation and personnel.

285 **Securing the seas; the Soviet naval challenge and Western Alliance options. An Atlantic Council policy study.**
Paul H. Nitze, Leonard Sullivan, Jr, edited by Albert P. Toner. Boulder, Colorado: Westview Press, 1979. 464p.

An expert analysis of the capabilities of the Western Alliance to defend essential sea lines of communication under various conditions of peace, tension and war. It includes a review of the economic potential of the Atlantic Ocean and its sensitivity to shipping interruptions.

286 **The widening Atlantic.**
Donald Nuechterlein. *World Today*, vol. 40, nos. 8-9 (Aug.-Sept. 1984), p. 321-26.

The author maintains that a fundamental divergence of American views over the Reagan administration's attitude to detente with the USSR may erode the concensus in basic Allied interests and result in a withering of the North Atlantic alliance.

287 **The Atlantic community; a complex imbalance.**
Robert L. Pfaltzgraff, Jr. New York: Van Nostrand Reinhold,
1969. 216p. (New perspectives in political science, no. 22).
A study of United States-West European relations and the future of the NATO
alliance.

288 **Time of fear and hope; the making of the North Atlantic Treaty
1947-1949.**
Escott Reid. Toronto: McClelland & Stewart, 1977. 315p.
bibliog.
A well-documented account of 'the first multilateral military alliance to span the
North Atlantic Ocean in time of peace'.

289 **Command of the sea; the history and strategy of maritime
empires.**
Clark G. Reynolds. London: Robert Hale, 1976. 642p. bibliog.
The aim of this broad sweep of maritime history is to attempt a definition of the
concept of sea power. The author examines such factors as geography, topography, political and economic aspects of empire building, culture and intellectual
manifestations, technology and the tactical evolution of naval forces. Aspects of
the Atlantic history reviewed include: the Viking raids in Northern Europe; the
rise and ascendancy of the Spanish and Portuguese empires in the Americas; the
struggle for maritime supremacy between England and Holland in the 17th and
18th centuries; the British empire in North America in the 18th century; and the
'Pax Britannica' in the 19th century. A general review of the naval strategy in two
World Wars, with reference to the Battle of the Atlantic in World War II, is
followed by a concluding section on contemporary problems and nuclear confron-
tation.

290 **EEC and the Third World: a survey 3. The Atlantic rift.**
Edited by Christopher Stevens. Sevenoaks, England: Hodder &
Stoughton in association with the Overseas Development Institute
and the Institute of Development Studies, 1983. 256p. bibliog.
The central theme of the articles which comprise this volume is the growing
division between the European Economic Community and the USA regarding
their policies toward the Third World. A range of contemporary issues is examined
at international level (including law of the sea, export credits, UN global negotiations), and at regional level (southern Africa, the Caribbean basin and the Middle
East). The contributors are all experts in their various fields. There is an introduction by Willy Brandt.

The Atlantic as a Strategic Military Area and Contemporary Foreign Relations

291 **Building the Atlantic world.**
Robert Strausz-Hupé, James E. Dougherty, William R. Kintner.
New York: Harper & Row, 1963. 400p. (Foreign Policy Research Institute Book).
An attempt to define the Atlantic community, and an analysis of its political, economic and strategic rationale, its institutions and future prospects.

292 **Maritime strategy and the nuclear age.**
Geoffrey Till. London: Macmillan, 1982. 74p. bibliog.
A survey of the historical axioms regarding the concept of sea power from Alfred Thayer Mahan onwards, with the object of raising issues of past and present that are relevant to presenting maritime strategy. The book includes seven contributions by experts, including naval historians and considerable attention is paid to the history of Atlantic strategy. Appended is a select critical bibliography followed by a list of books and articles cited in the text.

293 **The future of British sea power.**
Edited by Geoffrey Till. London: Macmillan, 1984. 265p.
Since the battle for the Falkland Islands in 1982 Britain's defence policy has been under continuing scrutiny. This series of articles by some of the country's leading experts explores, for example, aspects of defence policy, the British fishing and shipping industry, the Atlantic connection with the USA, the Soviet threat, and certain features of the Falklands campaign.

294 **The Atlantic alliance and its critics.**
Edited by Robert W. Tucker, Linda Wrigley. New York: Praeger, 1983. 192p. (A Lehrman Institute book).
The essays comprising this volume were initially presented at a seminar series on 'The Atlantic alliance' sponsored by the Lehrman Institute in 1981-82. The authors, three Americans and three Europeans, all recognised experts, discuss the present tendency towards instability in the Atlantic alliance and propose realistic prescriptions that would allow a revamped Atlantic relationship to function more efficiently.

295 **The southern oceans and the security of the free world; new studies in global strategy.**
Edited by Patrick Wall. London: Stacey International, 1977. 256p. maps.
Presents contributions from a conference of specialists appraising the prospects and problems of the southern oceans in general with special reference to southern Africa, all with a view to countering increasing Soviet influence in the area. In the final contribution, 'Argentina and the sea', Rear Admiral Mario Lanzarini stresses the strategic importance of the South Atlantic to Argentina, over which 90% of her foreign trade moves, and the need to counter the growing Soviet threat by a policy of maritime cooperation aimed at the economic development of the zone.

296   The Pentagon negotiations March 1948: the launching of the
      North Atlantic Treaty.
      Cees Wiebes, Bert Zeeman. *International Affairs*, vol. 59, no. 3
      (summer 1983), p. 351-63.
An account of the secret negotiations on a security treaty held at the end of
March 1948 in Washington DC by the USA, the United Kingdom and Canada
during which the North Atlantic Treaty was effectively conceived. The delay in
implementing these recommendations seems to have been due to internal
differences of opinion within the US State Department and the efforts required to
unite Congress behind the plan. It appears likely that the USSR was informed of
these negotiations via information leaked by the British spy Donald Maclean.

297   The Atlantic community; progress and prospects.
      Edited by Francis O. Wilcox, H. Field Haviland, Jr.   New York:
      Praeger, 1963. 294p.
A volume of contributions by European and American specialists on the furthering
of cooperative relations among the North Atlantic nations. The early chapters
reflect on the present and future development of the Atlantic community in
relation to the interests of the USA, Great Britain, France, West Germany, the
communist states, the neutral notions and the countries of the Third World.
Subsequent chapters deal with the functional aspects of the community,
economic, strategic and political, together with its relations with the European
Community and the United Nations.

298   The British nuclear defence option.
      Geoffrey Williams.   London: British Atlantic Publications, 1983.
      16p.
The author argues the case against a non-nuclear defence option for Britain as
pressed for by the unilateralists. He stresses that there is no alternative to Britain's
continued membership of NATO whose forces must be equipped with at least
the same type and number of nuclear weapon systems available to the Soviet
Union and the Warsaw Pact.

The influence of sea power upon history 1660-1805.
See item no. 212.

Atlantic meeting; an account of Mr. Churchill's voyage in H.M.S. *Prince
of Wales* in August 1941, and the conference with President Roosevelt
which resulted in the Atlantic Charter.
See item no. 238.

Law of the Sea

299 **The law of the sea.**
D. W. Bowett. Manchester, England: Manchester University
Press; Dobbs Ferry, New York: Oceana Publications, 1967. 117p.
(The Melland Schill Lectures).
An analysis of outstanding problems awaiting solution in the law of the sea.

300 **The law of the sea.**
R. R. Churchill, A. V. Lowe. Manchester, England: Manchester
University Press, 1983. 321p. bibliog.
A concise introductory survey of the 1982 United Nations Convention on the
Law of the Sea and of the customary and conventional law which supplements it.
An explanation is given of the rules applicable to the major maritime zones recog-
nized in international law and of the rules presently applicable to each zone
against the background of their historical development. Also discussed are the
rules relating to the various uses of the seas and referring, for example, to
pollution, fishing and navigation.

301 **The law of the sea.**
Alastair D. Couper. London: Macmillan Education, 1978. 28p.
bibliog. (Aspects of Geography).
A short introduction to the political and economic geography of the sea with
special reference to fisheries.

302 **Who owns the oceans?**
A. D. Couper. *Geographical Magazine*, vol. 55, no. 9 (Sept.
1983), p. 450-57. maps.
One of the main problems of ocean exploitation and management relates to the
ownership of resources outside the zones of national jurisdiction, a problem that
still defies international agreement. This article looks at the problems with
reference to fisheries and mineral resources in the North Atlantic.

303 **The sea: a select bibliography on the legal, political, economic and technological aspects 1978-1979.**
Dag Hammarskjöld Library. New York: United Nations, 1980.
46p. (ST/LIB/SER B/29. UN publication E/F 80.1.6).
A bibliography compiled in connection with the Ninth Session of the Third United Nations Conference on the Law of the Sea, New York, 3 March-4 April 1980, and supplementing five previous bibliographies prepared for the 1974, 1975, 1976, and 1978 conferences. The subject headings include law and politics, ocean science and technology, uses of the sea, marine pollution, bibliographies and reference works.

304 **The enclosure of ocean resources; economics and the law of the sea.**
Ross D. Eckert. Stanford, California: Hoover Institution Press, 1979. 390p. maps. bibliog.
Part 1 of this book describes some of the new property arrangements for important ocean resources that have been developed either by coastal state enclosure or by new international agreements, and outlines the implications for efficient resource use of institutions of each type, for example, the economic consequences of exclusive coastal control over hydrocarbon exploitation, fish and living resources. Part 2 evaluates the policies of the treaty negotiations determined by the United Nations Conference on the Law of the Sea.

305 **Law of the sea; oceanic resources.**
Erin Bain Jones. Dallas, Texas: Southern Methodist University Press, 1972. 162p. bibliog.
The author commences with an historical chapter reviewing concepts of law for oceanic areas from Roman times to the 20th century. This is followed by chapters dealing with the study of the problem by international organizations, the development and codification of the law of the sea, and finally community interests versus exclusive state policies.

306 **International regulation of marine fisheries; a study of regional fisheries organizations.**
Albert W. Koers. West Byfleet, England: Fishing News, 1973. 368p. bibliog.
The author argues that an analysis of the law of international fisheries organizations is of interest not only for the future of the international law of marine fisheries, but also for the future of the international law of the sea in general. Organizations concerned with Atlantic fisheries include the Regional Fisheries Advisory Commission for the South West Atlantic, the Fishery Committee for the Eastern Central Atlantic, the International Commission for the Conservation of Atlantic Tuna, the International Council for the Exploration of the Sea, the International Commission for the Southeast Atlantic Fisheries, the International Commission for the Northwest Atlantic Fisheries, the Northeast Atlantic Fisheries Commission and the International Whaling Commission.

Law of the Sea

307 **Law for the world ocean; Tagore law lectures.**
Gerard J. Mangone. London: Stevens & Sons; Calcutta: Eastern
Law House, 1981. 313p. bibliog.

A series of lectures delivered to the University of Calcutta Law Faculty reviewing
all aspects of maritime law including shipping, fisheries, exploitation of the seabed
and pollution. Chapter 3, which deals with the regulation of the world's merchant
marine is perhaps of special relevance to the North Atlantic where shipping lanes
are the most frequented. Here the author outlines the creation and operation of
the Intergovernmental Maritime Consultative Organization (IMCO), an agency of
the United Nations, with internationally recognized regulatory functions. Chapter
4 on fisheries reviews the various regulatory fisheries commissions including those
covering the various sectors of the Atlantic and chapter 5 contains much of
relevance to the exploitation and regulation of the Atlantic seabed under international law.

308 **Marine Affairs Bibliography; a Comprehensive Index to Marine
Law and Policy Literature.**
Halifax, Nova Scotia: Dalhousie Law School, 1980- . quarterly.

A classified cumulative bibliography with author and geographical indexes covering all aspects of the law of the sea, maritime transportation and communications,
and physical and geographical aspects of the sea. References to the Atlantic are
widely scattered under various headings including: 'Falkland Islands'; 'Continental
Shelf'; and 'Marine Resources'.

309 **Ocean Development and International Law Journal.**
New York: Crane, Russak, 1973- . quarterly.

The primary purpose of this journal is to promote responsible and informed
discussion of issues and policies concerning the development, use and regulation
of the ocean and its contents.

310 **The influence of law on sea power.**
D. P. O'Connell. Manchester, England: Manchester University
Press, 1975. 204p. bibliog.

The author states in his preface that this is not a textbook but rather an attempt
'to bring into focus the disparate questions that contemporary international law
poses for naval planning'. It is therefore essentially a book for students and for
naval officers. It is of special interest for its discussion of the legal problems of
maritime boundary fixing as the struggle for natural resources of the oceans
accelerates.

311   **The international law of the sea. Vols. I and II.**
D. P. O'Connell, edited by I. A. Shearer.   Oxford, England:
Clarendon Press, 1982, 1984. 2 vols. bibliog.
A comprehensive exposition of the principles and doctrines governing the international law of the sea as developed by jurists, law-making institutions and
diplomats during the past 400 years. This treatise by the late Chichele Professor
of Public International Law at the University of Oxford, and completed after his
death by Professor Shearer, takes account of recent major developments including
the United Nations Convention on the Law of the Sea in 1982.

312   **International law of the sea; a bibliography.**
Nikos Papadakis.   Alphen aan den Rijn, Netherlands: Sijthoff
& Noordhoff, 1980. 457p.
This comprehensive bibliography covers traditional areas and modern trends and
concepts in the law of the sea, and includes English and French language material.
The main classified divisions are as follows: the marine environment and the
international law of the sea; maritime zones and maritime jurisdiction; the legal
régime of the sea-bed and subsoil beyond the limits of national jurisdiction;
marine resources; protection and preservation of the marine environment; marine
scientific research; military uses and arms control; ocean policy making (by
country); and the settlement of disputes. An update to this work has now been
published: *International law of the sea and marine affairs: a bibliography;
Supplement to the 1980 edition*, edited by Nikos Papadakis, Martin Glassner
(The Hague: Martinus Nijhoff, 1984. 579p.). This supplementary volume covers
comprehensively all areas and concepts in the law of the sea and marine affairs
in the major languages. Also included are documents emanating from the United
Nations and other international organizations.

313   **The political geography of the oceans.**
J. R. V. Prescott.   Newton Abbot, England: David & Charles,
1975. 247p. maps. bibliog.
This work contains chapters covering the following topics: the concept and
measurement of the territorial sea; claims to territorial seas; fishing zones; continental shelves; claims to areas of the continental shelves; and the High Seas.
The book forms a useful introduction to the political significance of the world's
seas and ocean. Examples from Atlantic Ocean history abound; the North Atlantic
has proved a source of economic discord between the trading nations of Europe
since Denmark began to assert sovereignty over the area in the 16th century. More
recently Argentina's claims to sovereignty over the continental shelf in her sector
of the South Atlantic have been tied to her claim to the Falkland Islands. An
appendix shows national claims to territorial seas, continental shelves and exclusive
fishing zones.

314   **UN Convention on the Law of the Sea 1982.**
Kenneth R. Simmonds.   Dobbs Ferry, New York: Oceana
Publications, 1983. 312p.

A compilation of basic texts containing: the text of the Final Act of the Third
UN Conference on the Law of the Sea (UNCLOS III) with corrigenda; and the
text of the UN Convention on the Law of the Sea, 1982, with corrigenda. The
documents are prefaced by an introductory chapter.

Economic Resources

General

315 **Treaties and other international agreements on oceanographic
resources, fisheries, and wildlife to which the United States is
party . . . Prepared . . . for the use of the Committee on
Commerce, United States Senate.**
Washington, DC: US Government Printing Office, 1970. 672p.
map. (91st Congress, 2nd session, committee print).
This list is divided into three sections: 'Multilateral', subdivided by class, e.g.
conservation, desalination, fisheries, law of the sea, whaling; 'Bilateral', subdivided
by country; and 'Agreements not yet in force'. A valuable source of reference on
Atlantic fisheries.

Fisheries

316 **Atlantic Ocean fisheries.**
Edited by Georg Borgstrom, Arthur J. Heighway.   London:
Fishing News, 1961. 335p. maps.
A comprehensive account covering all aspects of fisheries in the North and South
Atlantic Ocean. It includes a list of common oceanic and freshwater food fishes
and is prefaced by a popular article covering the physical aspects of the Atlantic.

317 **Council of Europe colloquy on the conservation of the living resources in the north-east Atlantic and Mediterranean Sea, Malta, 26-28 October 1977.**
Marine Policy, vol. 2, no. 2 (April 1978), p. 112-67. bibliog.
The author of this review of the purposes of the colloquy is not named. The colloquy was organized by the Committee on Agriculture of the Parliamentary Assembly of the Council of Europe. The object was to have an exchange of opinion on fish conservation matters between various interested bodies and individuals from the nineteen member states. Answers to a questionnaire relating to conservation which were completed by fifteen members are reproduced.

318 **The Atlantic Fisheries Commissions.**
David H. Cushing. *Marine Policy*, vol. 1, no. 3 (July 1977), p. 230-38.
The author traces the development of the North East Atlantic Fisheries Commission and the International Commission for the North West Atlantic Fisheries from their origins in the International Council for the Exploration of the Sea to the present. He also discusses the problems of stock conservation in the North Atlantic and assesses the commissions' success in handling them.

319 **Fisheries resources of the sea and their management.**
David H. Cushing. London: Oxford University Press, 1975. 87p. bibliog.
The various techniques used for catching fish, their natural history, the dynamics of fish populations and measures for their conservation are outlined in this volume. The international structure of fisheries management is described with reference to the International Commission for Northwest Atlantic Fisheries and the North East Atlantic Fisheries Commission.

320 **The impact of climatic change on fish stocks in the North Atlantic.**
David H. Cushing. *Geographical Journal*, vol. 142, pt. 2 (July 1976), p. 216-27, map.
The author suggests that a study of periodic changes in the biological cycle of the North Atlantic ecosystem will suggest how such climatic factors as wind strength and solar radiation might affect the reproduction of living organisms in the sea.

321 **North Atlantic seafood.**
Alan Davidson. London: Macmillan, 1979. 512p. maps. bibliog.
A catalogue of sea fish, crustaceans, molluscs and miscellaneous seafoods indigenous to the North Atlantic and likely to be found in markets or restaurants. Marine mammals are excluded. Each fish is described briefly with a note on its use in the kitchen. A list of national recipes is included.

322 **Atlas of the living resources of the seas.**
Food and Agriculture Organization. Rome: Food and Agriculture
Organization of the United Nations, 1982. [72] p. maps.

The atlas comprises three series of maps: there are ten maps illustrating the geographical distribution and present state of exploitation of the living resources of
the world's oceans; seven maps giving characteristic examples of fish migration;
and forty-five regional maps presenting the geographical and vertical distribution,
as well as the abundance, of the main stocks in each ocean region, including
the Atlantic. An introductory section deals with the details of presentation.
An index of fish names is appended.

323 **Free-range salmon.**
The Economist, vol. 283, no. 7309 (1983), p. 82-84.

Advances in the techniques of salmon ranching in the open ocean are described.
Several countries are investigating the possibility of rasing salmon in the South
Atlantic.

324 **History of the swordfishery of the northwestern Atlantic.**
Charles Dana Gibson. *American Neptune* vol. 41, no. 1 (1981),
p. 36-65.

A brief history of this New England based industry from its beginnings in the
latter part of the 17th century.

325 **The fisheries resources of the ocean.**
Edited by J. A. Gulland.   West Byfleet, England: Fishing News,
1971. 255p. maps. bibliog.

This work includes six chapters on the Atlantic Ocean providing basic information
on its resources and indicating possibilities for the development of new fisheries.
It is the author's hope that the data given will help to provide early warning of the
need for conservation. The volume was published for the UN Food and Agriculture
Organization, Rome.

326 **Index and list of titles of ICNAF publications, 1951-79.**
Compiled by V. M. Hodder.   Dartmouth, Nova Scotia: International Commission for the Northwest Atlantic Fisheries, 1980.
193p. map. (Special Publication, no. 11 revised).

Subject and author indexes and lists of titles of the principal publications of the
ICNAF from 1951 to its termination in 1979 are included in this bibliography.

327 **Marine fisheries.**
S. J. Holt, C. Vanderbilt. *Ocean Yearbook*, no. 2 (1980), p. 9-56.

An overview of world fisheries catches concentrating on the nutritional use of
living resources. This is an update of Holt's paper in *Ocean Yearbook* no. 1 (1978),
p. 38-83 which covered the years 1938 to 1975.

328 **International Atlantic Salmon Foundation Special Publication Series.**
New York: International Atlantic Salmon Foundation, 1970- . irregular.

The Foundation, privately sponsored, has among its objectives the need to promote the appreciation, preservation and conservation of Atlantic salmon resources and to encourage and support scientific research in biology and management. This series is published by the IASF to diffuse information in all fields of Atlantic salmon research and management.

329 **Symposium on environmental conditions in the northwest Atlantic 1960-1969.**
International Commission for the Northwest Atlantic Fisheries. Dartmouth, Nova Scotia: International Commission for the Northwest Atlantic Fisheries, 1972. 254p. maps. bibliog. (Special publication, no. 8).

The eleven papers read at this conference cover aspects of the oceanography and climate of the North Atlantic as well as fish stocks and fish production.

330 **The biology, distribution and state of fish stocks in the ICES area part II.**
International Council for the Exploration of the Sea. Charlottenlund Slot, Denmark: ICES, 1979. 202p. maps.

A comprehensive and detailed report covering the exploitation and management of commercial fish stocks in the northeast Atlantic.

331 **Atlantic salmon; the leaper struggles to survive.**
Art Lee. *National Geographic Magazine*, vol. 160, no. 5 (Nov. 1981), p. 600-14.

This article covers aspects of commercial salmon conservation and management in Iceland and elsewhere and is of special interest to the angler.

332 **Marine Science Contents Tables.**
Rome: Food and Agriculture Organization of the United Nations. 1966- . monthly.

An international listing of the contents of selected periodicals in the field of marine biology and fisheries. Each issue lists the names of titles searched together with the name and address of the publisher.

333 **The living marine resources of the southeast Atlantic.**
Garth Newman. Rome: Food and Agriculture Organization of
the United Nations, 1977. 59p. bibliog. (FAO Fisheries Technical
Paper, no. 178).

This document reviews the nature, distribution and state of exploitation of
fishery resources in the International Commission for the Southeast Atlantic
Fisheries region, which is an area extending from the mouth of the River Congo
to Mozambique. The author reviews management schemes in force at national and
regional levels and priorities in research on the regions' resources are also
discussed.

334 **Northwest Atlantic Fisheries Organization Statistical Bulletin.**
Dartmouth, Nova Scotia: International Commission for the
Northwest Atlantic Fisheries Organization, 1980- . annual.

Provides annual tabulated statistics of commercial catches from the NAFO convention area as well as catches of harp and hooded seals.

335 **Fisheries ecology.**
Tony J. Pitcher, Paul J. B. Hart. London: Croom Helm;
Westport, Connecticut: Avi, 1982. 414p. bibliog.

A textbook dealing with the broader aspects of commercial fisheries, their stocks
and optimal management. The stocks of the various fishery zones of the Atlantic,
and their management commissions, are reviewed on p. 54-56. Further relevant
information can also be found, for example, in those chapters dealing with fishery
economics and fish farming. An index of fish names is appended.

336 **Fisheries conflicts in the North Atlantic: problems of
management and jurisdiction.**
Edited by Giulio Pontecorvo, Norma Hench Hagist. Cambridge,
Massachusetts: Ballinger, 1974. 203p.

The proceedings of the Law of the Sea Institute Workshop in Hamilton, Bermuda
in 1974. Chapter 1, 'Geography of the North Atlantic' by Lewis M. Alexander,
provides a succinct definition of the region and its conflicting economic interests.

337 **Proceedings of the conference on acid rain and the Atlantic
Salmon. Portland, Maine, November 22-23, 1980.**
Edited by Lee Sochasky. New York: International Atlantic
Salmon Foundation, 1981. 174p. maps. bibliog. (IASF Special
Publication Series, no. 10).

The object of this conference was to present current information on the present
and potential effects of acid precipitation on Atlantic salmon, the resulting
impact on the fisheries, and action being taken to examine or correct the situation.
A secondary objective was to educate the public on the northeast coast of the
USA and Canada on the action needed to halt or reverse the acidification trend.

338 **The role of the ICES in the north-east Atlantic.**
Hans Tambs-Lyche. *Marine Policy*, vol. 2, no. 2 (April 1978),
p. 127-41.

The author traces the development of the International Council for the Exploration of the Sea (ICES) since its inception in 1902. He then outlines, with special
reference to the northeast Atlantic, the machinery whereby the annual assessments
of the states of fish stocks are made within ICES and the means by which information is gathered.

339 **The politics of international fisheries management; the case of
the northeast Atlantic.**
Arild Underdal. Oslo: Universitetsforlaget, 1980. 239p. bibliog.

This is primarily a study of political processes which deals specifically with the
attempts at managing northeast Atlantic fisheries through a regional fisheries
commission (NEAFC).

340 **Atlantic salmon; its future.**
Edited by A. E. J. Went. Farnham, England: Fishing News,
1980. 252p.

The proceedings of the second International Atlantic Salmon Symposium, held in
Edinburgh, in 1978. Many important aspects of the Atlantic salmon and its future
role are discussed. A unanimous resolution called for the establishment of an
International Atlantic Salmon convention.

341 **The Atlantic salmon.**
Lee Wulff. New York: A. S. Barnes, 1967. 222p.

Examines the history and techniques of angling for salmon with special reference
to Maine and the Atlantic provinces of Canada.

342 **Yearbook of Fishery Statistics.**
Rome: Food and Agriculture Organization of the United Nations,
1953- . annual.

Annually updated statistics covering all aspects of world fisheries catches and
production.

The European fisheries in early modern history.
See item no. 125.

The law of the sea.
See item no. 300.

The law of the sea.
See item no. 301.

International regulation of marine fisheries; a study of regional fisheries organizations.
See item no. 306.

Law for the world ocean; Tagore law lectures.
See item no. 307.

The political geography of the oceans.
See item no. 313.

New world of the ocean.
See item no. 381.

Annales Biologiques. (Biological Annals).
See item no. 518.

The Faroese salmon fishing industry and its management.
See item no. 657.

Whaling

343 Kendal Whaling Museum paintings.
M. V. Brewington, Dorothy Brewington.   Sharon, Massachusetts: Kendal Whaling Museum, 1965. 137p.

The arrangement of this well-illustrated catalogue is by the nationality of the scene or vessel. Paintings of vessels include notes on both vessels and artists, along with bibliographical notes concerning published reproductions of the pictures. The coverage is whaling worldwide and the paintings include scenes of whaling by Dutch, British and American ships in North Atlantic waters.

344 Kendal Whaling Museum prints.
M. V. Brewington, Dorothy Brewington.   Sharon, Massachusetts, Kendal Whaling Museum, 1969. 209p.

Reproductions in both black-and-white and colour of the holdings of one of North America's largest collections on whaling. Besides whaling vessels and scenes the museum owns a large collection of views of ports visited by the whalers on both sides of the Atlantic.

Economic Resources. Whaling

345   **Modern whaling in Britain and the north-east Atlantic Ocean.**
      Sidney G. Brown. *Mammal Review*, vol. 6, no. 1 (March 1976),
      p. 25-36, maps. bibliog.
A review of the history of modern whaling in this zone of the Atlantic suggests
that the blue, humpback and right whale populations would not support con-
tinuous whaling on any great scale. Fin whales have also probably been overfished
in the Faroe whaling grounds and elsewhere, but there is no evidence that sei and
sperm whales have been overfished.

346   **Whale ships and whaling; a pictorial history of whaling during
      three centuries; with an account of the whale fishery in colonial
      New England.**
      George Francis Dow.   Salem, Massachusetts: Marine Research
      Society, 1925. 446p.
A classic history of the whaling industry in this part of the North Atlantic.

347   **Great waters; a voyage of natural history to study whales,
      plankton and the waters of the Southern Ocean in the old Royal
      Research Ship *Discovery* with the results brought up to date by
      the findings of the R. R. S. *Discovery II.***
      Sir Alister Hardy.   London: Collins, 1967. 542p. bibliog.
An account of a scientific expedition to the South Atlantic and Antarctic waters
based on the author's personal journals, but updated in the light of subsequent
research.

348   **Whales, whaling and whale research; a selected bibliography.**
      Compiled by L. R. Magnolia.   Cold Spring Harbor, New York:
      The Whaling Museum, 1977. 91p. (Publication no. WM-1).
This bibliography presents 1,000 English-language references on the cetacea,
whaling techniques, research and substitutes for whale-derived products.

349   **The whale.**
      Leonard Harrison Matthews.   London: Allen & Unwin, 1968.
      287p. maps. bibliog.
A splendidly illustrated general review of whales and whaling, including those
found in the Atlantic with contributions by various experts.

350   **A dead whale or a stove boat; cruise of *Daisy* in the Atlantic
      Ocean June 1912-May 1913.**
      Robert Cushman Murphy.   Boston, Massachusetts: Houghton
      Mifflin, 1967. 176p.
An illustrated account of the author's Atlantic cruise whose narrative was
published under the title *Logbook for Grace*, (q.v.).

80

351 **Logbook for Grace; whaling brig** *Daisy* **1912-1913.**
Robert Cushman Murphy, introduction by George Gaylord
Simpson. New York: Time, 1965. 371p.
A facsimile edition of the first edition (New York: Macmillan, 1947). An account
of the author's cruise in the Mid- and South Atlantic from Dominica to the Cape
Verde Islands, Fernando Noronha and South Georgia, returning via Trinidad to
Barbados.

352 **Lost leviathan.**
F. D. Ommanney. London: Hutchinson, 1971. 280p.
A history of whaling spiced with the author's personal observations as a zoologist
with the 'Discovery Investigations' at South Georgia and in Antarctic waters.

353 **Report of the International Whaling Commission.**
Cambridge, England: International Whaling Commission, 1st
report, 1950- . annual.
This annual report includes not only the various reports on the work of the Commission but also numerous scientific papers concerning conservation, whale
biology and population.

354 **Sea hunters; the New England whalemen during two centuries
1635-1835.**
Edouard A. Stackpole. Philadelphia: Lippincott, 1953. 510p.
A well-researched history of the establishment and perfection of the American
whaling industry.

355 **History of the American whale fishery from its earliest inception
to the year 1876.**
Alexander Starbuck. New York: Argos-Antiquarian, 1964.
2 vols.
A reprint of the original edition of 1878 published by the US Commission on Fish
and Fisheries. The work records nearly 12,000 voyages from American ports and
represents a compendium of knowledge on the whaling industry with contributions by every major writer on US maritime history.

356 **The history of modern whaling.**
J. N. Tønnessen, A. O. Johnsen. London: Hurst; Canberra:
Australian National University Press, 1982. 798p. maps. bibliog.
This translation of the Norwegian four volume edition of 1959-70 is a definitive
history of the industry. The source list and general references contained in the
original volumes are omitted but the work does include a comprehensive bibliography.

357 **Salvesen of Leith.**
Wray Vamplew. Edinburgh: Scottish Academic Press, 1975.
311p.

The second half of this specialised history of Christian Salvesen is devoted to the firm's involvement in Antarctic whaling based at Leith Harbour, South Georgia, in the South Atlantic.

International regulation of marine fisheries; a study of regional fisheries organizations.
See item no. 306.

The stocks of whales.
See item no. 548.

Give me a ship to sail.
See item no. 608.

A narrative of the cruise of the yacht Maria among the Feroe [*sic*] Islands in the summer of 1854.
See item no. 634.

Open boat whaling in the Azores; the history and present methods of a relic industry.
See item no. 677.

The hand of God; whaling in the Azores.
See item no. 678.

Baleia! the whalers of the Azores.
See item no. 680.

Sealing

358 **The life of the harp seal.**
Fred Bruemmer. Newton Abbot, England: David & Charles, 1978. 171p.

A first-hand account of the controversial harp seal fishery off the coast of Newfoundland and Labrador which is illustrated with the author's colour photographs.

359 **The living ice; the story of the seals and the men who hunt them in the Gulf of St. Lawrence.**
Pol Chantraine. Toronto: McClelland & Stewart, 1980. 238p.

A translation from the French. The author argues for controlled culling of harp seals as part of the way of life of the fishing communities of Newfoundland and the Magdalen Islands.

360 **Savage luxury; the slaughter of the baby seals.**
Brian Davies. London: Souvenir Press, 1970. 214p.
The story of a campaign to abolish the annual cull of harp seals in the Gulf of St.
Lawrence.

361 **Wake of the great sealers.**
Farley Mowat, prints and drawings by David Blackwood.
Toronto: McClelland & Stewart, 1973. 157p.
The story of the Newfoundland men of the 19th and 20th centuries who set out
in flimsy ships to hunt seals on the treacherous North Atlantic ice fields. A
superbly illustrated fictional account based partly on fact and folklore.

Northwest Atlantic Fisheries Organization Statistical Bulletin.
See item no. 334.

The fur seal of South Georgia.
See item no. 892.

The elephant seal industry at South Georgia.
See item no. 895.

Mineral resources

362 **Underwater minerals.**
D. S. Cronan. London: Academic Press, 1980. 362p. bibliog.
A text book aimed at a wide audience reviewing the nature, occurrence, origin
and exploitability of marine mineral deposits. An appendix contains chemical
analyses of manganese nodules from the Indian, Atlantic and Pacific oceans.

363 **Minerals from the marine environment.**
Sir Peter Kent. London: Edward Arnold, 1980. 88p. bibliog.
A useful introduction to the recoverable mineral resources available to man in the
deep sea and on the continental shelves, with special emphasis on resource conservation. Minerals range from bulk material such as sand and gravel to rare metals
including diamonds, titanium and gold. Other minerals include manganese, in the
form of nodules, as well as oil, gas and coal. A penultimate chapter reviews
regional exploitation including the Atlantic sectors where mineral exploitation
concentrates in the North Sea, the Baltic, the waters off Spitzbergen, Newfoundland, the Gulf of Mexico, Nigeria and off the east coast of South America.

364 **The mineral resources of the sea.**
John L. Mero. Amsterdam, The Netherlands: Elsevier, 1965.
312p. maps. bibliog.

This study of ocean-floor materials of general economic interest originated in a
Scripps Institution of Oceanography cooperative economic analysis of mining
manganese nodules of which the author was chief investigator. A chemical
analysis of these nodules from the Atlantic Ocean with a map showing their
location will be found on p. 234-41. The author expresses doubt as to the
practicability of their profitable recovery in the light of weather conditions in
the ocean.

365 **Exploitation of seabed resources and international law.**
Robert Stein, Ingo Walter. Aberdeen, Scotland: University of
Aberdeen, Department of Political Economy, 1977. 14p.
(Discussion Paper 77-14).

International waters have traditionally been free for all to use, whether for fishing
or for dumping waste. A world demand for the economic resources of the ocean
have triggered off a 'land-grab' by the creation of exclusive economic zones. This
paper outlines the economic gains involved and the state of play in the international legal arena. Relevant to the Atlantic economy are petroleum recovery
and mineral resources, especially manganese-oxide nodules. The authors express
doubts as to whether the United Nations Conference on the Law of the Sea
(UNCLOS) will be able to resolve the legal problems involved; these will more
probably be dealt with by intergovernmental agreements between the techno-
logically advanced nations.

New world of the ocean.
See item no. 381.

Ocean Science

General

366 **A voyage of discovery.**
Edited by Martin Angel. Oxford, England: Pergamon, 1977.
696p. maps. bibliog.
A Festschrift dedicated to the doyen of British oceanography, Sir George Deacon,
on his 70th birthday which contains several papers concerned with the hydrology
of the Atlantic Ocean.

367 **The great ocean business.**
Brenda Horsfield, Peter Bennet Stone. London: Hodder &
Stoughton, 1972. 360p. maps. bibliog.
A popular but extremely well-researched account of the development of scientific
ideas in the field of oceanography. Of special relevance are the chapters dealing
with research on the Mid-Atlantic Ridge and the consequent rise of studies concerning sea floor spreading which during the past decade have led to a more
profound understanding of the mechanics of the deep earth. Other chapters deal
with the farming of the ocean and Atlantic circulatory systems.

368 **The physical geography of the oceans.**
Charles H. Cotter. London: Hollis & Carter, 1965. 317p. maps.
bibliog.
A general textbook at first-year university level.

369 **Deep-Sea Research. Part A. Oceanographic Research Papers.
Part B. Oceanographic Literature Review.**
Oxford, England: Pergamon, 1953- . monthly.
Part A contains papers reporting on original research in a broad field of oceanog-
raphy. Part B lists references from recent literature with short annotations or
abstracts. Cumulated author and subject indexes are published annually.

Ocean Science. General

370 **Physical oceanography. Vols. 1 and 2.**
Alfred Defant. Oxford, England: Pergamon, 1961. 2 vols. maps.
bibliog.
Translated into English from the author's original manuscript in German, this
classic treatise is largely based on Defant's work on the *Meteor* expedition to
the South Atlantic in 1925-27. Its contents formed the basis of his lectures on
physical oceanography at the University of Berlin between 1927 and 1942. The
first part of vol. 1 deals with the spatial, material and energetical characteristics
of the earth's water envelope. The second part describes the physical and chemical
properties of, for example, seawater and sea ice. Vol. 2 is devoted to waves, tides
and related phenomena.

371 **The ocean.**
Edited by Dennis Flanagan. San Francisco: Freeman, 1969.
140p. bibliog.
This volume includes ten chapters by specialists dealing with various aspects of
ocean science and technology originally published in the September 1969 issue
of *Scientific American.*

372 **The dynamic ocean.**
New York: W. H. Freeman, 1983. 116p. map. bibliog.
A collection of articles by various authors reprinted from *Scientific American*,
vol. 249, no. 3 (Sept. 1983) presenting the latest theories regarding the dynamic
nature of the ocean floor and the dry land, and the nature of the forces originating
the Earth's mantle and core. These articles update J. Tuzo Wilson's theories on
continental drift published in the 1960s.

373 **The waters of the sea.**
P. Groen. London: Van Nostrand, 1967. 328p. maps. bibliog.
A translation of the Dutch language edition of 1961, this work is intended for the
general reader who is interested in the physical phenomena of the Atlantic and
other oceans.

374 **Oceanography: a view of the Earth.**
M. Grant Gross. Englewood Cliffs, New Jersey: Prentice-Hall,
1982. 3rd ed. 544p. maps. bibliog.
An introductory non-mathematical text for the general reader designed to present
the role of the sea in human affairs. Annotated reading lists and a glossary of
technical terms are included.

375 **The science of the sea; a history of oceanography.**
Edited by C. P. Idyll. London: Nelson, 1970. 271p. bibliog.
A well-illustrated series of contributions by experts written for the layman.

376   **The International Decade of Ocean Exploration 1971-80.**
Intergovernmental Oceanographic Commission.   Paris: UNESCO,
1974. 87p. maps. (IOC technical series, no. 13).
A current status report on this long-term programme of research designed 'to
increase knowledge of the ocean, its contents and the contents of its subsoil,
and its interfaces with the land, the atmosphere and the ocean floor . . . with the
goal of enhanced utilization of the ocean and the resources for the benefit of
mankind.'

377   **Oceanography for oceanographers.**
Cuchlaine A. M. King.   London: Edward Arnold, 1965. 337p.
bibliog.
All aspects of physical oceanography and marine biology are covered in this
valuable introductory textbook. A concluding chapter introduces such themes as
the role of the oceans in exploration and transport, their strategic importance and
their importance as a source of food.

378   **Introduction to physical and biological oceanography.**
Cuchlaine A. M. King.   London: Edward Arnold, 1975. 372p.
maps. bibliog.
This revised edition of the author's *Oceanography for geographers* (q.v.) deals in
a general way with physical, chemical and biological oceanography. It includes
some reference to applied oceanography, ocean technology and the future exploitation of the Atlantic and the other oceans.

379   **Sea-level changes.**
Eugenie Lisitzin.   Amsterdam, The Netherlands: Elsevier
Scientific Publishing, 1974. 286p. maps. bibliog.
A specialized treatise which includes a table of the harmonic constants of the
seasonal variations in sea level of the Atlantic Ocean (p. 112-13).

380   **Marine Policy.**
Guildford, England: IPC Science and Technology Press. 1977- .
quarterly.
An international journal dealing with the economics, planning and politics of
ocean exploitation.

381   **New world of the ocean.**
Samuel W. Matthews.   *National Geographic*, vol. 60, no. 6.
(Dec. 1981), p. 792-833. maps.
The present state of ocean science forms the subject of this well-illustrated review,
aimed at the general reader. A colour reproduction of a Coastal Zone Color
Scanner aboard a Nimbus 7 satellite shows the distribution of chlorophyll in the
western Atlantic and model diagrams explain concisely the geology of the ocean
floor and current flow. The article also reviews fisheries research and the mineral
potential of the ocean.

382 **The physical geography of the sea and its meteorology, being
a reconstruction and enlargement of the eighth edition of 'The
physical geography of the sea'.**
Matthew Fontaine Maury. London: Sampson Low, Son & Co.,
1860. 8th ed. rev. 485p. maps.

The author was superintendent of the US Depot of Charts and Instruments in
1842. Amongst oceanographers and meteorologists his classic textbook on oceanography, the first in its field, will always occupy an important place, although
many of his scientific ideas have been seriously modified in the light of subsequent
research. Maury's chart representing a bottom profile of the North Atlantic
between Europe and America demonstrated the practicability of laying a submarine cable across the ocean.

383 **Ocean science.**
Edited by H. W. Menard. San Francisco: W. H. Freeman, 1977.
307p. bibliog.

Reprints some articles originally published in *Scientific American* which reviewed
the achievements of oceanography during the previous 25 years.

384 **MIAS News Bulletin.**
Wormley, Godalming, England: Marine Information and Advisory
Service, Institute of Oceanographic Sciences. 1978- . annual.

This bulletin is distributed free to those with a professional or academic interest
in the marine environment. Its aim is to alert readers to progress in MIAS data
bank services and to research at the Institute of Oceanographic Sciences.

385 **Principles of physical oceanography.**
Gerhard Neumann, Willard J. Pierson, Jr. Englewood Cliffs,
New Jersey: Prentice-Hall, 1966. 545p. maps. bibliog.

A reference textbook for third-year undergraduates.

386 **McGraw-Hill encyclopaedia of ocean and atmospheric sciences.**
Edited by Sybil P. Parker. New York: McGraw-Hill, 1980. 580p.

An interdisciplinary treatment of the ocean and atmospheric sciences which
provides practical information on subjects such as weather forecasting, mining
and farming the seas, pollution, and deep-sea diving.

387 **Descriptive physical oceanography; an introduction.**
George L. Pickard, William J. Emery. Oxford, England:
Pergamon, 1982. 4th ed. 249p. maps. bibliog.
This textbook is intended for would-be oceanographers, or for those requiring
an introduction to the subject. The plan followed in the text is to describe briefly
the ocean basins and their topography as they affect ocean circulation, and then
to introduce the terminology of physical oceanography. There is a brief summary
of the properties of fresh-water and sea-water with a general description of the
distribution of water characteristics both in the vertical and in the horizontal.
This is followed by an account of the sources of gain or loss of heat and water to
the ocean, and a description of instruments and methods of data analysis. Water
characteristics of the currents in the world's oceans and in coastal regions are
described and the author concludes with comments on the present state of the
science.

388 **Proceedings of the Scientific Committee on Oceanic Research
(SCOR).**
Halifax, Nova Scotia: Scientific Committee on Oceanic Research,
1965- . annual.
This committee coordinates international scientific research in the oceans on
behalf of the International Council of Scientific Unions. The proceedings review
ongoing research and list current publications.

389 **Progress in oceanography.**
Oxford, England: Pergamon, 1963- . annual.
An annual volume of research papers designed to keep oceanographers and others
interested in the sea conversant with recent advances in the field. It includes
original research as well as reviews of fundamental problems.

390 **Ocean science.**
Keith Stowe. New York: John Wiley, 1979. 610p. map.
This is essentially a textbook for college students accompanied by questions and
answers. A glossary of technical terms is appended.

391 **The oceans; their physics, chemistry, and general biology.**
H. U. Sverdrup, Martin W. Johnson, Richard H. Fleming. New
York: Prentice-Hall, 1970. 1,087p. maps.
A classic amongst oceanography textbooks embracing all subjects pertaining to
the oceans and to marine organisms.

392 **Descriptive regional oceanography.**
P. Tchernia. Oxford, England: Pergamon, 1980. 253p. maps.
(Regional Marine Series, no. 3).
A translation from the French original, designed for undergraduate teaching.
Section 5 deals with all aspects of the topography, winds, climatology, currents
and hydrology of the Atlantic Ocean.

393 **Study of the sea; the development of marine research under the auspices of the International Council for the Exploration of the Sea.**
Edited by E. M. Thomasson. Farnham, England: Fishing News Books, 1981. 253p.
A review of some of the more significant activities in marine oceanographic science pursued by the ICES which represents eighteen member countries and is the main coordinating body for marine investigations in the North Atlantic Ocean and neighbouring seas.

394 **Oceans.**
Karl K. Turekian. Englewood Cliffs, New Jersey: Prentice-Hall, 1976. 2nd ed. 149p. map. bibliog.
A short introduction to oceanography with emphasis on geology and chemistry.

395 **Oceanographic atlas of the North Atlantic Ocean. Section II physical properties.**
United States. US Naval Oceanographic Office. Washington DC: Naval Oceanographic Office, 1967. 300p. maps. bibliog. (Pub. no. 700).
This atlas contains charts presenting data for sea surface temperature, salinity, density and bathythermograph observations.

396 **Oceanographic atlas of the North Atlantic Ocean. Section VI sound velocity.**
United States. US Naval Oceanographic Office. Washington DC: Naval Oceanographic Office, 1967. 44p. maps. (Pub. no. 700).
Seasonal data presented in the form of charts and graphs.

397 **Tales of an old ocean.**
Tjeerd van Andel. New York: W. W. Norton, 1977. 176p. bibliog.
Written by a professor of geology at Stanford University this is a stimulating but personal account of the author's interests in oceanography. In a final chapter the author draws on his diaries kept on two geological expeditions to the North Atlantic.

398 **The origin of continents and oceans.**
Alfred Wegener. New York: Dover Publications, 1966. 246p. maps. bibliog.
A translation of the 4th edition of the German original, written in 1915, which expounded the then revolutionary theory that the present continents are derived from one supercontinent which later broke apart. This theory was the key to understanding the process of the opening up of the Atlantic Ocean.

399 **Exploration of the oceans; an introduction to oceanography.**
John G. Weihaupt. London: Collier Macmillan; New York:
Macmillan, 1979. 589p. bibliog.
The book is designed to provide a broad but comprehensive introduction to oceanography in non-technical language.

400 **The evolution of the north-east Atlantic.**
C. A. Williams, Dan McKenzie. *Nature* (London), vol. 232,
no. 5307 (July 1971), p. 168-73. bibliog.
Magnetic data suggests that the formation of the northeast Atlantic began with the separation of Spain from North America and Europe in probably the Upper Jurassic and early Cretaceous Periods.

401 **Continents adrift.**
Edited by J. Tuzo Wilson. San Francisco: W. H. Freeman, 1972.
172p. maps. bibliog. (Readings from *Scientific American*).
A collection of articles from *Scientific American* published between 1952 and 1970 reflecting changing views on the behaviour of the Earth's surface. Five articles dealing with continental drift, sea-floor spreading and plate tectonics are of special relevance to the evolution of the Atlantic Ocean.

402 **Did the Atlantic close and then re-open?**
J. Tuzo Wilson. *Nature* (London), vol. 211, no. 5050 (Aug.
1966), p. 676-81, bibliog.
The author suggests that during Lower Palaeozoic times North America and Europe were approaching each other, that this motion stopped and that it later reversed itself. This reopening of the Atlantic Ocean must have been an event of major significance in world geology.

403 **International cooperation in marine science.**
Warren S. Wooster. *Ocean Yearbook*, 2, 1980, p. 123-36.
A review of formal international cooperation in marine science since 1902 following the establishment in Copenhagen of the International Council for the Exploration of the Sea (ICES). The author refers to the characteristics of cooperation and the roles played by international organizations.

404 **Oceanography.**
Edited by J. B. Wright. Milton Keynes, England: Open University Press, 1978. 7 vols. maps. bibliog. (Open University Science: a third level course S334, units 1-16).
A complete course in physical oceanography at undergraduate level which includes biological aspects and the law of the sea. Each section is written by a recognized expert and concludes with sample examination questions and comprehensive reference lists.

The depths of the ocean; a general account of the modern science of oceanography based largely on the scientific research of the Norwegian steamer *Michael Sars* in the North Atlantic.
See item no. 48.

The sea: a select bibliography on the legal, political, economic and technological aspects 1978-1979.
See item no. 303.

Proceedings of the Scientific Committee on Oceanic Research (SCOR).
See item no. 388.

The Mitchell Beazley atlas of the oceans.
See item no. 484.

The Times atlas of the oceans.
See item no. 485.

World atlas vol. 2. Atlantic and Indian Oceans.
See item no. 486.

Seafloor

405 **Photographic atlas of the Mid-Atlantic Ridge rift valley.**
Robert D. Ballard, James G. Moore. New York: Springer Verlag, 1977. 114p. maps. bibliog.

A series of annotated photographs of Atlantic sea-floor features on the Azores Plateau resulting from an American-French expedition (Project FAMOUS) using aircraft, ships and submersibles. The location chosen is typical of the zone in the central Atlantic where volcanic activity apparently creates all of the sea-floor, a region of great importance to earth scientists. Geologists systematically investigated large and small geologic features to learn their shape, properties and origin.

406 **Physiographic diagram of the South Atlantic Ocean; the Carribean Sea, the Scotia Sea, and the eastern margin of the South Pacific Ocean.**
Bruce C. Heezen, Marie Tharp. New York: Geological Society of America, 1961. 1 sheet. bibliog.

The map shows the major physiographic features of the South Atlantic including the continental shelf, the Mid-Oceanic Ridge and the ocean-basin floor. An explanatory note by the compilers is published on the verso of the sheet with a list of references.

407 **Physiographic diagram of the North Atlantic Ocean.**
Bruce C. Heezen, Marie Tharp. Boulder, Colorado: Geological
Society of America, 1968. rev. ed. 1 sheet.
Originally published in 1961 to complement the authors' diagram of the South
Atlantic Ocean (q.v.).

408 **General bathymetric chart of the oceans (GEBCO).**
Scale 1:10,000,000.
Intergovernmental Oceanographic Commission. Ottawa:
Canadian Hydrographic Service for the Intergovernmental
Oceanographic Commission, 1982. 5th ed. (Sheet 5.08).
This sheet covers the Atlantic Ocean between latitudes 0° − 46°N and carries a
list of references to soundings and surveys used in its compilation. Other latitudes
are covered as follows: lat. 46° − 72°N sheet 5.04 (1978); lat. 0° − 46°S sheet
5.12 (1978); lat. 40° − 72°S sheet 5.16 (1981).

409 **The American-Antarctic Ridge.**
Lawrence A. Lawver, Henry J. B. Dick. *Journal of Geophysical
Research*, vol. 88, no. B10 (Oct. 1983), p. 8,193-202. maps.
bibliog.
A discussion of the results of a survey carried out in 1980-81 by the research
vessel *Melville* of the Scripps Institution of Oceanography covering the topography, physical geography and tectonics of this submarine ridge which forms a
boundary between the South America and Antarctic plates in the South Atlantic.

410 **The ocean floor; Bruce Heezen commemorative volume.**
Edited by R. A. Scrutton, M. Talwani. Chichester, England:
John Wiley, 1982. 318p. bibliog.
A collection of papers on the morphology of the sea floor including the North
and South Atlantic. A bibliography of some 300 publications by Heezen is
included, many of which deal with the Mid-Atlantic Ridge and other aspects of
submarine geology.

411 **Gazetteer of undersea features. Names approved by the United
States Board on Geographic Names.**
United States Board on Geographic Names. Washington DC:
Defense Mapping Agency, 1981. 3rd ed. 250p.
This gazetteer contains approximately 6,000 names of undersea features of the
world with coordinates.

Geology

412 **A symposium on continental drift.**
P. M. S. Blackett, Sir Edward Bullard, S. K. Runcorn. London:
The Royal Society, 1965. 329p. maps. bibliog. (Philosophical
Transactions, no. 1088).

The symposium contains several papers which contribute to the theory of continental drift based on evidence from the Mid-Atlantic Ridge.

413 **200,000,000 years beneath the sea.**
Peter Briggs. London: Cassell, 1971. 228p. maps. bibliog.

The deep-sea cores drilled on the US research vessel *Glomar Challenger* in the
North and South Atlantic and the Pacific since 1968 have produced powerful
evidence regarding the movement of continents. This is a popular account of the
cruises of the ship, the scientists involved and their ideas.

414 **Hot spots on the Earth's surface.**
Kevin C. Burke, J. Tuzo Wilson. *Scientific American,* vol. 235,
no. 2 (1976), p. 46-57. maps.

These regions of unusual seismic activity record the passage of plates over the
Earth's surface. Several hot spots are recorded on or near the Mid-Atlantic Ridge.

415 **The growth of the North Atlantic Ocean by the spreading of its
floor.**
Peter F. Friend. *Polar Record,* vol. 13, no. 86 (May 1967),
p. 579-88. maps. bibliog.

This article emphasizes the potential of the North Atlantic and Arctic Oceans as
laboratories for the study of major crustal movements and processes.

416 **Paleomagnetic evidence for a proto-Atlantic Ocean.**
E. A. Hailwood, D. H. Tarling. In: *Implications of continental
drift to the earth sciences. Vol. 1.* Edited by D. H. Tarling, S. K.
Runcorn. London: Academic Press, 1973, p. 37-46. bibliog.

The authors provide evidence in support of J. Tuzo Wilson's theory that the site
of the present Atlantic Ocean was occupied by an earlier 'proto-Atlantic' ocean
during late Precambrian and Lower Palaeozoic times.

417 **A revolution in the earth sciences, from continental drift to plate tectonics.**
A. Hallam. Oxford, England: Oxford University Press, 1973. 127p. maps. bibliog.

This book, which is addressed to both students and the interested layman, aims to view the continental drift theory, and its sequel, in their scientific and historical context. The work constitutes a useful informed introduction to the geological history of the Atlantic Ocean.

418 **Atlantic Ocean.**
Bruce C. Heezen, Raymond P. Freeman-Lynde. In: *Geological world atlas 1:10,000,000.* Compiled by G. Choubert, A. Faure-Muret, P. Chanteux. Paris: UNESCO & Commission for the Geological Map of the World, 1976, sheet 22, [4] p. map. bibliog.

This geological map of the Atlantic Ocean floor (scale 1:34,100,000), indicates all holes drilled by the drilling vessel *Glomar Challenger* until the middle of 1977, the data being extracted from the publication *Initial Reports of the Deep Sea Drilling Project* (q.v.). The text is in English and French.

419 **The evolution of the North Atlantic Ocean.**
J. R. Heirtzler. In: *Implications of continental drift to the earth sciences. Vol. 1.* Edited by D. H. Tarling, S. K. Runcorn. London: Academic Press, 1973, p. 191-96. bibliog.

The author describes the evolution of the Atlantic Ocean from the time of the break of North America from Africa and Eurasia some 200 million years ago.

420 **The floor of the Mid-Atlantic Rift.**
J. R. Heirtzler, W. B. Bryan. *Scientific American*, vol. 233, no. 2 (1975), p. 79-91. maps.

A report on the work of a cooperative French-American project begun in 1971 to study the central part of the Mid-Atlantic Ridge, 400 miles southwest of the Azores.

421 **Project Famous – man's first voyage to the Mid-Atlantic Ridge.**
J. R. Heirtzler. *National Geographic Magazine*, vol. 147, no. 5 (May 1975), p. 586-603.

A well-illustrated report on the French-American Mid-Ocean Undersea Study of 1972-74 to investigate the behaviour of tectonic plates on a sea bed section of the Mid-Atlantic Rift some 400 miles southwest of the Azores.

422 **Petrology of the ocean floor.**
R. Hekinian. Amsterdam, The Netherlands: Elsevier, 1982.
393p. maps. bibliog.

Essentially this is a book for marine geologists, but the general reader will find
material of interest here concerning the Mid-Atlantic Ridge and the Atlantic Basin.

423 **Marine geology.**
James P. Kennett. Englewood Cliffs, New Jersey: Prentice-Hall,
1982. 813p. bibliog.

A comprehensive textbook covering the broad spectrum of marine geology
including rocks, sediments, geophysics, structure, microfossils and stratigraphy
together with a history of the ocean basins and their margins.

424 **Paleo-oceanography: global ocean evolution.**
James P. Kennett. *Reviews of Geophysics and Space Physics,*
vol. 21, no. 51 (June 1983), p. 1,258-74. bibliog.

Numerous references to the Atlantic Ocean are included in this global state-of-
the-art review of palaeoceanography.

425 **A schematic model of the evolution of the South Atlantic.**
X. Le Pichon, M. Melguen, H. C. Sibuet. In: *Advances in ocean-
ography.* Edited by Henry Charnock, Sir George Deacon. New
York: Plenum Press, 1978, p. 1-48. maps. bibliog.

A demonstration of the possibility of reconstructing the history of the ocean
basin presented by sedimentary evidence from deep holes made by the drilling
vessel *Glomar Challenger.*

426 **The morphostructure of the Atlantic Ocean: its development
in the Meso-Cenozoic.**
V. M. Litvin, translated from the Russian by V. M. Divid, N. N.
Protsenko, Yu U. Rodzhabov. Dordrecht, The Netherlands:
D. Reidel, 1984. 172p. maps. bibliog.

A study of the interrelationship between the submarine relief and the geological
structure of the Atlantic Ocean floor based on geological studies conducted on
board Soviet research vessels between 1967 and 1977. A number of new maps
based on the data collected have been compiled and these demonstrate the
different stages of Atlantic Ocean Development during the Cenozoic Period.

427 **The ocean basins and margins. Vol. I the South Atlantic.
Vol. II the North Atlantic.**
Edited by Alan E. M. Nairn, G. Stehli. New York: Plenum Press,
1973, 1974. 2 vols. bibliog.

Contains authoritative critical review articles presenting surveys of geological and
geophysical data.

428   **Atlas of continental displacement, 200 million years ago to the present.**
H. G. Owen.   Cambridge, England: Cambridge University Press, 1983. 159p. maps. bibliog.

The first volume of a two-part work designed to provide maps of the distribution of continental and oceanic crust during the last 700 million years of the Earth's history. The spreading of the North and South Atlantic is illustrated textually and in a series of maps.

429   **Sea-floor spreading in the North Atlantic.**
W. C. Pitman III, Manik Talwani. *Geological Society of America Bulletin*, vol. 83, no. 3 (March 1972), p. 619-46. maps. bibliog.

A history of the opening of the North Atlantic Ocean is deduced, primarily from a study of magnetic anomalies. This history is given in terms of a time sequence of poles and angles of rotation that describe the gradual separation of Europe and Africa from North America.

430   **A history of the formation of the Atlantic Ocean.**
A. T. S. Ramsay. *Advancement of Science*, (March) 1971, p. 239-49. maps.

Early theories of continental drift, in which the opening of the Atlantic Ocean is but one related event, relied on the geometrical fit of coastlines, particularly those of South Africa and South America, and certain palaeontological and stratigraphical similarities. These theories lacked a convincing mechanism to account for the initiation and maintenance of drift. This paper explains the opening up of the Atlantic in terms of the concept of the ocean floor spreading of oceanic crust from the mid-ocean ridges, and the partial resorbtion into the earth's mantle.

431   **Paleoceanography.**
Thomas H. M. Schopf.   Cambridge, Massachusetts: Harvard University Press, 1980. 341p. bibliog.

This volume is based on a course given by the author at the University of Chicago. Its aim is to treat succinctly each of the major topics of palaeoceanography with sufficient depth to enable the reader to understand the current literature.

432   **The history of the Atlantic.**
John G. Sclater, Christopher Tapscott. *Scientific American*, vol. 240, no. 6 (June 1979), p. 120-32. maps.

The Atlantic Ocean is 165 million years old. This article discusses its growth and the topography of its bottom in terms of plate-tectonic theory, deep probes of the bottom and measurements of heat flow and magnetism, illustrated with model diagrams and maps.

433 **The paleobathymetry of the Atlantic Ocean from the Jurassic to the present.**
John G. Sclater, Steven Hellinger, Christopher Tapscott.
Journal of Geology, vol. 85, no. 5 (Sept. 1977), p. 509-52. maps. bibliog.

A reconstruction in chart format of the bathymetry of the Atlantic Ocean at twelve specific times between the Jurassic and the present, based on published tectonic histories for the region south of latitude 35°N.

434 **Geological oceanography: evolution of coasts, continental margins and the deep-sea floor.**
Francis P. Shepard. London: Heinemann, 1978. 214p. maps. bibliog.

A useful introduction to the advances made in our knowledge of, for example, spreading sea floors and the nature of waves and currents, written by an emeritus professor of submarine geology at the Scripps Institution of Oceanography.

435 **Submarine geology.**
Francis P. Shepard. New York: Harper & Row, 1973. 3rd ed. 515p. maps. bibliog.

All aspects of submarine geology including the origins and topography of the Atlantic Ocean are dealt with in this textbook. Appended is an extensive bibliography and a gazetteer.

436 **Evolution of the South Atlantic.**
E. S. W. Simpson. *Transactions of the Geological Society of South Africa*, annexure to vol. 89 (1977), 15p. maps. bibliog. (Alex du Toit Memorial Lecture, no. 15).

A review of concepts of continental drift hypotheses since the publication of Alex L. du Toit's book *Our wandering continents* (1937), and a critical assessment of the evolution of the South Atlantic in the light of our present knowledge of plate tectonics.

437 **Continents in motion; the new earth debate.**
Walter Sullivan. London: Macmillan, 1977. 399p. maps. bibliog.

A popular account by the science correspondent of the *New York Times* of the evolution of the concept of continental drift including the birth and growth of the Atlantic Ocean.

438 **Deep drilling results in the Atlantic ocean: continental margins and paleoenvironment.**
Edited by Manik Talwani, William Hay, William B. F. Ryan.
Washington, DC: American Geophysical Union, 1979. 437p.
maps. bibliog. (Maurice Ewing Series, no. 3).
Presents papers read at the second Maurice Ewing Symposium devoted to the results of the first phase of the International Program of Ocean Drilling in the Atlantic. The papers are all concerned with aspects of the history of the formation of the Atlantic.

439 **Deep drilling results in the Atlantic Ocean: ocean crust.**
Edited by Manik Talwani, Christopher G. Harrison, Dennis E.
Hayes. Washington, DC: American Geophysical Union, 1979.
431p. maps. bibliog. (Maurice Ewing Series, no. 2).
Reproduces papers presented at the second Maurice Ewing Symposium assessing the results of the first phase of the International Program of Ocean Drilling as they relate to the Atlantic Ocean crust.

440 **Initial reports of the Deep Sea Drilling Project.**
United States. National Science Foundation. Washington, DC:
National Science Foundation, Ocean Sediment Coring Program,
1969- .
Funded by means of a contract with the University of California, and managed by the Scripps Institution of Oceanography, this international programme for the study of the age of the ocean basins and their processes of development has involved a series of reconnaissance voyages on the drilling ship *Glomar Challenger*. The analysis of the drilling and coring of the rocks and sediments beneath the Atlantic and elsewhere has been analysed in this series of publications.

441 **Oceanographic atlas of the North Atlantic Ocean. Section V marine geology.**
United States. US Naval Oceanographic Office. Washington DC:
Naval Oceanographic Office, 1975. 71p. maps. bibliog. (Pub. 700).
This atlas presents maps and charts dealing with the physiography, structure, lithology, sedimentary petrology, seismicity, volcanism and terrestrial magnetism, showing their distribution either in the oceans themselves or in the coastal regions, and sometimes inland, in order to demonstrate the continental and oceanic relationships.

442 **Depositional history of the South Atlantic Ocean during the last 125 million years.**
Tjeerd H. van Andel, Jörn Thiede, John G. Slater, William W. Hay.
Journal of Geology, vol. 85, no. 6 (Nov. 1977), p. 651-98. maps. bibliog.

A description of the depositional history of the South Atlantic Ocean as it is recorded in the Deep Sea Drilling Project (DSDP) data, and a tracing of the sedimentary consequences of the gradual change in width, depth and shape of the basin. An attempt is made to draw some conclusions about the evolving oceanic deep and shallow circulation during the last 100 million years.

North Atlantic biota and their history; a symposium held at the University of Iceland, Reykjavík July 1962.
See item no. 516.

Geology of the middle Atlantic islands.
See item no. 669.

Dynamics and chemistry

General

443 **Modern concepts of oceanography.**
Edited by G. E. R. Deacon, Margaret B. Deacon. Stroudsburg, Pennsylvania: Hutchinson Ross, 1982. 386p. bibliog.

A volume of reprinted key scientific papers in the field of oceanography containing several papers relating to Atlantic currents.

444 **Sargasso Sea expedition.**
John W. Foerster, Patricia M. Thompson. *Explorers Journal*, vol. 56, no. 4 (Dec. 1978), p. 181-85.

A general account of a six-weeks' expedition from Woods Hole, Massachusetts, in 1978 to gather information on the biological activity of the Sargasso Sea, a water mass bounded by the major North Atlantic current systems.

445 **The distribution of phosphorous and oxygen in the Atlantic Ocean, as observed during the I.G.Y., 1957-58.**
David A. McGill. *Progress in Oceanography*, vol. 2, 1964, p. 129-211. bibliog.

Data on total phosphorous distribution in the Atlantic Ocean presented for the first time and taken from a resurvey of the ocean during the International Geophysical Year, 1957-58.

446 **The anatomy of the Atlantic.**
Henry Stommel. *Scientific American*, vol. 192, no. 1 (Jan.
1955), p. 30-35. maps.

A review of our knowledge of Atlantic currents, temperature, saltiness and
oxygen content gained from oceanographic voyages during the period 1925-55.
It is estimated that even if all the winds were to stop and the atmosphere to fall
into a dead calm, the major surface circulations could draw enough energy from
the potential lens-shaped masses of warm water in certain regions of the ocean.

447 **The Sargasso Sea.**
John Teal, Mildred Teal. Boston: Little, Brown, 1975. 216p.
map. bibliog.

Presents excerpts from the journal of Dr. John Teal, the chief scientist on cruise
62 of the research vessel *Atlantic II* out of Woods Hole, Massachusetts, to the
Sargasso Sea in September 1971. This is a factual and personal account of life in,
above, around, and beneath the Sargasso Sea. The peculiar hydrology of this vast
whirlpool of currents is explained and there is a detailed account of the fauna and
flora. The book concludes with a discussion of the sea as a source of food for man
and the consequences of man-made pollution.

448 **Major currents in the North and South Atlantic Oceans between
64°N and 60°S.**
United States. US Naval Oceanographic Office. Washington DC:
Naval Oceanographic Office, 1967. 92p. (TR 193).

Identifies the major currents of the North and South Atlantic Oceans and
provides a comprehensive summary of their characteristics.

449 **Oceanographic atlas of the North Atlantic Ocean. Section I,
tides and currents.**
United States. US Naval Oceanographic Office. Washington DC:
Naval Oceanographic Office 1968. 300p. maps. bibliog.
(Pub. no. 700).

This atlas presents seasonal charts compiled from monthly or three-monthly
averages.

450 **Oceanographic atlas of the North Atlantic Ocean. Section IV,
sea and swell.**
United States. US Naval Oceanographic Office. Washington DC:
Naval Oceanographic Office, 1969. 227p. maps. bibliog.
(Pub. no. 700).

An atlas of monthly charts presenting winds, sea and swell, wave period-height
and period direction, ship routing feasibility and wave persistence.

451 **On the North Atlantic circulation.**
L. V. Worthington. Baltimore, Maryland: Johns Hopkins
University Press, 1976. 110p. maps. bibliog. (Johns Hopkins
Oceanographic Studies, no. 6).

The author's hypothesis is that the main circulation of the North Atlantic consists
of two separate anticyclonic gyres. Fresh evidence from the International
Geophysical Year, 1957-58, supports his theory.

Gulf Stream

452 **Wayward ocean river.**
Louis De Vorsey. *Geographical Magazine*, vol. 52, no. 7 (April
1980), p. 501-10. maps.

An examination of the first attempts to map the path of the Gulf Stream on early
charts.

453 **William De Brahm's 'Continuation of the Atlantic pilot', an
empirically supported eighteenth-century model of North
Atlantic surface circulation.**
Louis De Vorsey, Jr. In: *Oceanography: the past.* Edited by
Mary Sears and D. Merriman. New York: Springer-Verlag, 1980.
p. 718-33. map. bibliog.

De Brahm's *The Atlantic pilot*, published in 1772, contained the first published
chart to show the Gulf Stream as a major feature of the North Atlantic Ocean.
His unpublished *Continuation of the Atlantic pilot* (1775) based on a hydrographic survey in which De Brahm took part, and now in the Harvard University
Library, contains additional information on Atlantic currents, navigation and
meteorology.

454 **The Gulf Stream on eighteenth century maps and charts.**
Louis De Vorsey, Jr. *Map Collector*, issue no. 15 (June 1981),
p. 2-10, maps.

An account of the pioneer charting by Benjamin Franklin and others.

455 **Gulf Stream '60.**
F. C. Fuglister. *Progress in Oceanography*, vol. 1 (1963),
p. 265-373. maps. bibliog.

Presents the results of a comprehensive study of a large portion of the Gulf
Stream undertaken by the Woods Hole Oceanographic Institution, from April
to June 1960.

456 **The Gulf Stream.**
T. F. Gaskell. London: Cassell, 1972. 170p. maps.
A popular account which considers the history, geography, climate and meteorology, hydrography and political aspects of the Gulf Stream.

457 **The Benjamin Franklin and Timothy Folger charts of the Gulf Stream.**
Philip L. Richardson. In: *Oceanography: the past.* Edited by Mary Sears and D. Merriman. New York: Springer-Verlag, 1980. p. 703-17. maps. bibliog.
A description of an early chart first printed in 1769-70 in London and a copy discovered by the author in the Bibliothèque Nationale, Paris, in 1978. The article discusses its depiction of the Gulf Stream relative to later charts and recent measurements.

458 **Progress on the Gulf Stream.**
Philip L. Richardson. *Geographical Magazine*, vol. 52, no. 8 (May 1980), p. 575-81. maps.
An explanation of how the methods of oceanography have provided a better understanding of the Gulf Stream.

459 **The Gulf Stream; a physical and dynamical description.**
Henry Stommel. Berkeley, California: University of California Press; London: Cambridge University Press, 1965. 248p. illus. maps. bibliog.
The standard work on the Gulf Stream written for physical scientists.

Assault on the unknown; the International Geophysical Year.
See item no. 55.

Navigation of the Atlantic Ocean.
See item no. 502.

Ocean passages for the world.
See item no. 506.

Impingement of man on the oceans.
See item no. 559.

International Decade of Ocean Exploitation (IDOE). Progress Reports.
See item no. 561.

Tin in oceans.
See item no. 563.

Ice and Icebergs

460 **Icebergs: a new problem for oil exploration and production.**
Jean Duval. *Geological Survey of Canada. Paper 71-23* (1973),
p. 639-52.
This article discusses the problems presented by icebergs in the North Atlantic
Ocean as well as their frequency, detection, estimation of drift, and how to deal
with them during oilfield development.

461 **Ice at the end of . . . [month of the year].**
Great Britain. Meteorological Office, Bracknell, Berkshire,
England: Meteorological Office.
A monthly chart indicating the distribution of warm and cold water and ice
probability in the North Atlantic and Arctic Oceans.

462 **Ice conditions in areas adjacent to the North Atlantic Ocean from
June to August 1983.**
Marine Observer, vol. 54, no. 283 (1984), p. 45-48. maps.
Provides information in words and charts regarding: the position of ice edges; sea
surface and air temperatures, together with departures from the means; and
eastern iceberg limits in season (February-July). This information is reported
regularly in each quarterly issue of the *Marine Observer*.

463 **The International Ice Patrol.**
Marine Observer, vol. 51, no. 271 (1981), p. 20-31. maps.
An outline history of the development of this service with a description of the
behaviour of ice in the North Atlantic with special reference to iceberg drift.

464 **Eleven year chronicle of one of the world's most gigantic icebergs.**
E. Paul McClain. *Mariners Weather Log*, vol. 22, no. 5 (1978),
p. 328-33. map. bibliog.
Deals with the tracking by satellite of a vast tabular iceberg 'Trolltunga' from its
calving off the coast of Antarctica in August 1967 to its eventual drift past South
Georgia into the South Atlantic in April and May 1978.

465 **Long term trends in the iceberg threat in the northwest Atlantic.**
Charles W. Morgan. *US Coast Guard Bulletin*, no. 57 (1974),
p. 15-26. maps.
An analysis of records of icebergs drifting past the coast of Newfoundland since
1880 shows that the seasonal count has fallen by 55% in the past 30 years.

466   **Report of the International Ice Patrol in the North Atlantic.**
      Bulletin.
      Washington DC: United States Coast Guard, [1914?] - . annual.

The International Ice Patrol came into being as a result of the sinking of the
Titanic in 1912 and has been carried out ever since by the United States on behalf
of other maritime powers subscribing to the original convention of 1913. Originally
reports were made by US Coast Guard vessels during the ice season. Today the
work is largely carried out by aircraft in the region of the Grand Banks. Facsimile
broadcasting stations provide special forecasts.

467   **Iceberg dead ahead!**
      Leo Shubow.   Boston, Massachusetts: Bruce Humphries, 1959.
      203p.

A first-hand account of the International Ice Patrol in the North Atlantic.

468   **Oceanographic atlas of the North Atlantic Ocean. Section III, ice.**
      US Naval Oceanographic Office.   Washington DC: Naval Oceano-
      graphic Office, 1968. 156p. maps. bibliog. (Pub. no. 700).

Monthly charts present data on coastal ice, mean concentration, percentage
frequencies of occurrence, thickness, pressure ice, maximum limits and unusual
observations of ice.

Voyage of the iceberg; the story of the iceberg that sank the *Titanic*.
See item no. 158.

Meteorological aspects of the drift of ice from the Weddell Sea towards
the mid-latitude westerlies.
See item no. 479.

The Mariner's handbook.
See item no. 505.

Ocean passages for the world.
See item no. 506.

Weather and climate

469   **Atlantic hurricanes.**
      Gordon E. Dunn, Banner, I. Miller.   Baton Rouge, Louisiana:
      Louisiana State University Press, 1960. 326p. maps. bibliog.

The authors explain in layman's language how hurricanes occur, how they travel,
the physical processes involved in their formation and dissipation, methods of
tracking and forecasting procedures.

470   Tables of temperature, relative humidity, precipitation and
       sunshine for the world. Part I North America and Greenland
       (including Hawaii and Bermuda).
       Great Britain. Meteorological Office.   London: HM Stationery
       Office, 1980. 223p. maps. bibliog. (Meteorological Office Publica-
       tion OP 1100.12.023 (14)).
Provides average daily and monthly climatic tables.

471   Tables of temperature, relative humidity, precipitation and
       sunshine for the world. Part II Central and South America, the
       West Indies and Bermuda.
       Great Britain. Meteorological Office.   London: HM Stationery
       Office, 1958. 53p. map. bibliog. (Meteorological Office Publica-
       tion OP 1100.12.023 (2)).
Includes average daily and monthly tables for the Central West Atlantic, South
Atlantic, Falkland Islands and Dependencies and Fernando de Noronha.

472   Tables of temperature, relative humidity, precipitation and
       sunshine for the world. Part III Europe and the Azores.
       Great Britain. Meteorological Office.   London: HM Stationery
       Office, 1972. 228p. maps. bibliog. (Meteorological Office
       Publication 100.12.023 (16)).
Presents average daily and monthly climatic tables.

473   Tables of temperature, relative humidity, precipitation and
       sunshine for the world. Part IV Africa, the Atlantic Ocean south
       of 35°N and the Indian Ocean.
       Great Britain. Meteorological Office.   London: HM Stationery
       Office, 1983. 429p. maps. bibliog. (Meteorological Office
       Publication 1100.12.023 (17)).
Includes monthly tables for Madeira, the Canary Islands, Cape Verde Islands,
São Tomé, Ascension Island, St. Helena, Tristan da Cunha and Gough Island.

474   Atmosphere and ocean; our fluid environments.
       John G. Harvey.   Horsham, Sussex, England: Artemis, 1976.
       143p. maps. bibliog.
An integrated introduction to meteorology and physical oceanography, this book
is concerned mainly with the physical aspects of the atmosphere.

475 **Climatic atlas of the tropical Atlantic and eastern Pacific oceans.**
Stefan Hastenrath, Peter Lamb. Madison, Wisconsin: University
of Wisconsin Press, 1977. 112p. maps. bibliog.

A series of monthly charts showing values for the following meteorological
elements: sea level pressure; resultant wind vector; wind speed; sea surface
temperature; air temperature; dew point temperature; total cloud amount; and
low cloud amount and present weather types including drizzle, rain, rain showers,
thunderstorm phenomena and fog. The atlas presents a climatology based on data
for the period 1911-70.

476 **The Marine Observers' log.**
Marine Observer, vol. 54, no. 283 (1984), p. 8-11.

A quarterly selection of observations relating to such topics as weather phenomena
and marine life, reported by mariners navigating the North and South Atlantic
and other oceans.

477 **The world weather guide.**
E. A. Pearce, C. G. Smith. London: Hutchinson, 1984. 480p.
bibliog.

This simple guide to basic world weather contains statistical tables based on long-
term averages for every country in the world, including the principal Atlantic
islands covered by this bibliography. The tables clearly display: average daily
maximum and minimum temperatures in Centigrade and Fahrenheit; relative
humidity; average monthly precipitation in inches and millimetres; and latitude
and longitude and height above sea level. Concise notes on the climate of each
region supplement the information provided in the tables. An introductory
chapter explains the use of a 'comfort index' relating relative humidity to air
temperature, and a 'wind chill index' relating temperature to wind speed.

478 **The ocean-atmosphere system.**
A. H. Perry, J. M. Walker. London: Longman, 1977. 160p.
maps. bibliog.

This book is concerned with interactions between the atmosphere and the oceans
and with the interdependence of atmospheric and oceanic circulations. It is
addressed primarily to advanced students.

479 **Meteorological aspects of the drift of ice from the Weddell Sea
towards the mid-latitude westerlies.**
W. Schwerdtfeger. *Journal of Geophysical Research*, vol. 84,
no. C 10 (1979), p. 6321-28. bibliog.

A discussion of the effect of winds from the Antarctic ice shelf on the drift of ice
as far north as latitude 61°S which has a marked effect on temperature conditions
in the South Atlantic.

480   **Oceanography for meteorologists.**
      H. U. Sverdrup.   London: Allen & Unwin, 1952. 243p. maps.
      bibliog.
A valuable and authoritative introduction to the interrelationship between
physical processes in the ocean and the atmosphere.

481   **U. S. Navy marine climatic atlas of the world. Vol. I North
      Atlantic Ocean. Published by direction of the Chief of Naval
      Operations.**
      United States. Navy.   Washington DC: US Government Printing
      Office, 1955. 291p. maps. (NAVAER 50-1C-528).
Climatic data for the surface and upper air presented by monthly graphs, tables
and isopleths.

482   **U.S. Navy marine climatic atlas of the world. Vol. IV South
      Atlantic Ocean. Published by direction of the Chief of Naval
      Operations.**
      United States. Navy.   Washington DC: US Government Printing
      Office, 1958. 285p. maps. (NAVAER 50-1C-531).
Climatic data presented by graphs, tables and isopleths and separated into surface
and upper air observations.

483   **Climates of the oceans.**
      Edited by H. van Loon.   Amsterdam: The Netherlands: Elsevier,
      1984. 716p. maps. bibliog.
Chapter 1 'Climate of the South Atlantic Ocean', by O. Höflich, and Chapter 2
'Climate of the North Atlantic Ocean', by G. B. Tucker and R. G. Barry, constitute the best summaries of these topics to date. Climatic charts and maps are
appended.

**Symposium on environmental conditions in the northwest Atlantic
1960-1969.**
See item no. 329.

**The physical geography of the sea and its meteorology, being a recon-
struction of the eighth edition of 'The physical geography of the sea'.**
See item no. 382.

McGraw-Hill encyclopaedia of ocean and atmospheric sciences.
See item no. 386.

The mariner's handbook.
See item no. 505.

Atlases, Pilots, Charts and Handbooks

Atlases

484 **The Mitchell Beazley atlas of the oceans.**
Edited by Martyn Bramwell. London: Mitchell Beazley, 1977.
208p. maps.

A splendidly illustrated introduction to all aspects of the oceans with maps, diagrams and texts providing basic information on the bathymetry, circulation, evolution, mineral resources and living resources of the Atlantic.

485 **The Times atlas of the oceans.**
Edited by Alastair Couper. London: Times Books, 1983. 272p.
maps. bibliog.

This popular volume contains a wealth of colourful pictures of marine life and activities. The text and maps cover such topics as ocean environment, geography, atmosphere, biology, resources of the ocean, both living and mineral, ocean trade and shipping, strategic use and the law of the sea. A bibliography and glossary are appended.

486 **World atlas vol. 2. Atlantic and Indian oceans.**
Edited by Sergei G. Gorshkov with an introductory text and
a gazetteer translated into English, and a key for non-Russian-
speaking users. Oxford, England: Pergamon, 1978. 334p. maps.

An exceedingly comprehensive and up-to-date Soviet atlas of the Atlantic Ocean. The introduction and gazetteer, published as a separate 117 page booklet, sum- marizes each section of the atlas as follows: 1, 'History of the exploration of the ocean'; 2, 'The ocean floor'; 3, 'Climate'; 4, 'Hydrochemistry'; 5, 'Biogeography'; and 6, 'Reference and navigational and geographical charts'.

487 **Lloyds maritime atlas including a comprehensive list of ports and shipping places of the world.**
London: Lloyds of London Press, 1983. 14th ed. variously paged.

The ports and shipping places are listed geographically together with their approxi- mate latitude and longitude. A distance table is also included.

Atlas of maritime history.
See item no. 19.

Pilots

488 **Africa pilot vol. 1, comprising the Arquipélago da Madeira, Islas Canarias, Arquipélago de Cabo Verde, the west coast of Africa from Cabo Espartel to Bakasi Peninsula.**
Great Britain. Hydrographer of the Navy. Taunton, England: Hydrographer of the Navy, 1982; 13th ed. 364p. maps. (N.P.1).
In addition to the standard navigational information this pilot includes useful general information for visitors to Madeira, the Cape Verde Islands, and the Canary Islands.

489 **Africa pilot vol. 2, comprising the west coast of Africa from Bakasi Peninsula to Cape Agulhas; islands in the Bight of Biafra; Ascension Island; Saint Helena Island; Tristan da Cunha group and Gough Island.**
Great Britain. Hydrographer of the Navy. Taunton, England: Hydrographer of the Navy, 1977. 12th ed. 248p. maps. bibliog. (N.P.2).
This pilot contains useful background information on the South Atlantic islands.

490 **Newfoundland and Labrador pilot, coasts of Newfoundland including Ile Saint-Pierre and Miquelon; strait of Belle Isle and coast of Labrador to Cape Kakkiviak.**
Great Britain. Hydrographer of the Navy. Taunton, England: Hydrographer of the Navy, 1978. 10th ed. 443p. maps. (N.P.50).
The Saint Pierre and Miquelon archipelago constitutes the sole remaining French territory in North America.

491 **Nova Scotia and Bay of Fundy pilot, south-east coast of Nova Scotia and Bay of Fundy including Sable Island and outlying banks.**
Great Britain. Hydrographer of the Navy. Taunton, England: Hydrographer of the Navy, 1971. 11th ed. 188p. maps. (N.P.59).
The pilot includes a list of relevant Canadian and United States sources of information.

492 **South America pilot vol. 1, north-eastern and eastern coasts of South America, from Cabo Orange to Cabo Tres Puntas.**
Great Britain. Hydrographer of the Navy. Taunton, England: Hydrographer of the Navy, 1975. 11th ed. 318p. maps. bibliog. (N.P.5).
This pilot covers the section of the western South Atlantic Ocean from approximately northern Brazil southwards to Uruguay and central Argentina.

493 **South America pilot vol. 2, east, south and west coasts of South America from Cabo Tres Puntas to Cabo Raper, and Falkland Islands.**
Great Britain. Hydrographer of the Navy. Taunton, England: Hydrographer of the Navy, 1971. 15th ed. 313p. maps. bibliog. (N.P.6).
This work is valuable for general background information on the Falkland Islands.

494 **South American pilot vol. 4, comprising the islands of Tobago and Trinidad-north-eastern coast of Venezuela from Punta Pēnas to Cabo Orange, including Rio Orinoco-the northern coast of South America from Punta Pēnas to Punta Tirbi including Nederlandse Antillen.**
Great Britain. Hydrographer of the Navy. Taunton, England: Hydrographer of the Navy, 1982. 481p. maps. bibliog. (N.P.7).
This volume contains useful general background information on the area and includes a bibliography. It also includes specialised sailing directions.

495 **West coasts of Spain and Portugal pilot from Cabo Ortegal to Gibraltar, Strait of Gibraltar, north coasts of Africa from Cabo Espartel to Ceuta, and Arquipélago dos Açores.**
Great Britain. Hydrographer of the Navy. Taunton, England: Hydrographer of the Navy, 1972. 5th ed. 188p. maps. (N.P.67).
Chapter 7 (p. 131-52) deals with the Azores and with coastal views (p. 176-78).

Charts

496 **North Atlantic Ocean eastern portion.**
Great Britain. Hydrographer of the Navy. Taunton, England: Hydrographer of the Navy, 1975. Scale: 1:10,000,000. 1 sheet. (Chart 4014-International Chart Series).
This chart covers latitudes 5°S to 65°N, longitudes 10°E to 45°W. Depths are shown in metres and the directions of currents are indicated.

497 **North Atlantic Ocean western portion.**
Great Britain. Hydrographer of the Navy. Taunton, England: Hydrographer of the Navy, 1981. New ed. Scale: 1:7,500,000. 1 sheet. (Chart 2422-International Chart Series).
Covers latitudes 0°N to 65°N, longitudes 35°W to 90°W. Depths are shown in metres and the directions of currents are indicated.

498 **South Atlantic Ocean; from the latest information in the Hydrographic Department 1976, with additions and corrections to 1982.**
Great Britain. Hydrographer of the Navy. Taunton, England:
Hydrographer of the Navy, 1982. Scale: 12,900,000. 1 sheet.
(Chart 2203-International Chart Series).

A useful general chart south of the equator to latitude 60°S.

499 **South Atlantic Ocean eastern part.**
Great Britain. Hydrographer of the Navy. Taunton, England:
Hydrographer of the Navy, 1984. New ed. Scale: 1:10,000,000.
1 sheet. (Chart 4021-International Chart Series).

Covers latitudes 55°S to 15°N, longitudes 30°E to 25°W. Depths are shown in metres and the directions of currents are indicated.

500 **South Atlantic Ocean western portion.**
Great Britain. Hydrographer of the Navy. Taunton, England:
Hydrographer of the Navy, 1982. Scale: 1:10,000,000. 1 sheet.
(Chart 4020-International Chart Series).

Covers latitudes 60°S to 10°N, longitudes 10°W to 70°W. Depths are shown in metres and the directions of currents are indicated including the Antarctic Convergence.

501 **Islands and anchorages in the South Atlantic Ocean.**
Great Britain. Hydrographer of the Navy. Taunton, England:
Hydrographer of the Navy, 1963. Various scales. 1 sheet.
(Chart 1769-International Chart Series).

The islands depicted include Gough, Tristan da Cunha, Bouvetøya, and Saint Helena (James and Rupert's Bays).

History of cartography.
See item no. 12.

Explorers maps; chapters in the cartographic record of geographical discovery.
See item no. 29.

Handbooks

502 **Navigation of the Atlantic Ocean.**
A. B. Becher. London: J. D. Potter, 1892. 5th ed. 192p. maps.
An interesting handbook from the days of sailing ships with folding maps showing the direction of winds and currents.

503 **Admiralty distance tables Atlantic Ocean covering North Atlantic Ocean, South Atlantic Ocean, North-west Europe, Mediterranean, Caribbean, Gulf of Mexico.**
Great Britain. Hydrographer of the Navy. Taunton, England: Hydrographer of the Navy, 1978; 1st ed. rev. 231p. maps.
The tables in this compilation enable one to plot the shortest distance between the point of departure and destination, which can then be modified as circumstances require to find the quickest and most suitable route.

504 **Catalogue of Admiralty charts and other hydrographic publications.**
Great Britain. Hydrographer of the Navy. Taunton, England: Hydrographer of the Navy, 1984. 176p. maps. (N.P. 131).
A comprehensive guide to, and listing of, all British charts and allied publications (lists of lights, pilots, etc.) which is published annually.

505 **The mariner's handbook.**
Great Britain. Hydrographer of the Navy. Taunton, England: Hydrographer of the Navy, 1983. 5th ed. 163p. maps.
An essential work of reference for navigators with chapters on the sea and the sea bed, meteorology and ice hazards which includes an ice glossary. The handbook is periodically updated by supplements.

506 **Ocean passages for the world.**
Great Britain. Hydrographer of the Navy. Taunton, England: Hydrographer of the Navy, 1973. 3rd ed. 258p. maps (some in separate folder). (N.P. 136).
This publication contains information, based on the latest available material, relating to the planning and conduct of ocean voyages, and is kept up-to-date with periodical supplements. Part 1 refers to power vessels and part 2 to sailing vessels, with sections devoted to the North and South Atlantic. There are notes on weather and other factors affecting passages, directions for a number of recommended routes, and distance figures designed to help the planner calculate his voyage time. Charts in an accompanying folder show, for example, surface current distribution, world climate and the main ocean routes.

507 **Reed's nautical almanac 1985.**
London: Thomas Reed, 1984. 5th ed. 1,338p. maps.

A comprehensive annually up-dated handbook for mariners containing information on navigational aids, anchorages, port facilities and landmarks of especial interest to visiting yachtsmen, for the Azores, Madeira and the Canary Islands.

508 **South Atlantic official standard names approved by the United States Board on Geographic Names.**
United States. US Board on Geographic Names.   Washington DC: US Government Printing Office, 1957. 53p. (Gazetteer no. 31).

This gazetteer contains names and geographical coordinates for St. Helena, Ascension Island, Tristan da Cunha, the Falkland Islands, the South Orkney Islands, the South Shetland Islands and Bouvetøya.

Ocean Fauna

General

509 **A biography of the sea; the story of the world ocean, its animal populations and its influence on human history.**
Richard Carrington. London: Chatto & Windus, 1960. 286p. maps. bibliog.
A popular synthesis of knowledge of marine biology.

510 **The sea.**
Rachel Carson. London: Macgibbon & Kee, 1964. 611p.
This volume comprises the author's three published works: *The sea around us* (1951); *Under the sea-wind* (1952); and *The edge of the sea* (1955). A marine biologist with the US Fish and Wildlife Service, the author's trilogy constitutes an introduction to the life of the sea written with the insight of a poet.

511 **The ecology of the seas.**
Edited by D. H. Cushing, J. J. Walsh. Oxford, England: Blackwell Scientific Publications, 1976. 467p. bibliog.
A collection of scientific papers covering many aspects of marine biology including fish production, growth and food chains.

512 **Euphausids and pelagic amphipods distribution in North Atlantic and Arctic waters.**
Maxwell J. Dunbar. New York: American Geographical Society, 1964. 18p. maps. bibliog. (Serial Atlas of the Marine Environment, Folio 6).
Information concerning the geographic distribution of eight examples of northern North Atlantic and Arctic planktonic crustaceans presented in a series of maps.

Ocean Fauna. General

513 **The face of the deep.**
Bruce C. Heezen, Charles D. Hallister. New York: Oxford
University Press, 1971. 659p. maps.
An illustrated natural history of the ocean bottom derived from photographs
obtained on expeditions to the Atlantic, Pacific and Antarctic waters. An accom-
panying text explains and interprets the photographs.

514 **Journal of the Marine Biological Association of the United
Kingdom.**
Cambridge, England: Cambridge University Press, 1887- .
quarterly.
A journal for professional marine biologists covering all aspects of the zoology
and life history of fish and marine mammals, mainly in British waters and the
North Atlantic Ocean, together with related papers in physical oceanography.

515 **Marine ecology; a comprehensive, integrated treatise on life in
oceans and coastal waters. Vols. 1-5.**
Edited by Otto Kinne. London: Wiley-Interscience, 1970.
5 vols. in 12. maps. bibliog.
This all-embracing work covers the following broad topics: vol. 1, 'Environmental
factors'; vol. 2, 'Physiological mechanisms'; vol. 3, 'Cultivation'; vol. 4, 'Dynamics';
and vol. 5, 'Ocean management'.

516 **North Atlantic biota and their history; a symposium held at the
University of Iceland, Reykjavík, July 1962.**
Edited by Askell Löve, Doris Löve. Oxford, England: Pergamon,
1963. 430p. maps. bibliog.
These collected conference papers are largely concerned with the status of knowledge on the distribution and history of plants and animals in the North Atlantic
area and include reviews of the biogeographical and geological investigations concerning these problems.

517 **Oceanography and Marine Biology; an Annual Review.**
Aberdeen, Scotland: Aberdeen University Press, 1963- . annual.
A review for research scientists of basic aspects of marine biology dealing with
subjects of especial or topical importance.

518 **Annales Biologiques.** (Biological Annals.)
Edited by H. Tambs-Lyche. Copenhagen: Conseil International
pour l'Exploration de la Mer, 1943- . annual.
This periodical contains numerous English language papers; part 1 describes the
hydrographic situation in the northwestern Atlantic, especially the shelf and slope
waters; part 2 is devoted to plankton research; and part 3 deals with fish stocks.

Fish

519 **Check-list of the fishes of the north-eastern Atlantic and of the Mediterranean. Vols. 1-2.**
Edited by J. C. Hureau, Th. Monod. Paris: UNESCO, 1973.
2 vols. bibliog.
Vol. 1 includes the detailed text of the check-list and vol. 2 provides a bibliography with over 5,000 references.

520 **Fishes of the Atlantic coast of Canada.**
A. H. Leim, W. B. Scott. Ottawa: Fisheries Research Board of Canada, 1966. 485p. maps. bibliog.
An illustrated classification of fish species.

521 **Fishes of the world.**
Joseph S. Nelson. New York: John Wiley, 1976. 416p. maps. bibliog.
The main purpose of this textbook is to present an introductory systematic treatment of all major fish groups. A series of 45 maps present the world ocean distribution of fish. The bibliography includes some of the more important or useful works but it is not intended to be comprehensive.

Atlantic Ocean fisheries.
See item no. 316.

Fisheries resources of the sea and their management.
See item no. 319.

Birds

522 **Birds of the ocean, containing descriptions of all the sea-birds of the world, with notes on their habits and guides to their identification.**
W. B. Alexander. New York: G. P. Putnam's, 1963. 2nd ed. 306p.
An essential handbook for the identification of sea birds.

523 **The migration of birds.**
Jean Dorst. London: Heinemann, 1961. 476p. maps. bibliog.
Translated from the French edition of 1956, this work provides a scholarly and comprehensive review of the subject.

524 **Sea-birds; an introduction to the natural history of the sea-birds of the North Atlantic.**
James Fisher, R. M. Lockley. London: Collins, 1954. 320p. maps. bibliog.
Much of this book stems from the authors' own field work in the Eastern Atlantic. An appendix lists the sea-birds of the North Atlantic and their distribution.

525 **Southern albatrosses and petrels; an identification guide.**
Peter C. Harper, F. C. Kinsky, edited by Cleveland Duval. Wellington: Price Milburn for Victoria University Press, 1978. 2nd ed. 116p. map. bibliog.
A useful pocket guide with identification plates of southern hemisphere seabirds.

526 **The wandering albatross.**
William Jameson. London: Hart-Davis, 1958. 99p. maps. bibliog.
An introduction to the natural history of *Diomedea exulans* in the South Atlantic.

527 **Ocean birds; their breeding, biology and behaviour.**
Lars Löfgren. London: Croom Helm, 1984. 240p. maps. bibliog.
A comprehensive popular guide to all aspects of seabird life covering: evolution and taxonomy; methods of feeding and flying; weather protection; migration; distinctive habitats; and plumage and relationship to marking and behaviour. The book is illustrated with over 200 colour plates in addition to line drawings.

528 **Penguin; adventures among the birds, beasts and whales of the far south.**
Leonard Harrison Matthews. London: Peter Owen, 1977. 165p.
An autobiographical account of this distinguished British naturalist's observations on the penguin species of the Falkland Islands, South Georgia and the Antarctic during the 1920s.

529 **The bird faunas of Africa and its islands.**
R. E. Moreau. New York: Academic Press, 1966. 424p. maps. bibliog.
Chapter 16 describes the bird faunas of the west coast islands including the Canaries and the Cape Verde Islands.

530 **Distribution of North Atlantic pelagic birds.**
Robert Cushman Murphy. New York: American Geographical Society, 1967. 20p. maps. bibliog. (Serial Atlas of the Marine Environment, Folio 14).
A listing of sea-birds with notes on their distribution and migration followed by eight plates containing maps showing the range and breeding sites of the various species.

118

531   Oceanic birds of South America; a study of species of the related coasts and seas. Vols. 1 and 2.
Robert Cushman Murphy. New York: American Museum of Natural History, 1936. 2 vols. maps. bibliog.
An indispensable work which covers the birds of the Mid-Atlantic and South Atlantic. Part 1 describes the physical environment and part 2 the life histories of the oceanic birds.

532   Penguins past and present, here and there.
George Gaylord Simpson. New Haven, Connecticut: Yale University Press, 1976. 150p. maps. bibliog.
An entertaining, informative and wide-ranging account by one of the world's experts on penguins.

533   Penguins.
John Sparks, Tony Soper. Newton Abbot, England: David & Charles, 1967. 263p. map. bibliog.
A comprehensive account of the life histories of the various species of penguin with helpful line illustrations.

534   Birds of the Atlantic Ocean.
Ted Stokes. Feltham, England: Country Life Books, 1968. 156p. maps.
Well-illustrated in colour by the well-known bird artist Keith Shackleton this naturalist's guide to the ocean birds is arranged in classified order with distribution maps accompanying each species.

535   A sailor's guide to ocean birds Atlantic and Mediterranean.
Ted Stokes. London: Adlard Coles; New York: John de Graff, 1963. 64p.
The book consists of three sections: first-sighting recognition tables; the most common birds of the Atlantic; a classified list of Atlantic ocean birds. The recognition sketches are by Keith Shackleton.

536   Penguins.
Bernard Stonehouse. London: Arthur Barker; New York: Golden Press, 1968. 96p.
Seventeen species of penguin in the southern hemisphere are described in this popular account of penguins by an acknowledged expert in the field. References to his own research on heat balance and the significance of size and shape are included.

537   A guide to seabirds on the ocean routes.
G. S. Tuck. London: Collins, 1980. 144p. map.
Includes observations along several transatlantic and Atlantic coastal routes.

538 **Seabirds of the tropical Atlantic Ocean.**
George E. Watson. Washington DC: Smithsonian Press, 1966.
120p. maps.
This monograph is especially valuable for the plates which show in-flight drawings
of the various sea-bird species. The text deals in detail with the identification of
the 115 species normally encountered in the tropical Atlantic.

539 **On the habits and distribution of birds on the North Atlantic.**
V. C. Wynne-Edwards. *Proceedings of the Boston Society of
Natural History*, vol. 40, no. 4 (1935) p. 233-46. maps. bibliog.
This article is based on the author's observations on eight consecutive trans-
atlantic voyages in 1933. The birds described are mainly northern hemisphere
breeding species but also included are observations on the northern migration of
Wilson's Petrel (*Oceanites oceanicus*).

The bird faunas of Africa and its islands.
See item no. 670.

Bird faunas of the Atlantic islands. Vols. 1-4.
See items no. 676, 681, 687, 700.

**Wandering albatross; adventures among the albatrosses and petrels in
the Southern Ocean.**
See item no. 898.

Marine mammals

540 **The encyclopedia of sea mammals.**
David J. Coffey. London: Hart-Davis, MacGibbon, 1977. 223p.
This is a well-illustrated popular account of whales, seals, sirenia and sea otters
by a veterinary clinician specializing in animal behaviour.

541 **Marine mammals.**
Richard J. Harrison, Judith E. King. London: Hutchinson
University Library, 1965. 192p. bibliog.
A general account for the layman of the whales, seals and dugongs, their appear-
ance, classification and anatomical and physiological adaptation to life in sea
water.

542   **Handbook of marine mammals. Vol. 1, the walrus, sea lions, fur seals and sea otter. Vol. 2, seals.**
Edited by Sam E. Ridgway, Richard J. Harrison.   London:
Academic Press, 1981. 2 vols. bibliog.
A guide to marine mammal types for use in the field and laboratory as a practical aid to identification, and to provide useful basic information. Individual chapters are written by subject specialists.

543   **A natural history of marine mammals.**
Victor B. Scheffer.   New York: Charles Scribner's, 1976. 157p.
bibliog.
An introductory account of, for example, seals and sea otters, whales, and dugongs and their adaptation to the ocean environment. The author is an internationally recognised expert in the field. Appendixes list habitats in North American waters and a classification.

Whales

544   **Whales.**
W. Nigel Bonner.   Poole, England: Blandford Press, 1980. 278p.
bibliog.
A general account of whales and the whaling industry written by the head of the Life Sciences Division of the British Antarctic Survey.

545   **The life and death of whales.**
Robert Burton.   London: Andre Deutsch, 1973. 159p. bibliog.
A popular review of the larger cetaceans with an account of the whaling industry and the problems of conservation.

546   **The book of whales.**
Richard Ellis.   New York: Knopf, 1982. 202p. bibliog.
A general account in words and pictures by a marine artist.

547   **The ecology of whales and dolphins.**
D. E. Gaskin.   London: Heinemann, 1982. 459p. bibliog.
A reference work for teachers and researchers covering distribution, migration, feeding, behaviour, social organization and population studies.

548 **The stocks of whales.**
N. A. Mackintosh. London: Fishing News, 1965. 232p. bibliog.

A seminal work in the field of conservation covering: all aspects of the migration and life cycles of whales; analysis of stocks; and the regulation of the whaling industry.

549 **Whales.**
E. J. Slijper. London: Hutchinson, 1962. 475p. bibliog.

Translated from the Dutch edition of 1958, this is a standard textbook on whale physiology, anatomy and behaviour.

550 **Sea guide to whales of the world.**
Lyall Watson. London: Hutchinson, 1981. 302p. bibliog.

This well-illustrated review of the cetacea contains summaries of all known information including distribution and habitat.

Kendal Whaling Museum paintings.
See item no. 343.

Kendal Whaling Museum prints.
See item no. 344.

Whales, whaling and whale research; a selected bibliography.
See item no. 348.

The whale.
See item no. 349.

Report of the International Whaling Commission.
See item no. 353.

Seals

551 **Seals.**
K. M. Backhouse. London: Arthur Barker; New York: Golden Press, 1969. 96p.

A popular account of seals which concentrates mainly on the grey seal.

552 **Seals and man; a study of interactions.**
W. Nigel Bonner. Seattle, Washington: University of Washington Press, 1982. 170p.

A series of nine lectures on seals of the world which lays special emphasis on their interaction with man and the problems of their conservation.

553 **The life of the harp seal.**
Fred Bruemmer. Newton Abbot, England: David & Charles,
1978.
This first-hand account of the controversial harp seal fishery off the coast of
Newfoundland and Labrador, is illustrated with the author's colour photographs.

554 **Grey seals and the Farne Islands.**
Grace Hickling. London: Routledge & Kegan Paul, 1962. 180p.
bibliog.
A study of a colony of grey seals (*Halichoerus grypus*) on the Farne Islands off
the coast of Northumberland. The chief object was to investigate the seals'
migration patterns. A general review of seals is contained in an appendix.

555 **The world of the walrus.**
Richard Perry. London: Cassell, 1967. 162p. map. bibliog.
Provides a popular account of the life histories of the Atlantic and Pacific walrus,
with chapters on the walrus industry and on the geographical range of the species.

556 **An annotated bibliography on the pinnipedia.**
Compiled by K. Ronald, L. M. Hanby, P. J. Healey, L. J. Selley.
Charlottenlund, Denmark: International Council for the Explora-
tion of the Sea, 1976. 785p.
A computer-set listing of some 9,500 references on seals, sea lions and walruses
arranged under authors and subjects.

557 **Seals, sea lions and walruses.**
Victor B. Scheffer. Stanford, California: Stanford University
Press; London: Oxford University Press, 1958. 179p; bibliog.
An authoritative account of the pinnipedia, their characteristics, evolutionary
history and classification.

The fur seal of South Georgia.
See item no. 892.

Utilization of the Ocean by Man. Pollution

558 The international law of pollution.
James Barros, Douglas M. Johnston. New York: Free Press; London: Collier Macmillan, 1974. 476p.

A practical research tool for students and researchers which includes a chapter on marine pollution with reading lists on multilateral and unilateral measures to combat it.

559 Impingement of man on the oceans.
Edited by Donald W. Hood. New York: Wiley-Interscience, 1971. 738p. bibliog.

This volume contains specialist contributions on: oceanic transport processes and reservoirs; chemical models of the ocean; chemical contamination by man; and the legal and philosophical implications of man's activities.

560 Report of the ICES Advisory Committee on Marine Pollution 1982.
International Council for the Exploration of the Sea. Copenhagen: International Council for the Exploration of the Sea, 1983. 74p. bibliog. (Cooperative Research Report, no. 120).

This report covers several aspects of pollution in the North Atlantic Ocean and the Baltic including: monitoring; the dumping of waste; biological effects (e.g. fish diseases and pollution); and the transport of lead in the marine environment.

561 **International Decade of Ocean Exploration (IDOE) Progress Reports.**
Washington DC: National Oceanic and Atmospheric Administration, National Oceanographic Data Center, 1973- .

Summary reports of this long-term international cooperative programme to enhance the utilization of the oceans and their resources for the benefit of mankind. The reports include, for example, studies of the distribution pattern of selected chemical pollutants in the Atlantic Ocean.

562 **The feasibility of ocean disposal of high-level radioactive waste.**
H. J. Richards, S. G. Carlyle. *MIAS News Bulletin*, no. 7 (May 1984), p. 2-6. map.

A series of engineering feasibility studies has been carried out on behalf of Great Britain's Department of the Environment to consider the use of certain identified sites in the North Atlantic Ocean as repositories for storing encased radioactive waste products. This will require extensive and specialized research on physical, biological and chemical oceanographic investigations.

563 **Tin in oceans.**
B. T. Richman. *EOS, Transactions, American Geophysical Union*, vol. 64, no. 31 (1983), p. 482.

Concentrations of tin in the North Atlantic Ocean are shown to be twenty times greater than in the uncontaminated tropical Pacific Ocean. This phenomenon has been linked with the burning of fossil fuels in North America and Europe.

International law of the sea; a bibliography.
See item no. 312.

Proceedings of the conference on acid rain and the Atlantic Salmon. Portland, Maine, November 22-23, 1980.
See item no. 337.

Trade and Communications

564 **GATT plus-a proposal for trade reform with the text of the General Agreement; report of the special advisory panel to the trade committee of the Atlantic Council.**
Atlantic Council of the United States. New York: Praeger, publishers for the Atlantic Council of the United States, 1975. 196p.
This monograph proposes a code of trade liberalization which it is hoped would be of benefit to the developing countries.

565 **Chisholm's handbook of commercial geography tentatively rewritten by Sir Dudley Stamp.**
Revised by G. Noel Blake, Audrey N. Clark. London: Longman, 1975. 19th ed. 984p.
An invaluable work not only of reference but also for the stimulation of ideas. It is subdivided as follows: 1, 'General factors affecting the production and distribution of commodities', e.g. climate, soil, and labour; 2, 'Circumstances connected with the exchange of commodities', e.g. transport, communications, and commercial countries; 3, 'Commodities classified climatically'; and 4, 'Regional geography', in which brief details of the geography and commerce of (inter alia) the Atlantic islands will be found.

566 **The changing framework of shipping; trends in trade, technology, and policies.**
Hans Böhme. *Marine Policy*, vol. 8, no. 3 (July 1984), p. 229-38.
An analysis of the prospects and policy options for shipping in the context of three major influences: changes in seaborne trade; technical and organizational innovation; and changes in the political environment of shipping. The author stresses the need to remove the tonnage surplus as an essential feature of any restoration of equilibrium between supply and demand.

567 **The economics of interdependence; economic policy in the Atlantic community.**
Richard N. Cooper. New York: McGraw-Hill, 1968. 302p. bibliog. (Atlantic Policy Studies).

Written by a professor of economics at Yale University this book analyses the growing economic interdependence among the members of the Atlantic community. It poses the problem of how nations may enjoy the many benefits of international commerce while preserving the freedom to set and pursue objectives. The author makes the case for close international cooperation to prevent the uncontrolled use of restrictions from negating the principal benefits of trade.

568 **Ancient trade in a modern form.**
Sharon Cox. *Geographical Magazine*, (Oct. 1984), p. 521-26. map.

The concept of the unit-load has had an enormous influence on transportation in general and shipping lines in particular. This article reviews the changes in world fleet organization in recent years. World commodity trade flows and the composition of world fleets are shown graphically.

569 **Kemps directory 1982-83 vol. 3, international information.**
London: The Kemps Group (Printers and Publishers), 1982. variously paged.

This directory contains essential information for British business men, concerning, for example, imports, exports, banks and trade representation. This volume covers the following Atlantic islands: the Azores; the Canary Islands; the Cape Verde Islands; the Falkland Islands; the Faroe Islands; Madeira; and St. Helena.

570 **Lloyd's nautical yearbook 1984.**
London: Lloyd's of London Press, 1984. 608p.

A vast amount of practical current information relating to shipping is arranged under the following headings: 1, 'Lloyd's', covering their organization and services; 2, 'Salvage and cargo carriage, including the Carriage of Goods by Sea Act, 1971'; 3, 'Maritime organizations, national and international'; 4, 'Safety at sea'; 5, 'General articles' e.g. shipping companies – their histories, flags and funnels; and 6, 'Facts and figures' including tidal constants, sea distance tables and standard times.

571 **Fairplay world shipping year book 1984.**
Edited by William Peach. London: Fairplay Publications, 1984. 940p.

This yearbook contains a wide selection of current information on matters relating to the shipping industry world-wide including: a list of shipping companies and their routes; information on marine insurance rates; towage and salvage; ship finance, marine equipment suppliers; ship brokers; shipping statistics; and ship surveyors and marine engineers.

572 **Greenwich forum IX. Britain and the sea, future dependence — future opportunities.**
Edited by M. B. F. Ranken. Edinburgh: Scottish Academic Press, 1984. 364p.

Reproduces the papers read at the Greenwich Forum's 9th conference held in London in 1983, together with 16 background papers. In his introductory remarks Lord Shackleton has some pertinent comments to make relating to the economic status of the Falkland Islands. The Forum itself covers the field of British marine activities including trade and shipping, mineral exploitation, the fishing industry and defence — particularly in the light of recent technological developments.

573 **Trade and investment policies for the seventies; new challenges for the Atlantic area and Japan.**
Edited by Pierre Uri. New York: Praeger, 1971. 286p.

A volume of papers read at a conference held in Tokyo in 1971. The papers cover topics in the general field of trade and investment in the 1970s in the light of both the experiences of the Atlantic Alliance and of Japan.

International Affairs.
See item no. 273.

Marine Affairs Bibliography; a Comprehensive Index to Marine Law and Policy Literature.
See item no. 308.

Ocean Development and International Law Journal.
See item no. 309.

Hints to exporters: Portugal, Madeira and the Azores.
See item no. 665.

Tourism

574 The 1985 South American handbook.
Edited by John Brooks. Bath, England: Trade & Travel Publications, 1985. 1,438p. maps.

This annually updated guide provides basic factual information about the Latin American countries for transatlantic travellers. The introduction contains general travel hints followed by a section on health. Tables of climatic averages precede the detailed descriptions of individual countries which provide information about everything the average tourist and traveller needs to know. The Falkland Islands (Islas Malvinas) are covered on p. 925-29 together with a note on South Georgia.

575 How to fly the Atlantic; a traveller's guide.
Peter Combes, John Tiffin. London: Kogan Page, 1980. 160p. maps.

Contains useful tips on buying tickets; passport and money problems; baggage; customs; reservations; and lists of United Kingdom, US and Canadian gateway airports.

576 Hickmans international air traveller.
Edited by R. H. Hickman, M. E. Hickman. London: Mitchell Beazley, 1982. 4th ed. 335p. maps.

A valuable guide for the transatlantic jet traveller listing which airlines have direct flights from each airport listed to other cities in the gazetteer. There is information on: local time; airline reservations; transport from airports to city centres; international flight information; and terminal facilities such as shops, snackbars, car rental and duty-free shops.

577 The business of tourism.
J. Christopher Holloway. Plymouth, England: Macdonald & Evans, 1983. 246p. maps. bibliog.

This is a textbook intended to help students in the systematic study of tourism as a business. Transatlantic tourism is steadily increasing in both directions, and this work contains a great deal of relevant information, including: the history of tourism; forms of mass tourism; passenger transport (sea and air); and the economic, social and environmental effects of tourism.

578 **A geography of tourism.**
H. Robinson. London: Macdonald & Evans, 1976. 476p. maps. bibliog. ('Aspect' Geographies).
This study is organized into five parts: 1, 'The historical background'; 2, 'The dimensions of tourism and its spatial patterns'; 3, 'Transport, the significance of tourism and its planning'; 4, 'The tourist and the environment', with special reference to the United Kingdom; and 5, 'Regional tourism', in for example, the USA and Latin America.

579 **Heathrow-Chicago.**
Stanley Stewart. Shepperton, Middlesex, England: Ian Allan, 1984. 81p. maps.
Few transatlantic passengers give thought to the complex network of procedures that guarantee their comfort and safety in the air. This slim volume provides a fascinating insight into a typical British Airways Boeing 747 flight from London, Heathrow to Chicago, with an account of, for example: checking in; the procedures on the flight-deck; the operations of air traffic conrol; and the duties of the cabin services crew.

580 **Cook's tours; the story of popular travel.**
Edmund Swinglehurst. Poole, England: Blandford Press, 1982. 192p.
A splendidly illustrated history of the travel agents Thomas Cook and Son, with much about transatlantic cruising in chapter 7 entitled 'A life on the ocean wave'.

The geography of air transport.
See item no. 197.

The world weather guide.
See item no. 477.

Small Boat Voyages and Racing

581 Vinland voyage.
J. R. L. Anderson. London: Eyre & Spottiswoode, 1967. 278p. map.

An account of the author's voyage with five companions on board the cutter *Griffin* from Scarborough, England, to Martha's Vineyard, Massachusetts, in order to demonstrate that the northeast coast of America was discovered and temporarily colonized by Vikings from Greenland. The expedition owes some of its inspiration to the publication of the Vinland map, see *The Vinland map and the Tartar relation* (q.v.).

582 Atlantic adventures; voyages in small craft.
Humphrey Barton. Southampton, England. Adlard Coles, 1962. 254p. maps. 2nd ed. New York: John de Graff, 1962.

A definitive record of voyages across the Atlantic in small boats in both directions, including tabulated detailed summaries.

583 Airborne; a sentimental journey.
William F. Buckley, Jr. New York: Macmillan, 1976. 252p.

The narrative of a transatlantic crossing from Miami, Florida, to Gibraltar via Bermuda and the Azores on the schooner *Cyrano* in 1975. Chapter 9 contains useful practical hints on navigation.

584 Alone across the Atlantic.
Sir Francis Chichester. London: Allen & Unwin, 1961. 191p. maps.

An account of a race between Sir Francis Chichester in *Gypsy Moth III*, Colonel H. G. ('Blondie') Hasler in *Jester*, and David Lewis in *Cardinal Vertue* from Plymouth, England to New York, in June and July 1960. This was the first race of any kind east to west across the Atlantic, and was accomplished by Chichester in forty and a half days.

Small Boat Voyages and Racing

585   *Gypsy Moth* circles the world.
Sir Francis Chichester.   London: Hodder & Stoughton, 1967.
269p.

Sir Francis Chichester's solo voyage in *Gypsy Moth IV* traversed the Atlantic on both outward and home passages in 1966-67.

586   **The romantic challenge.**
Sir Francis Chichester.   London: Cassell, 1971. 194p. maps.

The author's account of his 1970 solo run in *Gypsy Moth V* from Bissau, West Africa, to San Juan del Norte, Nicaragua during which he covered 4,000 miles in 23 days.

587   **Race under sail.**
Peter Hambly.   London: Stanford Maritime, 1978. 144p.

An account of the Tall Ships Races organized by the Sail Training Association in England. The author took part in the 1976 race in *Gypsy Moth V* the course being Plymouth, England, to Santa Cruz de Tenerife, Tenerife to Bermuda, Bermuda to Newport, Rhode Island and Boston, Massachusetts and from there back to Plymouth.

588   **High latitude crossing; the Viking route to America.**
Peter Haward.   London: Adlard Coles, 1968. 146p. maps. bibliog.

A voyage in 1966 from Scarborough, England, to Martha's Vineyard, Massachusetts, following the Vikings' track. The author was a crew member serving under J. R. L. Anderson (see item no. 581). There are descriptions of the North Atlantic from the yachtsman's viewpoint and an examination of the Vikings' means of transport and their navigational ability.

589   **The RA expeditions.**
Thor Heyerdahl.   London: Allen & Unwin. 334p. map.

In 1969 ethnologist Thor Heyerdahl, with a small crew, crossed the Atlantic Ocean from Morocco to the region of Central America in *RA*, a reconstruction of an ancient Egyptian reed boat, thus strengthening the possibility that pre-Columbian cultures in America were influenced by Egyptian civilization.

590   **Atlantic cruise in *Wanderer III*.**
Eric C. Hiscock.   London: Oxford University Press, 1968. 159p.

A narrative description of a cruise made by the author and his wife on their 30-foot sloop *Wanderer III* from England to Maine, USA via Brittany, Spain, the Canary Islands, Barbados, the Bahamas and home via the Intracoastal Waterway, USA, and the Azores. The circuit covered was 15,000 miles.

591 **Small boat against the sea; the story of the first trans-world rowing attempt.**
Derek King, Peter Bird. London: Paul Elek, 1976. 244p.
The narrative of a non-stop rowing-boat voyage across the Atlantic in 1974 from Gibraltar to St. Lucia, 3,545 miles in 93 days and 7 hours.

592 **Across the oceans.**
Conor O'Brien. London: Granada Publishing, 1984. 272p. map.
A reprint of the 1927 edition. The author left Dublin on 20th June 1923 in the twenty ton *Saoirse* with a crew of two and crossed the Atlantic to Pernambuco, Brazil, then sailed on to Durban and across the Indian Ocean to Melbourne. On the way home he spent Christmas in the Falkland Islands which he describes in lively detail.

593 **The voyage of the 'Girl Pat'.**
George 'Dod' Orsborne. Maidstone, England: George Mann, 1974. 234p.
An account of the transatlantic voyage of the fishing vessel *Girl Pat* from Grimsby, England, to Georgetown, British Guiana, made by Captain Orsborne and three companions navigating with the aid of a 'sixpenny atlas'. The illegal use of the vessel earned the author a prison sentence on his return. This is a reprint of the 1937 edition.

594 **Alone against the Atlantic; the story of the Observer Single-handed Transatlantic Race 1960-80.**
Frank Page. London: Observer, 1980. 127p. map.
This well-illustrated summary of OBSTAR (from Plymouth, England to Newport, Rhode Island) includes a list of the results of every race from 1960 to 1980, including names of skippers, yachts and the time taken.

595 **The Atlantic challenge; the story of trimaran FT.**
David Palmer. London: Hollis & Carter, 1977. 187p. maps.
The story of the planning and building of this multihull and its eventual partici-pation in the Observer Singlehanded Transatlantic Race (OBSTAR) in 1976.

596 **Around the world single-handed; the cruise of the 'Islander'.**
Harry Pidgeon. London: Hart-Davis, 1950. 215p. map. (The Mariners Library, no. 12).
The author sailed from Los Angeles on 18 November 1921 bound for the Marquesas Islands. His cruise took him across the Pacific and Indian oceans to the South Atlantic where he paid brief visits to St. Helena and Ascension. He sailed close in to Fernando Noronha but did not land there.

Small Boat Voyages and Racing

597 **Adventures under sail; selected writings of H. W. Tilman.**
Edited by Libby Purves. London: Gollancz, 1982. 254p. maps.

A useful introduction to the writing of this indefatigable small-boat navigator whose voyages in the North and South Atlantic aboard *Mischief* have become legendary.

598 *Jester's* **transatlantic passage, 1972.**
Michael Richey. *Journal of Navigation*, vol. 26, no. 2 (1973),
p. 176-88. maps. bibliog.

The author's account of his participation in the east-to-west Observer Singlehanded Transatlantic Race (OBSTAR) in 1972 in *Jester*. There are comments on the route, weather encountered and the human problems involved in small boat navigation in Atlantic waters.

599 **Storm passage.**
John Ridgway. London: Hodder & Stoughton, 1975. 221p.
maps.

An account of a family cruise on the sailing boat *English Rose V* from Ardmore, Scotland, to Madeira, the Canary Islands; the Sahara and the Cape Verde Islands in 1974. Specifications of the boat are provided in an appendix.

600 **A fighting chance.**
John Ridgway, Chay Blyth. London: Hamlyn, 1967. 255p.
maps.

A running commentary on a 91-day rowing boat voyage from Cape Cod, Massachusetts, to Kilronan in Eire. There is some detail on equipment and stores.

601 **Erik the Red; the Atlantic alone in a home-made boat.**
Donald Ridler. London: William Kimber, 1972. 208p. maps.

Describes the author's voyage in the 26-foot long dory *Erik the Red* from Falmouth, England, to Spain, the Azores, Antigua, Bermuda and home in 1971.

602 **The walkabouts.**
Mike Saunders. London: Gollancz, 1975. 285p. map.

An account of the author's voyage of 1972-73 aboard the yacht *Walkabout* in the North and South Atlantic.

603 **The Brendan voyage.**
Tim Severin. London: Hutchinson, 1978. 292p. maps.

Describes the author's transatlantic voyage in 1976-77 from Southwest Ireland to Newfoundland in the *Brendan*, a boat made from oxhide. The object was to test the theory that the 6th-century Irish monk, St. Brendan, may have voyaged to North America in such a vessel.

604 Alone against the Atlantic.
Gerry Spiess, Marlin Bree. London: Souvenir Press, 1982.
224p. map.
An account of the voyage of the small boat *Yankee Girl* across the North Atlantic
from Norfolk, Virginia, to Falmouth, England, in June-July, 1979.

605 Children of Cape Horn.
Rosie Swale. London: Paul Elek, 1974. 242p. maps.
A description of a voyage made by the author, her husband and two small
children from London across the Atlantic to Australia via the Panama Canal and
back via Cape Horn aboard the 30-foot twin-hull *Anneliese*.

606 *Mischief* goes south.
H. W. Tilman. London: Hollis & Carter, 1968. 190p. maps.
The author's account of a voyage in the small boat *Mischief* in 1966-67 across the
Atlantic to Montevideo, Punta Arenas (Chile) and South Georgia.

607 The strange voyage of Donald Crowhurst.
Nicholas Tomalin, Ron Hall. London: Hodder & Stoughton,
1970. 317p. maps.
The story of an attempt to fake a world circumnavigation leading to the suicide of
Crowhurst in mid-Atlantic in July 1969.

608 Give me a ship to sail.
Alan Villiers. London: Hodder & Stoughton, 1958. 256p.
An account of the author's experiences both aboard a mock-up of *Pequod*,
Captain Ahab's whaler in the classic *Moby Dick* by Herman Melville, and during
an expedition with a reconstruction of the *Mayflower* in 1957 which followed in
the tracks of the Pilgrim Fathers' voyage of 1620.

609 Moxie, the American challenge.
Philip S. Weld. London: Bodley Head, 1981. 245p. map.
The author broke all previous records with his crossing of the Atlantic in under 18
days with the 50 foot trimaran *Moxie* in the 1980 Observer Singlehanded Transatlantic Race (OSTAR).

Early man and the ocean.
See item no. 63.

**Trans-ocean rowing boats and Portuguese working craft: major
collections at Exeter Maritime Museum.**
See item no. 628.

The Atlantic in Fantasy and Fiction

Fantasy

610 **Legendary islands of the Atlantic; a study in medieval geography.**
William H. Babcock. New York: American Geographical Society, 1922. 196p. maps. (American Geographical Society Research Series, no. 8).
A scholarly investigation of the evidence relating to such mythical Atlantic islands as Atlantis, the Island of Brazil and Markland.

611 **The Bermuda Triangle.**
Charles Berlitz. London: Souvenir Press, 1975. 203p. bibliog.
A study of the conceptual area of sea located off the southeast coast of the United States noted for a high incidence of unexplained losses of ships and aircraft.

612 **Without a trace.**
Charles Berlitz. London: Souvenir Press, 1977. 180p. bibliog.
An examination of unrecorded and new incidents in the Bermuda Triangle, the area between Florida, the Sargasso Sea and Bermuda where ships and aircraft have repeatedly disappeared without trace.

613 **Secrets of the Bermuda Triangle.**
Alan Landsburg. New York: Warner Books, 1978. 219p.
The author submits his theories concerning the mysterious disappearance of aircraft over this area of the Atlantic.

614 **Voyage to Atlantis.**
James W. Mavor, Jr. London: Souvenir Press, 1969. 252p.
maps. bibliog.
The author, an oceanographic engineer from the Woods Hole Oceanographic Institution, describes in this book two expeditions to the volcanic island of Thera which, he asserts, is the site of the lost continent of Atlantis.

615 **Atlantis: from legend to discovery.**
Andrew Tomas. London: Sphere Books, 1974. 155p. bibliog.
This book traces various concepts of the sunken continent from Plato onwards.

616 **Mysteries of the lost lands.**
Eleanor Van Zandt, Roy Stemman. London: Aldus Books, 1976. 256p.
A well-illustrated book which includes several chapters dealing with the supposed submerged city of Atlantis.

617 **They found Atlantis.**
Dennis Wheatley. London: Arrow Books, 1979. 352p.
A fictional account of an expedition to the lost continent of Atlantis.

Fiction

618 **Sea of darkness.**
Roland Huntford. London: Collins, 1975. 255p.
An imaginative recreation of Christopher Columbus' life as an explorer in which he is shown to have discovered North America on a voyage with the Norsemen before his later 'official' discovery in 1492. A wealth of historical detail makes the whole story most convincing. The publishers' blurb claims that 'fiction—if it is such—is for once as strange as truth and twice as entertaining'.

619 **Prince Habib's iceberg.**
Edward Hyams. London: Allen Lane, 1974. 288p.
Habib, the youthful and sybaritic potentate of an independent oil kingdom on the west coast of Africa, comes to London to find the engineer who can realize his dream of irrigating his desert lands with ice from the Arctic. As a result a million cubic miles of iceberg are navigated across the Atlantic — but not without complications!

The Atlantic in Fantasy and Fiction. Fiction

620 **Atlantic fury.**
Hammond Innes. London: Collins, 1978. 318p. (Collected edition).
Against the onslaught of a hurricane, seamen must evacuate a British guided missile unit from Laerg in the Western Isles of Scotland.

621 **A book of sea journeys.**
Compiled by Ludovic Kennedy. London: Collins, 1981. 395p.
A book about sea journeys, rather than the sea itself, selected from works of both fact and fiction. The authors have been chosen because of their sharp eye for character and situation or for their portrayal of courage, or because they are simply a joy to read. A whole section entitled 'Voyaging in style' is devoted to the life-style on the transatlantic liners in their hey-day.

622 **Moby Dick or the white whale.**
Herman Melville, with an introduction by J. N. Sullivan.
London: Collins, 1953. 479p.
First published in London in 1851 this is one of the greatest literary masterpieces of the sea. It is made up of three separate but related elements which are combined to produce a marvellous story. There is a contemporary view of the 1840s American whaling industry and the natural history of the sperm whale; an exciting narrative of a sea hunt by a deranged skipper named Ahab; and the novel ends with a philosophical and psychological commentary upon human life and fate.

623 **The cruel sea.**
Nicholas Monsarrat. London: Cassell, 1979. 416p. map.
Probably the best naval novel to emerge from the Second World War, this is the story of *Compass Rose*, a corvette plying the North Atlantic during the early months of the German U-boat campaign.

624 **Sea fiction guide.**
Myron J. Smith, Jr., Robert C. Weller. Metuchen, New Jersey: Scarecrow Press, 1976. 256p.
An annotated bibliography of 2,525 novels relating to the sea by British and American authors. There are indexes of pseudonyms and joint authors, titles and general subjects.

625 **Atlantic convoy.**
David Williams. London: Pan Books, 1979. 237p.
A gripping novel about a Second World War transatlantic convoy in the autumn of 1942.

Wake of the great sealers.
See item no. 361.

Research Institutions, Libraries, Art Galleries, Museums and Archives

626 The official museum directory 1984.
American Association of Museums. Wilmette, Illinois: National Register Publishing, 1983. 1,026p.

A comprehensive guide to the museums of the USA including maritime and naval museums and historic ships.

627 The *American Neptune* list of maritime titles in print by member organizations of the Council of American Maritime Museums.
American Neptune, vol. 39, no. 1 (Jan. 1979), p. 58-77.

A cooperative listing to increase the public's knowledge of museum sponsored publications. This list reflects works available from 1 January 1979. Addresses of the several museums covered are provided.

628 Trans-ocean rowing boats and Portuguese working craft: major collections at Exeter Maritime Museum.
B. A. Fyfield-Shayler, D. A. Manley. *Maritime History*, vol. 5, no. 2 (1977), p. 165-74.

A description of this museum and its collection of boats, several of which have been used in transatlantic ventures.

629 Oceanographic institutions; science studies the sea.
Peter R. Limburg. New York: Elsevier-Nelson Books, 1979. 252p. bibliog.

A general introduction to research institutions in the USA with a chapter on related institutions in other countries. Two introductory chapters are concerned with the history of oceanography.

Kendal Whaling Museum paintings.
See item no. 343.

Kendal Whaling Museum prints.
See item no. 344.

International cooperation in marine science.
See item no. 403.

Atlantic Islands in General

630 Islands time forgot.
Lawrence G. Green. London: Putnam, 1962. 269p.
An island traveller's reminiscences of islands visited in the Atlantic and off the west coast of Africa. These include Tristan da Cunha, Gough Island, St. Helena, Ascension Island, the Canary Islands, Madeira, and St. Paul's Rocks. In conclusion there is some speculation on the lost continent of Atlantis.

631 Island life or the phenomena and causes of insular faunas and floras including a revision and attempted solution of the problem of geological climates.
Alfred Russel Wallace. London: Macmillan, 1902. 3rd rev. ed. 563p. maps.
Wallace was co-originator with Charles Darwin of the idea of the survival of the fittest. This account of the importance of islands in any study of the distribution of plants and animals around the world contains chapters on the Azores and St. Helena.

The three voyages of Edmond Halley in the *Paramore* 1698-1701.
See item no. 38.

Darwin and the Beagle.
See item no. 43.

Log letters from 'The Challenger'.
See item no. 45.

North Atlantic Islands

Faroe Islands

The islands and their people

632 **The Faroes and Iceland: studies in island life.**
Nelson Annandale. Oxford, England: Clarendon Press, 1905.
238p. bibliog.
A general account of island life based on visits made between 1896 and 1903.

633 **Færo, and Færoa referata: that is a description of the islands
& inhabitants of Foeroe [sic]; being seventeen islands subject to
the King of Denmark, lying under 62 deg. 10 min. of north
latitude. Wherein several secrets of nature are brought to light,
and some antiquities hitherto kept in darkness discovered . . .**
Lucas Jacobson Debes. London: Printed by F. L. for William
Iles, 1676. 408p. maps.
A translation from the original Danish. Debes was provost of the church in the
Faroes.

634 **A narrative of the cruise of the yacht Maria among the Feroe [sic]
Islands in the summer of 1854.**
[E. H. Greig]. London: Longman, Brown, Green, & Longmans,
1855. 89p. map.
Although the author was in the Faroes for only a week, this account includes
much accurate information and is illustrated by eleven coloured lithographs, one
depicting whale hunting.

635 **The Faroe Islands.**
G. H. Harris. Birmingham, England: Cornish Brothers, publisher to the university, 1927. 119p.
A general description of the islands based on the author's visit in 1923.

636 **A description of the Feroe Islands containing an account of their situation, climate and productions; together with the manners and customs of the inhabitants, their trade, &c. Translated from the Danish.**
G. Landt. London: Longman, Hurst, Rees, & Orme, 1810. 426p. map.
A very thorough and comprehensive account of the Faroe Islands by a Danish pastor who lived on the islands for seven years.

637 **Nagel's encyclopedia-guide Denmark Greenland.**
Preface by Sven Acker. Geneva: Nagel Publishers, 1980. 543p. maps.
The guide contains information on the Faroe Islands (p. 321-36) and covers geography, the way of life and practical information for the visitor.

638 **An historical and descriptive account of Iceland, Greenland and the Faroe Islands; with illustrations of their natural history.**
[James Nicol]. Edinburgh: Oliver & Boyd, 1840. maps.
(Edinburgh Cabinet Library, vol. 28).
A good short account which has frequently been reprinted.

639 **Pen and pencil sketches of Faroe and Iceland.**
Andrew James Symington. London: Longman, Green, Longman, & Roberts, 1862. 315p.
An account based on the author's diaries written during a visit in 1859.

640 **Recent anthropological studies of the Faroe Islands (1971-1975).**
Ian Whitaker. *Folk Life*, vol. 16 (1978), p. 78-84. bibliog.
A review of fourteen publications in the field of Faeroese anthropology and sociology.

641   **The Atlantic islands; a study of the Faroe life and scene.**
Kenneth Williamson.   London: Routledge & Kegan Paul, 1970.
385p. maps. bibliog.

A naturalist's very comprehensive account of the Faroes, first published in 1948 and here updated by a chapter 'The Faroes today' by Einar Kallsberg, with appendixes on mammals and birds and a glossary of Faroese words. Written during and immediately after the Second World War, it became the definitive work on Faroese social history. The book includes information on, for example, folklore, language and place-names and has been quoted as 'probably the best account of the islands published in English this century'.

642   **Denmark.**
In: *Worldmark encyclopaedia of the nations vol. 5 Europe.*
New York, Worldmark Press, distributed by John Wiley, 1984.
6th ed., p. 57-68. bibliog.

This article on Denmark contains a brief guide to the history and present-day economy of the Faroe Islands (p. 67-68).

643   **The ring of dancers; images of Faroese culture.**
Jonathan Wylie, David Margolin.   Philadelphia: University of
Pennsylvania Press, 1981. 182p. maps. bibliog.

A collection of essays dealing with aspects of Faroese geographical idioms, literature, language, government and culture.

Nature and wildlife

644   **The zoology of the Faroes. Vols. I-III.**
Edited by Ad. S. Jensen, W. Lundbeck, Th. Mortensen, R. Spärck,
S. L. Tuxen.   Copenhagen: Andr. Fred. Høst, 1928-71. 3 vols. in
6 parts.

This thorough survey of the land and freshwater fauna of the Faroes and of the benthos fauna of the coastal waters is of special significance in resolving problems relating to the immigration of the insular fauna, and the problem of the land connection between Greenland and the European continent in the Quaternary period. A description of the birds and mammals is contained in Vol. III, together with a list of Faroese animal names.

645   **The Faroese bird names.**
W. B. Lockwood.   Copenhagen: Ejnar Munksgaard, 1961. 100p.
(Færoensia vol. V).

A full listing of traditional Faroese bird names with a philological commentary. A concluding chapter refers to the occurrence of bird names in toponyms, plant nomenclature and proverbial and other expressions.

646 **The flora of Iceland and the Faeroes.**
C. H. Ostenfeld, Johs. Gröntved. Copenhagen: Levin & Munks-gaard; London: Williams & Norgate, 1934. 195p. maps.

A descriptive account of the vascular plants with notes on their habitats and geographical distribution intended as a guide for botanists and amateurs in the field.

647 **Faeröe Islands.**
Jóannes Rasmussen. In: *Lexique stratigraphique international.*
Vol. 1 Europe, fasc. 1b Islande, 1c Iles Faeröe, 1d Svalbard.
Edited by P. Pruvost. Paris: Centre National de la Recherche
Scientifique, 1956, p. 13-17. map. bibliog.

An English dictionary of the stratigraphy of the Faroe Islands. The Faroe Islands, which are part of the North Atlantic basalt region, are built up of strata from the Eocene-Oligocene age. The sequences and intrusive rocks are briefly described.

648 **Geology of the Faroe Islands (pre-Quaternary).**
Jóannes Rasmussen, Arne Noe-Nygaard. Copenhagen:
C. A. Reitzels Forlag, 1970. 142p. map. bibliog. (Geological
Survey of Denmark 1. Series no. 25).

An introduction to the geology of the Faroe Islands which also contains a description of the stratigraphic map of the islands which is attached.

History

649 **Faroe; the emergence of a nation.**
John F. West. London: Hurst; New York: Paul S. Eriksson,
1972. 312p. map. bibliog.

A valuable historical introduction to the Faroe Islands and their people which is aimed at the general reader. The critical bibliography includes a separate listing of books in English.

650 **The journals of the Stanley expedition to the Faroe Islands and
Iceland in 1789. Vols. 1-3.**
Edited by John F. West. Torshavn, Iceland: Føroya Froðskapar-
felag, 1970. 3 vols.

The journals of an expedition that sailed from Leith, Scotland, in May 1789 and visited Orkney, Faroe, Iceland and Copenhagen. The leader was John Thomas Stanley, later 1st Baron Stanley of Alderley. Vol. 1 contains the journal of James Wright, a medical student; vol. 2 that of Isaac Benners, a planter; and vol. 3 that of John Baine, a Scotsman acting as a surveyor. The journals, which are of especial interest for Faroese history, are illustrated with sketches from the diaries, and are fully annotated.

North Atlantic Islands. Faroe Islands. Trade and industry

651 **From the Vikings to the Reformation; a chronicle of the Faroe Islands up to 1538.**
G. V. C. Young. Douglas, Isle of Man: Shearwater Press, 1979. 184p.

A well-documented history of this obscure and little recorded period of history. An appendix lists the Scandinavian monarchs connected with the Faroes prior to the Reformation.

Language

652 **An introduction to modern Faroese.**
W. B. Lockwood. Copenhagen: Ejnar Munksgaard, 1955. 244p. (Færoensia vol. IV).

The first attempt at an all-round description of Faroese with examples of idiomatic conversation and a Faroese-English glossary.

653 **Dictionarium færoense; færøsk-dansk-latinsk ordbog. [vol] 1 Ordbogen; [vol] 2 Inledning og registre.** (Faroese dictionary; Faroese-Danish-Latin wordbook. [vol] 1 wordbook; [vol] 2 introduction and index.)
J. C. Svabo. Copenhagen: Munksgaard, 1966, 1970. 2 vols. bibliog. (Færoensia vols. VII and VIII).

A definitive Faroese language dictionary with Danish and Latin equivalents.

Trade and industry

654 **Faerøerne og Grønland statistiske efterretninger.** (Faeroe Islands and Greenland statistical information.)
Copenhagen: Danmarks Statisk, 1983- . monthly.

Provides import and export statistics relating to the Faeroe Islands and Greenland.

655 **Fåreavl på Faerøerne.**
Robert Joensen. Copenhagan: C. A. Reitzels Boghandel, 1979. 310p. map. bibliog. (Faeroensia vol. XII).

A detailed account by a native of the Faroes of the sheep farming industry as carried out by Faroese peasant society before 1950. The work is based on conversations with members of the farming community over many years. English summaries of each chapter are found on p. 284-306.

146

656   **The Faroes: today's problems.**
Aa H. Kampp. *Inter-Nord*, no. 9 (March 1967), p. 83-97.

A survey by a leading geographical authority. Largely autonomous since 1948, improvements in social conditions in the Faroes since the Second World War have had to be paid for by increased economic development. Fishing products, especially cod and herring, account for 95% of the value of trade. Statistical tables are appended.

657   **The Faroese salmon fishing industry and its management.**
Alfred L. Meister.   New York: The Atlantic Salmon Federation, 1983. 36p. map. (ASF Special Publication Series, no. 11).

A joint Atlantic Salmon Federation and Atlantic Salmon Trust (Great Britain) team visited the Faroes in March 1982 and this is a report of their findings and recommendations for management of a common resource. There are also suggestions for a cooperative exchange of programmes that will maintain stocks and avoid over exploitation.

658   **The economic importance of sea-fowl in the Faroe Islands.**
Kenneth Williamson. *Ibis*, vol. 87 (1945), p. 249-69. bibliog.

A full account, including techniques, fowling rights and folklore.

Literature

659   **Faroese short stories.**
Translated from the Faroese and the Danish, with introduction and notes by Hedin Brønner.   New York: Twayne and the American Scandinavian Foundation, 1972. 267p. (The Library of Scandinavian Literature, vol. 16).

The introduction to these stories sketches the growth of the Faroese novel as a framework for the understanding and development of the short story, and includes notes on translated works of Faroese fiction.

660   **The saga of the Faroe islanders.**
Translated by Muriel A. C. Press.   London: Dent, 1934. 113p.

The manuscript of this saga is to be found in the Flat Island Book ms. which was written between 1387 and 1394.

661   **Saga-Book.**
London: University College, Viking Society for Northern Research, 1895 - . annual.

A journal devoted, for example, to the history of the Vikings and their language, and their folklore. There are related articles on the Faroes and Greenland.

662 **Faroese folk-tales & legends.**
    John F. West. Lerwick, Shetland: Shetland Publishing, 1980. 173p.

A collection of historical legends, tales of the supernatural ('huldumen stories'), and folk-tales.

663 **The Faroese saga freely translated with maps and genealogical tables.**
    G. V. C. Young, Cynthia R. Clewer. Belfast: Century Services, 1973. 60p. maps.

A free translation of the *Faereyínga Saga* with maps showing places mentioned in the saga, and genealogical tables.

Rockall

664 **Rockall.**
    James Fisher. London: Geoffrey Bles, 1956. 200p. maps. bibliog.

The author, a well-known ornithologist, accompanied the British government mission which formally annexed the island of Rockall, 220 miles west of the Outer Hebrides, on 18 September 1955. This book tells the story of the landing and in addition attempts to trace all recorded observations and notes concerning the position, size, geological origin and natural history of this uninhabited island.

Azores, Cape Verde Islands, Madeira, Canary Islands

General

665 **Hints to exporters: Portugal, Madeira and the Azores.**
    British Overseas Trade Board. London: British Overseas Trade Board 1984-85. 72p. bibliog.

In addition to specialized information on regulations, economic factors and methods of doing business, this booklet also contains up-to-date information on, for example, geography, population, climate, clothing and hotels.

North Atlantic Islands. Azores, Cape Verde Islands,
Madeira, Canary Islands. General

666 **Atlantic islands; Madeira, the Azores and the Cape Verdes in
seventeenth-century commerce and navigation.**
T. Bentley Duncan. Chicago: University of Chicago Press,
1972. 291p. maps. bibliog.

A discussion of the important and influential role of these islands situated at the
centre of a network of shipping routes reaching the Atlantic maritime communities
of four continents.

667 **Fodor's Portugal 1985.**
Edited by Susan Lowndes. London: Hodder & Stoughton, 1985.
312p. maps.

This guide book includes sections on Madeira (p. 275-91) and the Azores (p.292-
303). Comprehensive information for tourists includes a general description of
the region, local handicrafts, island tours, hotels and restaurants, shopping and
useful addresses.

668 **Canary Island hopping: the Azores-Madeira, a handbook for the
independent traveller.**
Judith Hayter. London: Sphere Books, 1982. 319p. maps.
bibliog.

Provides all the traveller needs to know about these Atlantic islands: how to get
there and travel around; where to stay and eat; what to do and see; together with
some history and basic Spanish and Portuguese phrases.

669 **Geology of the middle Atlantic islands.**
Raoul C. Mitchell-Thomé. Berlin: Gebrüder Borntraeger, 1976.
382p. maps. bibliog. (Beiträge Zur Regionalen Geologie Der Erde
Band 12).

A review of the geology of the Azores, Madeira, the Selvagens, Canary Islands and
Cape Verde Islands, prefaced by chapters dealing with their general geography and
geology as a group. Contains an extensive bibliography and an index to plants and
fossils.

670 **The bird faunas of Africa and its islands.**
R. E. Moreau. New York: Academic Press, 1966. 424p. maps.
bibliog.

Chapter 16 describes the bird faunas of the west coast islands including the
Canary Islands and Cape Verde Islands.

671 **Nagel's encyclopedia-guide Portugal, Madeira, The Azores.**
Geneva: Nagel Publishers, [n.d.] 3rd ed. 495p. maps.

At the time of going to press the most recent edition of this reliable guide with
sections on, for example, how to get there, geography, history, handicrafts,
excursions, and tourism. Madeira is covered (p. 358-89), as are the Porto Santo
Islands (p. 389-90) and the Azores (p. 391-414).

149

North Atlantic Islands. Azores, Cape Verde Islands,
Madeira, Canary Islands. General

672   **See Madeira & the Canaries; a complete guide with maps.**
      Annette Pink, Paul Watkins.   London: Format Books, 1980.
      144p. maps.

Includes historical introductions to the Canary Islands and Madeira and descriptions of the climate, the cultivation of plants and flowers, and plants of special
interest. There are also sections providing information on air travel, motoring, bus
services, tourist agencies, accommodation, food and drink and local weather.

673   **Frommer's dollarwise guide to Portugal, Madeira and the Azores,
      1984-85.**
      Edited by Darwin Porter.   New York: Frommer/Pasmantier,
      1984. 300p.

This volume contains basic information for tourists but lacks maps for the islands.

674   **Four island studies.**
      Hugh Prince, J. M. Callender, J. D. Henshall, C. Delano Smith,
      M. E. Caistor.   Bude, Cornwall, England: Geographical Publi-
      cations, 1968. [94] p. maps. bibliogs.

Four studies of agricultural land use: 1, the land use of Santa Maria in the Azores
(Prince) is a reissue of a 1953 monograph; 2, the land use of Faial in the Azores
(Callender and Henshall) is the report of an Oxford University expedition to the
island in 1960; 3, the land use of eastern Madeira (Smith) is the report of an
Oxford University expedition to the island in 1961; and 4, the land use of Zanzi-
bar (Caistor).

675   **Atlantic islanders of the Azores and Madeiras.**
      Francis M. Rogers.   North Quincy, Massachusetts: Christopher
      Publishing House, 1979. 464p. maps. bibliog.

This, as the author stresses, is essentially a subjective study about the background
of the Azoreans and Madeirans, their history, culture, way of life, economy and
the part they have played in transatlantic trade and commerce.

**The principall navigations voiages and discoveries of the English
nation . . . imprinted at London, 1589 . . . Vols. 1, 2.**
See item no. 16.

**The age of reconnaissance; discovery, exploration and settlement
1450-1650.**
See item no. 24.

The discovery of the sea.
See item no. 25.

**Atlantide-report. Nos. 1-12. Scientific results of the Danish expedition
to the coasts of tropical West Africa 1945-1946.**
See item no. 53.

Tables of temperature, relative humidity, precipitation and sunshine
for the world. Part IV Africa, the Atlantic Ocean south of 35°N and the
Indian Ocean.
See item no. 473.

Africa pilot vol. 1, comprising the Arquipélago de Madeira, Islas
Canarias, Arquipélago de Cabo Verde, the west coast of Africa from
Cabo Espartel to Bakasi Peninsula.
See item no. 488.

Reed's nautical almanac.
See item no. 507.

Atlantic cruise in Wanderer III.
See item no. 590.

Storm passage.
See item no. 599.

Azores

676   Birds of the Atlantic islands, Vol. 3, a history of the birds of the
Azores.
David Armitage Bannerman, W. Mary Bannerman.   Edinburgh:
Oliver & Boyd, 1966. 262p. maps. bibliog.
Introductory chapters describe the topography and natural features of the Azores
archipelago and their influence on the bird life as well as accounts of separate
islands and their birds. This is followed by a full description of breeding and
migration. There are indexes of scientific and English names and of Portuguese
bird names. The colour plates are by D. M. Reid-Henry and George Lodge.

677   Open boat whaling in the Azores; the history and present
methods of a relic industry.
Robert Clarke.   Cambridge, England: Cambridge University
Press, 1954. bibliog. (*Discovery Reports*, vol. XXVI, p. 281-354).
The most comprehensive account in English of the Azores whaling industry and
its history. A chapter on whaling from Madeira is appended.

678   The hand of God; whaling in the Azores.
Trevour Housby.   London: Abelard-Schuman, 1971. 95p.
The author lived for several months in 1969 with the open-boat whalers of Pico
Island in the Azores. In this book which is illustrated with his own photographs,
he gives an account of this dying industry.

North Atlantic Islands. Azores, Cape Verde Islands, Madeira, Canary Islands. Cape Verde Islands

679 **The Azores, nine islands in search of a future.**
Don Moser. *National Geographic Magazine*, vol. 149, no. 2 (Feb. 1976), p. 261-88.
A general account of the islands' economic status with some emphasis on the whaling industry. The relationship with Portugal is also discussed with reference to the movement for autonomy. There are some excellent photographs and much about island life and customs.

680 **Baleia! the whalers of the Azores.**
Bernard Venables. London: Bodley Head, 1968. 206p. map.
An account of the whale fishery based at Horta on the island of Fayal in the Azores.

The United States and six Atlantic outposts; the military and economic considerations.
See item no. 258.

Tables of temperature, relative humidity, precipitation and sunshine for the world. Part III Europe and the Azores.
See item no. 472.

West coasts of Spain and Portugal pilot from Cabo Ortegal to Gibraltar, Strait of Gibraltar, north coasts of Africa from Cabo Espartel to Ceuta, and Arquipélago dos Açores.
See item no. 495.

Erik the Red; the Atlantic alone in a home-made boat.
See item no. 601.

Cape Verde Islands

681 **Birds of the Atlantic islands, Vol. 4, a history of the birds of the Cape Verde Islands.**
David Armitage Bannerman, W. Mary Bannerman. Edinburgh: Oliver & Boyd, 1968. 458p. maps. bibliog.
A systematic list of the birds arranged by families and species is preceded by chapters describing: the geography and natural history of the islands; the history of their discovery and the explorers of bird life since 1784; zoological considerations of the fauna and vegetation; and an account of the journeys made by the authors. An appendix lists addenda to vol. 2 of this monograph (q.v.). The colour plates are by D. M. Reid Henry and P. A. Clancey.

682 **The voyages of Cadamosto and other documents on western Africa in the second half of the fifteenth century.**
Alvise Ca' da Mosto, translated and edited by G. R. Crone.
London: Hakluyt Society, 1937. 159p. maps. bibliog.
Alvise da Ca' da Mosto (1432?-1511), or Cadamosto as he is known to English writers, was a Venetian explorer and trader who visited the Canary Islands in 1455 on board a Portuguese caravel. His description of the islands is one of the earliest, and includes accounts of the native Guanches. In 1456 Cadamosto sailed on a second voyage equipped by Prince Henry of Portugal and sighted and examined the Cape Verde Islands. His claim to have discovered them is, however, disputed. Though Cadamosto made no new discoveries his account was comprehensive and well-informed. His work was for a considerable period the primary authority on this region of the Atlantic.

683 **The people of the Cape Verde Islands; exploitation and emigration.**
António Carreira. London: Hurst; Hamden, Connecticut:
Archon Books, 1982. 224p. maps. bibliog.
A translation from the Portuguese edition by Christopher Fyfe. This is a study of voluntary and forced migration to the islands based on legislative records, together with the history of settlement, the development of society, the organization of the economy and the development of the social structure.

684 **No fist is big enough to hide the sky: the liberation of Guine and Cape Verde; aspects of an African revolution.**
Basil Davidson. London: Zed Press, 1981. 187p. map.
A book about the struggle of Guine (Guinea-Bissau) and the republic of Cape Verde for independence from Portugal. A short reading list of books in English is appended.

685 **Traveller's guide to west Africa.**
Edited by Alan Rake. London: IC Magazines, 1983. 272p. map.
Essential facts for intending travellers to the Cape Verde Islands are to be found on p. 81-83.

686 **Cape Verde.**
In: *Worldmark encyclopaedia of the nations vol. 2 Africa.* New York: Worldmark Press, distributed by John Wiley, 1984. 6th ed.
p. 45-48. map. bibliog.
A brief guide to the geographic, historic, political, social and economic status of the Republic of Cape Verde.

Madeira

687 **Birds of the Atlantic islands, Vol. 2, a history of the birds of Madeira, the Desertas and Porto Santo Islands.**
David Armitage Bannerman, W. Mary Bannerman. Edinburgh: Oliver & Boyd, 1965. 207p. maps. bibliog.

This very full description of the avifauna of Madeira includes a comprehensive bibliography, an historical introduction and a chapter on the natural features and climate of the Madeira archipelago by G. E. Maue. The colour plates are by D. M. Reid-Henry. Appendix C contains addenda to Vol. 1 of this monograph, *Canary Islands* (q.v.).

688 **Madeira.**
Lausanne, Switzerland: Berlitz, 1977. 130p. maps.

A compact pocket guidebook for the tourist.

689 **Portugal: Madeira.**
London: Michelin [1982], 3rd ed. 162p. maps.

This *Michelin Green Guide* is essentially a sightseeing and route planning book. Madeira is covered on p. 144-62 with notes on, for example, history, geography, natural history, wines and handicrafts.

Canary Islands

The islands and their people

690 **Island of eternal spring.**
Brian Dicks. *Geographical Magazine*, vol. 53, no. 4 (Jan. 1981), p. 277-82. map.

A general account of the Canary Islands, their topographical features, climate and vegetation.

691 **The wild Canary.**
Brian Dicks. *Geographical Magazine*, vol. 55, no. 6 (June 1983), p. 322-27. map.

An account of San Miguel de la Palma, the fifth largest island of the Canaries archipelago, with special reference to: its volcanicity; its varied and complex landscapes; the scientifically important Taburiente National Park; and the sequence of vegetation zones.

692 **Fodor's Spain.**
London: Hodder & Stoughton. annual. maps.

Includes tourist information on the Canary Islands on p. 242-50.

693 **The Canary Islands.**
John Mason, Anne Mason. London: Batsford, 1976. 180p.
maps.
A factual account for visitors based on the authors' personal knowledge of the
islands over many years.

694 **The Canary islanders; their prehistory, conquest and survival.**
John Mercer. London: Rex Collings, 1980. 285p. maps. bibliog.
An anthropological study of the prehistoric islanders and their residual survival
at the present time, with an appendix on the pro-independence extremist
movement and its evolution.

695 **The Canary Islands.**
Henry Myhill. London: Faber & Faber, 1968. 205p. bibliog.
A readable and informative travelogue based on the author's residence in the
islands during three winters.

696 **Gran Canaria, Lanzarote, Fuerteventura.**
Manuel González Sosa. Madrid: Editorial Everest S.A., [1983].
4th ed. 208p. maps.
A well-illustrated pocket guide book in English to this group of the Canary Islands.
A section on the general history and geography of the group is followed by a
more detailed account of the island of Gran Canaria and its chief town, Las
Palmas, for which a street map and gazetteer is added. Separate sections cover
Fuerteventura and Lanzarote.

697 **Tenerife and other Canary Islands.**
Norah B. Spowart. Brentford, England: Roger Lascelles, 1984.
120p. maps.
This pocket handbook by a seasoned visitor to Tenerife provides the basic information essential to an enjoyable visit including background history, geography
and flora and fauna. This is followed up with practical information on accommodation, food and drink, entertainment, shopping, health and transport. Suggested
island tours are provided.

698 **Gran Canaria and the eastern Canary Islands.**
Mary Tisdall, Archie Tisdall. Brentford, England: Roger
Lascelles, 1984. 223p. maps. bibliog.
This pocket guide, written by two dedicated British travellers, is a mine of infor-
mation on this group of the Canary Islands with sections on how to get there,
where to stay, what to see, food, drink and practical information of all kinds.
Separate sections include suggested tours of Gran Canaria, Lanzarote and Fuerte-
ventura. Relevant *Firestone Hispanic* maps are listed.

North Atlantic Islands. Azores, Cape Verde Islands, Madeira,
Canary Islands. Canary Islands. History

699   **Canary Islands.**
       Eileen Yeoward. Ilfracombe, England: Arthur H. Stockwell,
       1975. 149p. map. bibliog.
A factual account of the islands, their people and their way of life along with
some useful basic statistics.

Nature and wildlife

700   **Birds of the Atlantic islands, Vol. 1, a history of the birds of the
       Canary Islands and of the Salvages.**
       David Armitage Bannerman. Edinburgh: Oliver & Boyd, 1963.
       358p. map. bibliog.
An attempt to collate all that has been learned about the natural history of the
birds inhabiting the seven large islands of the Canary archipelago with their
satellites and the Salvage Islands. A full description is given of the breeding birds
and migrant birds, and the work is illustrated with colour plates by D. M. Reid-
Henry. An appendix containing addenda is included in *Birds of the Atlantic
islands*. Vol. 2 (q.v.).

701   **Biology and ecology in the Canary Islands.**
       Edited by G. Kunkel. The Hague: W. Junk, 1976. 511p. maps.
       bibliog. (Monographiae Biologicae, vol. 30).
A collection of contributions by various specialist authors covering aspects of the
natural history of the Canary Islands including a general review, the prehistoric
population, place-names, geology and climate, flora and fauna.

History

702   **The Canarian or, book of the conquest and conversion of the
       Canarians in the year 1402 by Messire Jean de Bethencourt, Kt . . .**
       Composed by Pierre Bontier, Jean Le Verrier, translated and
       edited by Richard Henry Major. London: Hakluyt Society,
       1872. 229p. map. (Hakluyt Society First Series, no. 46).
The earliest authenticated distant voyage made by Frenchmen to the south. The
colonization of the Canary Islands from which the present European population
sprang originated from this expedition. A history of what was previously known
about the islands is dealt with in the introduction. Bethencourt led a body of
adventurers from Normandy in May 1402 and conquered and baptised the natives.
He was eventually appointed governor of the islands by Isabella of Castile.

703 **The Guanches of Tenerife, the holy image of Our Lady of Candelaria and the Spanish conquest and settlement by the Friar Alonso de Espinosa.**
Alonso de Espinosa, translated and edited with notes and an introduction by Sir Clements Markham. London: Hakluyt Society, 1907. map. bibliog. (Hakluyt Society Second Series, vol. 21).
Originally published in Seville in 1594, this account of Tenerife contains a description of the island and a history of its native people, the Guanches, and their customs. A bibliography of the Canary Islands is appended and a Guanche vocabulary and examples of Guanche sentences preface the work.

704 **The Canary Islands after the conquest; the making of a colonial society in the early sixteenth century.**
Felipe Fernández-Armesto. Oxford, England: Clarendon Press, 1982. 244p. maps. bibliog.
A scholarly history of the early settlements by Portuguese, Italians, Castilians and others. The work is based on original archive material.

705 **Historia de la conquista de las siete islas de Canaria.** (History of the conquest of the seven Canary Islands.)
Abreu Galindo, edited by Alejandro Cioranescu. Santa Cruz de Tenerife: Goya Ediciones, 1977. 367p.
An annotated edition of this classic history of the Canary Islands by Father Abreu Galindo which was first published in 1632.

706 **Apuntes para las historia de las Islas Canarias 1776-1868.** (Notes on the history of the Canary Islands 1776-1868.)
Francisco Maria de León. Santa Cruz de Tenerife: Aula de cultura de Tenerife, 1978. 2nd ed. 404p. bibliog.
An edition of Francisco Maria de León y Xvárez's 19th-century manuscript.

707 **Canary Islands: Fuerteventura.**
John Mercer. Newton Abbot, England: David & Charles; Harrisburg, Pennsylvania: Stackpole Books, 1973. 215p. maps. bibliog.
A general study of the island of Fuerteventura and its people, early history, geography, customs, crafts and industries.

708 **Historia general de las Islas Canarias.** (General history of the
Canary Islands.)
Agustin Millares Torres. Las Palmas de Gran Canaria: EDIRCA,
Editora Regional Canaria S.L., 1977-81. 6 vols. maps.

A definitive history of the Canary Islands first published in 1893-95 and here
reissued with numerous colour plates, a volume of biographies, and indexes.

Trade and industry

709 **Canary Islands shipping handbook 1983/84.**
Edited by James Moriarty. Downham Market, England: Charter
Publications, 1983. 40p.

This annually updated handbook contains essential information for the shipping
industry. It outlines the chief characteristics of the islands' ports, including Las
Palmas, Tenerife and Santa Cruz de la Palma and provides information concerning
ship repair and maintenance, specialist services, shipbrokers and agents.

St. Paul's Rocks

710 **Voyage to St. Paul's Rocks.**
Alasdair Edwards, Roger Lubbock. *Geographical Magazine*,
vol. 52, no. 8 (May 1980), p. 561-67. maps.

An account of the University of Cambridge Underwater Exploration Group's
expedition to these islets in 1979. St. Paul's rocks are all that is visible of the
Mid Atlantic Ridge at what is the easternmost point of South America, being
politically part of Brazil. This article gives an account of the group and their
remarkable terrestrial and marine life.

711 **The fishes of Saint Paul's Rocks.**
Roger Lubbock, Alasdair Edwards. *Journal of Fish Biology*,
vol. 18, no. 2 (Feb. 1981), p. 135-57. map. bibliog.

A report of the work of a University of Cambridge expedition to St. Paul's Rocks
in 1979. Fifty species of fishes are recorded in a checklist with notes on ecology
and behaviour. The shore fish fauna of the Rocks appears to be dominated by
Western Atlantic and Brazilian forms.

South Atlantic Islands

General

712 **A year book of the Commonwealth 1984.**
Great Britain. Foreign and Commonwealth Office, 1984. 539p.
maps.

This annual publication contains basic geographical, demographic, economic, financial, governmental and other essential information about Commonwealth countries including the following British Dependent Territories in the South Atlantic: St. Helena (with Ascension and Tristan da Cunha); and the Falkland Islands and Dependencies (South Georgia and the South Sandwich Islands).

713 **Geology of the South Atlantic islands.**
Raoul C. Mitchell-Thomé. West Berlin: Gebrüder Borntraeger, 1970. 367p. maps. bibliog.

A summary of existing knowledge based on scattered literature going back over a period of 140 years. The islands under consideration are all volcanic with the exception of the Falkland Islands. Included are the following: Saint Paul's Rocks; Fernando de Noronha; Ilha Trinidade (South Trinidad Island); Martin Vaz archipelago; Ascension Island; St. Helena; the Tristan da Cunha group; Gough Island; and the Falkland Islands. In addition to full geological descriptions of each group brief general accounts of the geography, physical features and climate are added.

714 **Slow boats home.**
Gavin Young, illustrations by Salim. London: Hutchinson, 1985. 442p. illus.

The author is a former foreign correspondent of *The Observer* newspaper and a professional travel writer. This book, a sequel to his *Slow boats to China* (Harmondsworth, Middlesex: Penguin, 1981. 489p.) is a vivid description of Gavin Young's voyage home from China on board a series of assorted container ships and 'rustbuckets' by way of Polynesia, Cape Horn, Rio de Janeiro and St. Helena in the South Atlantic. On St. Helena he spent some time with the governor and visited the museum at Longwood, the house where Napoleon languished in final exile. The book concludes with a brief visit to neighbouring Ascension Island.

The Three voyages of Edmond Halley in the *Paramore* 1698-1701.
See item no. 38.

Journal of researches into the natural history and geology of the countries visited during the voyage round the world of H.M.S. 'Beagle' under the command of Captain Fitz Roy R.N.
See item no. 41.

Charles Darwin and the voyage of the *Beagle*.
See item no. 42.

Darwin and the *Beagle*.
See item no. 43.

Tables of temperature, relative humidity and precipitation for the world. Part II Central and South America, the West Indies and Bermuda.
See item no. 471.

Africa pilot vol. 2, comprising the west coast of Africa from Bakasi Peninsula to Cape Agulhas; islands in the Bight of Biafra; Ascension Island; Saint Helena Island; Tristan da Cunha group and Gough Island.
See item no. 489.

South Atlantic official standard names approved by the United States Board on Geographic Names.
See item no. 508.

Around the world single-handed; the cruise of the 'Islander'.
See item no. 596.

Ice Cap News.
See item no. 804.

South Trinidad Island (Ilha Trinidade)

715 **Ilha da Trinidade (South Trinidad) September 1901 and July
1910.**
Edward Adrian Wilson. In: *Edward Wilson's birds of the
Antarctic.* Edited by Brian Roberts. Poole, England: Blandford
Press, 1980, p. 143-48.

Dr. Wilson was a zoologist on Captain R. F. Scott's two expeditions to the
Antarctic in 1901-04 and 1910-12. On both occasions brief visits were made to
South Trinidad, a remote island in the South Atlantic Ocean off the coast of
Brazil in lat. 20° 29′ S., long. 29° 20′ W. These extracts from Wilson's manuscript
diaries, now in the Scott Polar Research Institute at Cambridge, England, give a
vivid picture of the difficulties encountered in landing on the island through the
immense surf and swell, and of the unique bird and shore life found there. Wilson's
own watercolour sketches of the Trinidad Petrel (*Pterodroma arminjoniana*)
are reproduced on p. 108-110.

St. Helena

The island and its people

716 **Back in St. Helena with 512 STRE.**
A. H. Bayliss. *Royal Engineers Journal,* vol. 94, no. 3 (Sept.
1980), p. 152-56.

This article is based on work on a Doppler survey station completed by Specialist
Team Royal Engineers in 1979 and contains much general information about the
island of St. Helena.

717 **Isle of St. Helena.**
Oswell Blakeston. London: Sidgwick & Jackson, 1957. 189p.
map.

A personal and highly readable account of the island and its people.

718   **St. Helena including Ascension Island and Tristan da Cunha.**
Tony Cross.   Newton Abbot, England: David & Charles, 1980.
192p. maps.

An up-to-date account of St. Helena with a chapter on tourism. A chapter is also
devoted to Ascension Island, and there is a summary account of Tristan da Cunha.
Appendixes include a list of the endemic plants of St. Helena.

719   **Conditions and cost of living in St. Helena.**
Great Britain. Ministry of Overseas Development.   London:
Ministry of Overseas Development, 1965. 10p.

A mimeographed document giving brief details of climate and health, communications, housing and hotel accommodation, the cost of living, taxation, dental and
medical treatment, banking, and social and sports amenities.

720   **St. Helena and dependencies.**
Great Britain. Central Office of Information, 1983. 10p. maps.

Provides general information about St. Helena and its dependencies, Ascension
Island and Tristan da Cunha, concerning, for example, government, economic
conditions and social welfare provisions.

721   **St. Helena: a physical, historical, and topographical description
of the island including its geology, fauna, flora and meteorology.**
John Charles Melliss.   London: L. Reeve & Co., 1875. 426p.
maps.

A very thorough and comprehensive account of the natural history of the island
prefaced by an historical introduction. A list of the flora and fauna distinguishes
indigenous species and an appendix contains climatic tables, demographic and
other information.

722   **Broadcasting (sound) on the island of St. Helena.**
St. Helena Government.   Jamestown: St. Helena Information
Office, 1976. 7p.

Presents general facts about the St. Helena Government broadcasting service.

723   **The island of St. Helena, South Atlantic, notes for visitors and
prospective residents.**
St. Helena Government.   Jamestown: St. Helena Government,
1983. 12p.

Provides concise basic information including details of ship fares from the United
Kingdom.

724 St. Helena Government Gazette.
Jamestown: St. Helena Government, 1847- . weekly.
This official journal covers all manner of information ranging from the appointment of officials, to road traffic regulations, rainfall figures and the arrival and departure of ships.

725 Serendipity in St. Helena; a genetical and medical study of an isolated community.
Ian Shine, Reynold Gold. Oxford: Pergamon Press, 1970. 187p.
Dr. Shine was medical officer on St. Helena from 1960 to 1963. During this tour of duty he became interested by the variety of genetic anomalies that he found among his patients, and carried out a genetic survey of 4,500 islanders. This survey, the first ever, revealed an atypical pattern of disease including several diseases hitherto undescribed. The results are presented with much personal and anecdotal detail.

726 St. Helena; ocean roadhouse.
Margaret Stewart Taylor. London: Robert Hale, 1969. 192p. map. bibliog.
A general account of the island based on a fifteen weeks' visit which took place between November 1967 and March 1968.

727 In mid Atlantic; the islands of St. Helena, Ascension, and Tristan da Cunha.
C. C. Watts. London: Society for the Propagation of the Gospel, 1936. 64p.
A brief popular account of this group of islands.

728 Notes for newcomers to St. Helena.
Women's Corona Society. London: Women's Corona Society, 1979. 6p.
Supplies basic information essential to successful adjustment to island life.

729 St. Helena.
In: *Worldmark encyclopaedia of the nations* vol. 2. Africa. New York: Worldmark Press, distributed by John Wiley, 1984. 6th ed. p. 345-46. map.
A brief guide to the geographic, historic, political, social and economic status of this United Kingdom colony with its dependencies, Ascension Island and Tristan da Cunha.

Nature and wildlife

730 **St. Helena's ancient shores.**
Patrick D. Nunn. *Geographical Magazine*, vol. 55, no. 5 (May 1983), p. 252-57. maps.
The author discusses the work of a scientific expedition to the island of St. Helena in 1981 to investigate the geomorphology in the light of current theories relating to Pleistocene sea-level changes and plate tectonics. It would seem that there is a strong possibility that the island's coastline was once at a much higher level.

History

731 **St. Helena.**
Octave Aulry, authorised translation by Arthur Livingston.
London: Gollancz, 1937. 640p. bibliog.
The author investigates in detail the 'tedious and sad unrolling' of Napoleon's life on St. Helena. Published and archival sources, both French and British, have been consulted including the archives of the governor, Sir Hudson Lowe (1769-1844).

732 **St. Helena story.**
Mabel Brookes. London: Heinemann, 1960. 309p. map. bibliog.
The author's family had associations with Napoleon on St. Helena and her account is based on private records which throw new light on the emperor.

733 **St. Helena 1502-1938.**
Philip Gosse. London: Cassell, 1938. 447p. map. bibliog.
A well-researched history of the island aimed at the general reader. The concluding chapter is devoted to some speculation on the island's economic future. Included among the appendixes are examples from the island's past legislation, including the regulation of slaves, as well as a review of St. Helena's printing presses and local publications.

734 **St. Helena; postal history and stamps.**
Edward Hibbert. London: Robson Lowe, 1979. 200p. maps. bibliog.
The first full account published in this field. There is a useful historical and descriptive chapter prefacing an account of the island's postal history and that of the various stamp issues. Among the appendixes are lists of ships visiting the island, a list of postmasters, a quick reference guide to the first issues with comparative rarity, cancellations, forgeries and postcards.

735 **St. Helena during Napoleon's exile; Gorrequer's diary.**
Edited by James Kemble. London: Heinemann, 1969. 298p.
map.
An edited edition of the personal diary of Major Gideon Gorrequer, aide-de-camp
to Sir Hudson Lowe, Governor of St. Helena during the period of Napoleon's
banishment. It includes biographical notes on Napoleon and Sir Hudson Lowe.

736 **The last years of Napoleon; his captivity on St. Helena.**
Ralph Korngold. London: Gollancz, 1960. 429p. bibliog.
The author takes the view that the Governor of St. Helena during Napoleon's
exile, Sir Hudson Lowe, suffered from a severe personality disorder.

737 **Napoleon's St. Helena.**
Gilbert Martineau. London: John Murray, 1968. 241p. map.
bibliog.
A translation of the French original published in 1966, revised and enlarged. The
author provides an account of Napoleon's last years of exile on St. Helena,
1815-21.

738 **Napoleon in exile, St. Helena (1815-1821), Vols. 1-2.**
Norwood Young. London: Stanley Paul & Co., 1915. 2 vols.
bibliog.
A definitive and well-illustrated history with a bibliography containing details of
172 publications.

Agriculture

739 **A review of agriculture & forestry in the island of St. Helena.**
Norman Humphrey. London: Crown Agents for Overseas
Governments and Administrations on behalf of the Government
of St. Helena, 1957. 88p. map. bibliog.
A review by the island's agricultural and forestry officer of the state of agriculture
and forestry against the background of the past. It is particularly concerned with
the effects of deforestation, problems of soil erosion and stock improvement.

Ascension Island

740 **Ascension; the story of a South Atlantic island.**
Duff Hart-Davis. London: Constable, 1972. 244p. map. bibliog.
A good general account of the island, which is a British dependency of St. Helena,
containing a useful reading list.

741 **Ascension Island and the British Ornithologists' Union centenary
expedition 1957-59 [reports].**
Bernard Stonehouse (et al.). *Ibis*, vol. 103 b, no. 2 (1962),
p. 107-295; no. 3 (1962), p. 297-482. map. bibliog.
A collection of scientific reports on the investigations of the British Ornithologists'
Union expedition to Ascension Island, 1957-59, to study the breeding cycles and
breeding seasons of fifteen species of sea birds and introduced land birds.

742 **Wideawake island; the story of the B.O.U. centenary expedition
to Ascension.**
Bernard Stonehouse. London: Hutchinson, 1960. 224p. map.
A general narrative by the leader of the British Ornithologists' Union expedition
to Ascension Island, 1957-59, to study the breeding habits of the wideawake tern
and other sea birds.

Tristan da Cunha and Gough Island

The island and its people

743 **Rock of exile; a narrative of Tristan da Cunha.**
D. M. Booy. London: J. M. Dent, 1957. 196p. map.
An account of a visit in 1942-43 by a member of a South African Navy party
sent to establish an outpost on the island.

744 **Tristan da Cunha, the lonely isle.**
Erling Christophersen. London: Cassell, 1940. 243p. maps.
An account by the leader of the Norwegian Scientific Expedition to Tristan da
Cunha, 1937-38.

745 **I went to Tristan.**
Allan B. Crawford. London: Hodder & Stoughton, 1941. 268p.
maps.
An account of the author's experiences on the island of Tristan da Cunha as a
surveyor with the Norwegian Scientific Expedition of 1937-38.

746 **Tristan da Cunha and the Roaring Forties.**
Allan B. Crawford. Edinburgh: Charles Skilton; Cape Town:
David Philip, 1982. 256p. map. bibliog.
A personal account of Tristan da Cunha by one who first visited the island in
1937 and knows it intimately having spent four and a half years there over a
period of four decades. Accounts of visits to Marion Island, Bouvetøya, Gough
Island and Antarctica are also provided.

747 **Narrative of a residence in New Zealand, journal of a residence in
Tristan da Cunha.**
Augustus Earle, edited by E. H. McCormick. Oxford: Clarendon
Press, 1966. 270p. bibliog.
Earle resided on Tristan da Cunha from March to November 1824 and his book
was first published in 1832. This new edition is embellished with reproductions of
Earle's original watercolour sketches.

748 **Back to Tristan.**
Arne Falk-Rønne. London: George Allen & Unwin, 1967. 149p.
bibliog.
An account of the attempt to resettle the inhabitants of Tristan da Cunha after
their temporary evacuation to Great Britain following the volcanic eruption of
1961.

749 **Tristan da Cunha; an empire outpost and its keepers with
glimpses of its past and consideration of the future.**
Douglas M. Gane. London: Allen & Unwin, 1932. 173p. bibliog.
A personal account of the island with a report on the physical condition of the
inhabitants.

750 **So this is Tristan da Cunha; a photo guide to the world's loneliest
island in the South Atlantic Ocean, with philatelic notes.**
Nigel Humphries. Aston, Oxford, England: Nigel & Gillian
Humphries, 1982. 25p. maps.
A first-hand account of a visit to the island in 1974-78 where the author served as
head teacher of St. Mary's School. There are well-illustrated brief descriptions of
the island and its history, the present way of life of its people, its government and
communications, the school and the church. Brief philatelic notes accompany
some of the photographs.

South Atlantic Islands. Tristan da Cunha and Gough Island.
The island and its people

751 **Crisis in Utopia.**
Peter A. Munch. London: Longman, 1971. 324p. maps. bibliog.
A social history of the British community on Tristan da Cunha. Special emphasis is placed on the social problems posed by the temporary evacuation of the islanders to Great Britain after the volcanic eruption of 1961 and their subsequent demand to be returned home.

752 **The song tradition of Tristan da Cunha.**
Peter A. Munch. Bloomington, Indiana: Indiana University
Research Center for the Language Sciences; The Hague: Mouton,
1970. 176p. bibliog. (Indiana University Folklore Institute
Monograph Series, vol. 22).
A collection of traditional songs and dance tunes recorded by the author during a four months' stay on Tristan da Cunha in 1938 with a Norwegian scientific expedition. The work is updated by an epilogue containing an account of further recordings in the 1960s.

753 **The lonely island.**
Rose Annie Rogers. London: Allen & Unwin, 1927. 223p. map.
An account of life on Tristan da Cunha during the period 1922-25 by a missionary's wife.

754 **The English of Tristan da Cunha.**
Arne Zettersten. Lund, Sweden: C. W. K. Gleerup, 1969. 179p.
maps. bibliog. (Lund Studies in English, no. 37).
A study of the dialect of Tristan da Cunha based on interviews with the islanders during their temporary evacuation to England in 1961. The monograph contains much information on the history of the island as well as the islanders' vocabulary, the names of topographical features and persons, and details gleaned from the censuses for 1875, 1906 and 1966.

Nature and wildlife

755 **The volcanological report of the Royal Society expedition to Tristan da Cunha, 1962.**
F. E. Baker, I. G. Gass, P. G. Harris, R. W. Le Maitre.
Philosophical Transactions of the Royal Society of London, Series A, Mathematical and Physical Science, no. 1075, vol. 256, (Nov. 1964), p. 439-578. maps. bibliog.

In November 1961 the Royal Society agreed to send an expedition to study the recently erupted volcano on Tristan da Cunha. This official report is based on seven weeks' field work on Tristan, and Inaccessible and Nightingale Islands. A geological survey of Tristan da Cunha was made and the effect of the eruption on the fauna and flora examined.

756 **Results of the Norwegian Scientific Expedition to Tristan da Cunha 1937-1938, Vols. 1-5.**
Edited by Erling Christophersen. Oslo: Det Norske Videnskaps-Akademi i Oslo, 1946. 5 vols. maps. bibliog.

A collection of specialised reports on botany and zoology as well as medical and sociological surveys.

757 **The biological report of the Royal Society expedition to Tristan da Cunha.**
J. H. Dickson, N. M. Wace, Martin Wyatt Holdgate, D. E. Baird.
Philosophical Transactions of the Royal Society of London, Series B. Biological Sciences, no. 795, vol. 249 (Oct. 1965), p. 257-434. bibliog.

A collection of scientific reports on terrestrial botany and fauna, and the effects on these of the volcanic eruption of 1961.

758 **Mountains in the sea; the story of the Gough Island expedition.**
Martin Wyatt Holdgate. London: Macmillan; New York: St. Martin's Press, 1958. 222p. maps.

A popular account of the Gough Island Scientific Survey, 1955-56, an expedition from the University of Cambridge to a small sub-Antarctic island in the Tristan da Cunha group. A list of Gough Island place-names is appended.

759 **Man and nature in the Tristan da Cunha islands.**
N. M. Wace, Martin Wyatt Holdgate. Morges, Switzerland:
International Union for Conservation of Nature and Natural
Resources, 1976. 114p. maps. bibliog. (IUCN Monograph, no. 6).

This comprehensive report describes the scientific interest of the Tristan da
Cunha-Gough Island group; summarizes current knowledge of the four main
islands; outlines the history of their human utilization; analyses the impact of
man upon the biota; and sets out proposals for future management and conservation.

History

760 **Tristan da Cunha 1506-1902.**
J. Brander. London: Allen & Unwin, 1940. 336p. maps. bibliog.

A history of the island documented by reference to British, Dutch and Cape
Colonial papers.

761 **The history and postal history of Tristan da Cunha.**
George Crabb. Ewell, England: George Crabb, 1980. 347p.

A factual history based on original research with an evaluation of some earlier
accounts. The book is available from the author's address: 'Charlwood', Howard
Avenue, Ewell, Epsom, Surrey, England.

762 **The glass island; the story of Tristan da Cunha.**
Nancy Hosegood. London: Hodder & Stoughton, 1964. 192p.
map.

A history of the island before the volcanic eruption in October 1961, followed
by an account of the eruption itself, the evacuation of the inhabitants to England,
and the eventual return of many of the islanders.

763 **Angry island: the story of Tristan da Cunha (1506-1963).**
Margaret Mackay. London: Arthur Barker, 1963. 288p. map.
bibliog.

A history of the island from its discovery by the Portugese admiral Tristão da
Cunha in 1506 to the volcanic eruption of 1961 which resulted in the temporary
evacuation of the islanders to England.

Ice Cap News.
See item no. 804.

Polar Post.
See item no. 805.

Falkland Islands

The islands and their people

764 **Antarctic diary; a letter to her family.**
Maria Buxton. Lavenham, England: Terence Dalton, 1983. 78p.
map.

Written mainly for her children, this diary covers the author's visit to the Falkland Islands, South Georgia and the Antarctic Peninsula, February-March 1982, shortly before the Argentine invasion.

765 **Tierra del Fuego, Argentina. 1979.**
Rae Natalie Prosser de Goodall. Buenos Aires; Ushuaia,
Argentina: Ediciones Shanamaiim, 1978. 3rd ed. 329p. maps.
bibliog.

An invaluable handbook for the visitor to these parts with parallel Spanish and English texts. A separate chapter deals with the Falkland Islands (Malvinas) on p. 305-24.

766 **Scientific papers and publications relevant to the Falkland Islands.**
J. H. McAdam. *Falkland Islands Journal* (1984), p. 11-15.

A continuing annotated bibliography, commencing with this issue of the *Journal*, of articles and books in the following fields: general science; fisheries; and agriculture and forestry.

767 **The meteorology of the Falkland Islands and Dependencies. 1944-1950.**
J. Pepper. London: Falkland Islands Dependencies Survey, 1954. 249p.

A compilation of meteorological records including a discussion of the data and tabulated summaries of meteorological variants.

768 **Bibliografía de las Islas Malvinas, obras, mapas y documentos.**
(Bibliography of the Malvinas Islands, publications, maps, documents.)
José Torre Revello. Buenos Aires: Imprenta de la Universidad, 1953. 260p. maps. (Universidad de Buenos Aires, Facultad de Filosofía y Letras, Publicaciones del Instituto de Investigaciónes Historicas, no. 99).

A comprehensive annotated bibliography of the Falkland Islands (Islas Malvinas) with special reference to historical and geographical works before 1900. It includes a list of early maps including those in the Ministerio de Marina, Madrid.

769 **The geography of the Falkland Islands.**
Lord Shackleton, Richard Johnson, Charles Swithinbank, James Fawcett, Sir George Deacon, Huw Ll. Williams, Patrick Vincent, Bernard Stonehouse, Inigo Everson. *Geographical Journal*, vol. 149, part 1 (March 1983), p. 1-21. maps.
Nine contributions to a symposium on the geography of the Falkland Islands held at the Royal Geographical Society in May 1982. These papers cover: the political and legal aspects of the British claim to the Falklands; the history, physical geography and the present social scene; an updating of earlier proposals for improving the Islands' economic prospects; the need for the conservation of resources; the sheep farming potential; and the economic possibility of krill fishing.

770 **Falkland Islands.**
Ian J. Strange, Bob Elliott, Lord Shackleton. *Geographical Magazine*, vol. 55, no. 1 (Jan. 1983), p. 30-39. maps.
Ian Strange reflects on the passing of the Falklands' way of life as it was before the Argentine invasion of 1982; Bob Elliott discusses the problems involved in fighting a war 12,600 kilometers from Britain; and Lord Shackleton summarizes the economic problems facing the islanders.

771 **The Falkland Islands.**
Ian J. Strange. Newton Abbot, England: David & Charles, 1983. 3rd ed. 328p. maps. bibliog.
This is the standard textbook on the islands of which the author has considerable personal experience. This edition included two chapters dealing with the invasion of the islands by Argentina in 1982.

772 **Focus on the Falkland Islands.**
Margaret Stewart Taylor. London: Robert Hale, 1971. 191p. map. bibliog.
An account of life in the islands based on a three-month visit by the author in 1966, a year after Argentina had brought her claims to sovereignty over the island group before the United Nations.

South America pilot vol. 2, east, south and west coasts of South America from Cabo Tres Puntas to Cabo Raper, and Falkland Islands.
See item no. 493.

Across the oceans.
See item no. 592.

Nature and wildlife

773 **Survival: South Atlantic.**
Cindy Buxton, Annie Price. London: Granada, 1983. 235p.
maps. bibliog.
Illustrated with first-rate colour photographs, this book describes two seasons
spent by the authors filming wildlife on the Falkland Islands followed by a seven
months' sojourn on South Georgia where both authors were caught up in the
Argentine invasion of March 1982.

774 **Notes on Falkland Islands fishes and vertebrates.**
S. Graham. *Falkland Islands Journal*, (1977), p. 43-52. bibliog.
These notes are based on results emanating from studies of over 2,300 specimens
collected in the Falklands in 1967.

775 **Penguin summer; an adventure with the birds of the Falkland
Islands.**
Eleanor Rice Pettingill. New York: Clarkson N. Potter, 1960.
197p. map.
The author visited the islands in 1953-54 with her husband, a professional ornithologist. This is a general account of their experiences there and their work
among the penguin and other bird colonies. A British edition of this book (reset)
was published by Cassell in 1962.

776 **Another penguin summer.**
Olin Sewall Pettingill, Jr. London: Harrap, 1975. 80p.
The author and his wife returned to the Falkland Islands in 1971-72 to follow up
their photographic work of 1953-54. This well-illustrated narrative looks in
particular at the gentoo, macaroni, rockhopper, king and jackass penguins.

777 **Beauchêne Island.**
R. I. Lewis Smith. *Polar Record*, vol. 22, no. 137 (May 1984),
p. 159-168. maps. bibliog.
Beauchêne is the southernmost of the Falkland Islands and is now a wildlife
reserve with large penguin and albatross populations. This article draws attention
to early reports of the island and outlines what is known of its history.

778 **Illustrations of the flowering plants and ferns of the Falkland
Islands.**
E. F. Vallentin, E. M. Cotton. London: L. Reeve, 1921. 73p.
The standard descriptive flora of the islands. The text is by E. F. Vallentin and is
illustrated with sixty-four fine colour plates from illustrations by E. M. Cotton.

779 **The birds of the Falkland Islands.**
Robin W. Woods. Oswestry, England: Anthony Nelson, 1975.
240p. maps. bibliog.

The author worked in the Falkland Islands between 1956 and 1963 and the
introduction to this work describes the physical features, climate and vegetation
of the islands. The *Field Guide* constitutes a major part of the book listing
eighty-seven species, with records for a further sixty-two species formerly breeding on the islands.

780 **Falkland Islands birds.**
Robin W. Woods, photographs by Cindy Buxton, Annie Price.
Oswestry, England: Anthony Nelson, 1982. 79p. bibliog.

A well-illustrated popular guide to Falkland Islands birds with a checklist of the
species that occur there.

History

781 **Historia completa de las Malvinas. Tomos I-III.** (Complete history
of the Malvinas. Vols. I-III.)
José Luis Muñoz Azpiri. Buenos Aires: Editorial Oriente, 1966.
3 vols. maps. bibliog.

A very thoroughly documented history of the Falkland Islands (Malvinas), though
biased towards Argentina's territorial claims. Volume I consists of the history of
the islands, a full bibliography, and reproductions of various official documents.
Volume II is devoted to reproducing various official and unofficial documents –
Spanish, English, Argentinian and North American – relating to the conflict of
claims. Volume III is made up of a number of separate articles dealing with
territorial claims to the Falklands. Each volume is accompanied by a set of
coloured transparencies.

782 **The Falkland Islands; with notes on the natural history.**
V. F. Boyson, Rupert Vallentin. Oxford, England: Clarendon
Press, 1924. 414p. map.

Despite its age, this is still the best historical account of the islands prior to 1914.
There are additional chapters on industries and natural history, the latter by
Vallentin.

783   **Byron's journal of his circumnavigation 1764-1766.**
Edited by Robert E. Gallagher. Cambridge, England: Cambridge
University Press for the Hakluyt Society, 1964. 230p. maps.
bibliog. (Hakluyt Society, Second Series, no. 122).

Captain John ('Foul-weather Jack') Byron's voyage with the *Dolphin* and *Tamar*
was commissioned by the Admiralty primarily for the advancement of British
trade. On 12 January 1765 Byron made a landfall on the northwest corner of the
Falkland Islands and formally took possession in the name of King George III on
22 January 1765. The Admiralty believed that the islands were the key to the
whole Pacific Ocean.

784   **Commodore Byron, letters to Lord Egmont, and letters of the
same year following up the proposed action—1765.**
Introduced by Jack Abbot. *Falkland Islands Journal*, (1975),
p. 14-23.

Provides copies of three letters describing the first settlement of the Falkland
Islands by Commodore John Byron at Port Egmont. Lord Egmont was at this
time First Lord of the Admiralty.

785   **The Falkland story 1592-1982.**
Mary Cawkell. Oswestry, England: Anthony Nelson, 1983. 90p.
map.

An abridged and updated edition of the author's *The Falkland Islands* (London:
Macmillan, 1960) covering the history of their discovery on 14 August 1592 by
John Davies on the ship *Desire* down to the Argentinian invasion of 2 April 1982.
The author lived in the Falklands during the 1950s.

786   **The Antarctic problem; an historical and political study.**
E. W. Hunter Christie. London: Allen & Unwin, 1951. 336p.
maps. bibliog.

A history of the discovery of the Falkland Islands and their dependencies, South
Georgia and the South Sandwich Islands, which is intended to serve as a back-
ground to the political dispute in the area involving Argentina, Chile and Great
Britain. Although now over thirty years old, this is still essential reading.

787   **The history of the Falkland Islands Company.**
W. M. Dean, edited by S. Miller. *Falkland Islands Journal*,
(1980), p. 10-19; (1981), p. 37-44; (1982), p. 32-44; (1983),
p. 28-36; (1984), p. 43-50.

An on-going account of the developments leading up to the incorporation of the
Company by Royal Charter in January 1851 and its subsequent history. In
addition to a detailed account of Company business there is much information
about sheep farming and its problems.

788 Falkland Islands: a bibliography of 50 examples of printed maps
bearing specific reference to the Falkland Islands.
Angela Fordham. London: Map Collectors' Circle, 1964. 18p.
maps.
An annotated list of maps from 1597 to 1885 preceded by a brief cartographic
history of the islands.

789 Raising the flag in the Falklands; an account of the annexation
of the islands in 1836 from the private journals of Capt. George
Grey, R.N.
George Grey. *Observer Review*, (2 May 1982), p. 25-26.
In 1836 Captain (later Admiral) Grey was ordered to proceed to the Falkland
Islands to make a survey and to reaffirm British possession. These previously
unpublished extracts are taken from long, vivid letters home. Details are given
of the condition of the islanders and their way of life, the natural products of the
islands and the advantages to Britain of access to the great quantity of cattle.

790 The history of place-names in the Falkland Islands Dependencies
(South Georgia and South Sandwich Islands).
Geoffrey Hattersley-Smith. Cambridge, England: British
Antarctic Survey, 1980. 112p. maps. (British Antarctic Survey
Scientific Reports, no. 101).
The objective of this work is to provide a complete history of place-names in the
Falkland Islands Dependencies found in a search of more than 400 published
sources in eight languages.

791 Thoughts on the late transactions respecting Falkland's Islands.
Samuel Johnson. Leigh-on-Sea, England: Thames Bank
Publishing, 1948. 44p.
A reprint of this famous pamphlet which was first published in 1771 at a time of
crisis when Spain and Great Britain were at loggerheads over the sovereignty of
the Falkland Islands. Johnson counselled against the folly of unnecessary war
for the sake of an island 'which not the southern savages dignified with habitation;
where a garrison must be kept in a state that contemplates with envy the exiles of
Siberia, of which the expence will be perpetual and the use only occasional'.

792 The history of a voyage to the Malouine (or Falkland) islands,
made in 1763 and 1764, under the command of M. de Bougainville
in order to form a settlement there and of two voyages to the
Streights of Magellan with an account of the Patagonians. Translated from Dom Pernety's historical journal written in French.
Antoine Joseph Pernety. London: printed for William Gold-
smith and David Steel, 1773. 2nd ed. 294p. maps.
It was on this expedition that the French took possession of the Falkland Islands,
prior to Commodore Byron's voyage of 1764-65.

793 *The Great Britain.*
K. T. Rowland. Newton Abbot, England: David & Charles, 1971. 132p.

A history of the first Atlantic liner built of iron and having a screw propeller, built by Sir Marc Isambard Brunel in 1843. She became a rusting hulk at Port Stanley, Falkland Islands, where she was scuttled in 1937 but was eventually salvaged and returned to Britain where she is now a floating museum.

794 **The Falkland Islands and Antarctica.**
Lord Shackleton. *Proceedings of the Royal Institution of Great Britain*, vol. 56 (1984), p. 147-60.

Outlines the political and economic history of the Falkland Islands, South Georgia and the Antarctic from ca. 1690 to the present day. The author pays particular attention to the issue of the sovereignty of the Falkland Islands.

795 **The Falklands story.**
John Skelly. *Falkland Islands Journal*, (1984), p. 4-10.

An account of the events leading up to the hoisting of the Union Jack and taking possession of the Falkland Islands at Port Louis, Berkley Sound, on 10 January 1834 by the first British Lieutenant-Governor, Henry Smith.

796 **A two years' cruise off Tierra del Fuego, the Falkland Islands, Patagonia, and in the River Plate: a narrative of life in the southern seas. Vols. I and II.**
W. Parker Snow. London: Longmans, Brown, Green, 1857. 2 vols. map.

An account of two years work in Patagonia between 1854 and 1856 when the author commanded the South American Missionary Society's vessel *Allen Gardiner* used to carry missionaries between Tierra del Fuego and the Falkland Islands, and stations on the mainland.

797 **The Falkland Islands crisis of 1770; use of naval force.**
Nicholas Tracy. *English Historical Review*, vol. 90, no. 354 (Jan. 1975), p. 40-75, bibliog.

The crisis arose from the seizure of the British fort in the Falklands in 1770 by Spanish troops. British policy was to assert its interests without resorting to war. This was achieved by insisting that the base be restored to British sovereignty, while secretly agreeing to abandon it after peace was restored. Thus, the author maintains, did Britain fail to crush the Bourbon revival, and thereby only deferred eventual hostilities.

798   **Falkland heritage; a record of pioneer settlement.**
      Mary Trehearne.   Ilfracombe, England: Arthur H. Stockwell,
      1978. 201p. maps.

The story of two early settlers in West Falkland, Ernest Holmested and Robert
Blake, who established sheep farming and agriculture in this remote region after
1868. The account is based on original diaries and letters.

Coronel and the Falklands.
See item no. 217.

**The enemy fought splendidly, being the 1914-1915 diary of the
Battle of the Falklands & its aftermath.**
See item no. 218.

The Great War at sea 1914-1918.
See item no. 221.

Coronel and the Falklands.
See item no. 222.

**From the Dreadnought to Scapa Flow; the Royal Navy in the Fisher
era, 1904-1919.**
See item no. 223.

Command the far seas; a naval campaign of the First World War.
See item no. 224.

**Before Jutland; Admiral von Spee's last voyage. Coronel & the battle
of the Falklands.**
See item no. 225.

The battle of the Falkland Islands before and after.
See item no. 226.

Philately

799   **The cancellations of the Falkland Islands and Dependencies and
      the handstruck stamps; with notes on the British, Argentine
      and Chilean post offices in the Antarctic.**
      James Andrews.   London: Robson Lowe, 1956. 56p. maps.
      bibliog.

The standard work on the subject complementing B. S. H. Grant's historical
review entitled *The postage stamps of the Falkland Islands and Dependencies*
(q.v.). A chapter on Argentine and Chilean post offices in the Falkland Islands
Dependencies is included together with a list of post offices.

800 **The postal service of the Falkland Islands including South Shetlands (1906-1931) and South Georgia.**
Robert Barnes. London: Robson Lowe, 1972. 96p. bibliog.

A history of the postal service of the Falkland Islands with information on the producers of stamps, where and how they were used, postal rates, cancellations, and dates and names of mail boats from 1888 to 1970.

801 **Argentina's 'philatelic annexation' of the Falklands.**
Peter J. Beck. *History Today*, vol. 33 (Feb. 1983), p. 39-44.

The author discusses the propaganda role of postage stamps portraying the Falkland Islands as Argentine territory since the 1930s.

802 **The Falklands war; postal history and stamps of the Argentine occupation 1982.**
J. D. Davis. Thruxton, Andover, England: J. D. Davis, [n.d.]. [88] p.

A study of postal operations at Port Stanley and of internal mail services with the islands during the Argentine occupation made by Wing Commander John Davis during a visit to the Falklands shortly after the cessation of hostilities. It makes a unique record of the conflict through philatelic eyes. In addition to much information about stamps and cancellations, there is a catalogue section with general price guidelines for some of the material available and a great deal about life at Stanley before and during the invasion.

803 **The postage stamps of the Falkland Islands and Dependencies.**
B. S. H. Grant. London: Stanley Gibbons, 1952. 140p. bibliog.

A definitive history starting with the first postage stamps issued in 1878-79 and concluding with the Pictorial Issue of 1952. The text also covers overprints from South Georgia, Port Foster (Deception Island) and Graham Land and an appendix lists governors of the Falkland Islands. This work is complementary to James Andrews's book on the Falkland Islands cancellations entitled *The cancellations of the Falkland Islands and Dependencies and the handstruck stamps . . . .* (q.v.).

804 **Ice Cap News.**
El Paso, Texas: American Society of Polar Philatelists, 1956- . bimonthly.

Primarily concerned with the polar regions, this publication does feature occasional articles and notes of a philatelic nature on such South Atlantic islands as Tristan da Cunha and the Falkland Islands.

805 **Polar Post.**
York, England: Polar Postal History Society of Great Britain, 1958- . quarterly.

A society journal which includes philatelic and historically related articles on the polar regions, the Falkland Islands, Tristan da Cunha and South Georgia.

806 **The 1933 centenary issue of the Falkland Islands.**
R. N. Spafford. Chippenham, England: Picton Publishing, 1972.
84p. maps. bibliog.

A history of this issue designed to celebrate the centenary of permanent British settlement of the Falkland Islands in 1833. The detailed description of the various issues contain a great deal of historical background material and a history of the Battle of the Falkland Islands on 8 December 1914 is appended.

807 **The Upland Goose; journal of the Falkland Islands Philatelic Study Group.**
Baldock, England: Falkland Islands Philatelic Study Group.
1972?- . biannual.

The aim of the group is to research into all aspects of philately connected with the Falkland Islands and their dependencies, and to publish the findings.

Economic development

808 **Economic survey of the Falkland Islands.**
Lord Shackleton, chairman. London: Economist Intelligence Unit, 1976. 2 vols. maps. bibliog.

This committee report was a milestone in the economic history of the Falkland Islands. Wholly independent of government its aim was to provide an overall examination of the islands' economic prospects in all sectors. The committee's recommendations contained in volume 2 are presented with a plan of action for their implementation as well as a broad estimate of their financial implications. The report was updated by the *Falkland Islands Economic Study of 1982* (q.v.).

809 **Falkland Islands economic study 1982, presented to the Prime Minister.**
Lord Shackleton, chairman. London: HM Stationery Office, 1982. 137p. 3 maps. (Cmnd. 8653).

A re-examination of the resources of the islands and their dependencies and the prospects for their future economic development, together with a review of government services and an assessment of the financial, manpower and social obligations of any recommended strategy. This is an updating of Lord Shackleton's 1976 report in the light of the Argentine invasion of the islands in 1982.

Falklands War (1982)

British official sources

810 **Falkland Islands review; report of a committee of privy counsellors.**
Lord Franks, chairman. London: HM Stationery Office, 1983.
105p. map. (Cmnd. 8787).

The Franks report is probably the best single source for understanding the extent to which the British contributed to the Falkland crisis. The committee was appointed by the government in July 1982 'to review the way in which the responsibilities of government in relation to the Falkland Islands and their Dependencies were discharged in the period leading up to the Argentine invasion'. A detailed account of the dispute from 1965 to 1979 is followed by a re-examination of the present government's policy towards Argentina and the Falklands in the period immediately preceding the war. The report also attempts to answer such questions as 'could the invasion have been foreseen?'.

811 **Britain and the Falklands crisis; a documentary record.**
Great Britain. Central Office of Information. London:
HM Stationery Office, 1982. 95p.

The collection of documents in this pamphlet, together with a short account of the Falklands crisis, is designed to show the development of British policy in response to Argentina's invasion of the islands. It also explains Britain's subsequent refusal to withdraw her forces, in compliance with a mandatory resolution of the United Nations Security Council. The work also covers the support given by Britain to the USA and other intermediaries in their efforts to promote a negotiated settlement and describes how Britain was finally compelled to use force to secure the islanders' freedom to determine their own future.

812 **The Falklands campaign; a digest of debates in the House of Commons 2 April to 15 June 1982.**
Great Britain. House of Commons. London: HM Stationery Office, 1982. 361p.

A summary of the part played by the British Parliament in influencing negotiations over the Falkland Islands. Some of the speeches are creative and responsible, others are ill-informed and jingoistic.

South Atlantic Islands. Falkland Islands. Falklands War (1982).
British official sources

813 **The Falklands campaign: the lessons; presented to Parliament by the Secretary of State for Defence.**
Great Britain. Ministry of Defence. London: HM Stationery Office, 1982. 46p. maps.

A brief outline of the events leading to the Falklands campaign followed by a description of the principal lessons learned and the steps being taken to apply them in the fields of maritime and land operations, equipment, logistics and personnel. Annexes tabulate: the composition of the task force and supporting elements; weapons systems performance against enemy aircraft; and ship and aircraft losses.

814 **House of Commons. First report from the Defence Committee, Session 1982-83, the handling of press and public information during the Falklands conflict. Vol. I report and minutes of proceedings, Vol. II minutes and evidence.**
Great Britain. House of Commons. London: HM Stationery Office, 1982. 2 vols. (Publication no. 490).

An investigation into the manner in which the Ministry of Defence dealt with information concerning the Falklands conflict and the way in which the media described and interpreted the conflict to the public. Evidence was invited from the Ministry of Defence, national provincial and foreign press bodies, the British Broadcasting Corporation, Independent Television News, and the journalists who went to the Falklands. A number of unsolicited memoranda and letters were also received. Visits to the USA and Japan elicited further opinions on how these countries viewed Britain's handling of information. There appears to have been a failure to project the British case in South America and in third world countries.

815 **The future defence of the Falkland Islands; observations presented by the Secretary of State for Defence on the third report from the Defence Committee, House of Commons paper 154, 1982-83.**
Great Britain. Ministry of Defence. London: HM Stationery Office, 1983. 11p. (Cmnd. 9070).

The report restates Britain's commitment to NATO and adds that this will not be prejudiced by measures in hand to protect the Falkland Islands. Other points dealt with include: airfield construction on the islands; coordination of military and civil projects; conditions of service; welfare and accommodation; and observance of environmental and conservation regulations.

816 **House of Commons. Minutes of the proceedings of the Foreign Affairs Committee, session 1982-83.**
Great Britain. House of Commons. London: HM Stationery Office, 1983. 101. (Publication no. 380).

The committee's brief in July 1982 was to consider the future of British foreign policy in relation to the Falkland Islands and Dependencies, the Antarctic and adjacent South American states 'making use of the Franks report and evidence from government departments and other sources at home and overseas including the Falkland Islands themselves'. This draft report concentrates on future policy towards the Falklands rather than re-examining the events leading up to the Argentine invasion. It concludes that any immediate consideration of a transfer of sovereignty must be ruled out but that serious consideration must be given to securing the islands' long-term future. A leaseback arrangement with Argentina should not be discounted. The committee does not yet recommend a resumption of negotiations on the sovereignty issue.

817 **House of Commons. Third report from the Defence Committee, session 1982-83, the future defence of the Falkland Islands.**
Great Britain. House of Commons. London: HM Stationery Office, 1983. 226p. map.

An examination, based on evidence taken in the Falkland Islands, of the future defence requirements of the islands. The report explores the nature of possible threats from Argentina, the size of the force required to deter such threats, problems of military infrastructure and the impact of all this on the islanders themselves.

818 **House of Commons. Fifth report from the Foreign Affairs Committee session 1983-84, Falkland Islands report with annexes; together with the proceedings of the committee, Vol. 1. report and minutes of proceedings. Vol. 2. minutes of evidence and appendices.**
Great Britain. House of Commons. London: HM Stationery Office, 1984. 2 vols. maps. (HC 268).

A re-examination of the dispute between Argentina and the United Kingdom over the Falklands, originally investigated by the Foreign Affairs Committee of the previous Parliament but without an agreed report. This report summarizes the history of the dispute and examines the options now open to HM Government in the search for a lasting settlement of the dispute. Evidence was also taken concerning the sinking of the Argentine cruiser *Belgrano* on 2 May 1982 which allegedly precipitated the collapse of peace negotiations then being conducted by the President of Peru. The report contains a wealth of up-to-date information on such subjects as the Falkland Islands' economy, the system of government, and life on the islands. The minutes of evidence are contained in eight separate supplements (HC 268 i-viii).

British unofficial sources

819   **Above all, courage: the Falklands front line – first hand accounts.**
Max Arthur.   London: Sidgwick & Jackson, 1985. 338p. map.
This illustrated volume brings together thirty first-hand accounts of the Falklands
War by Royal Navy, Royal Marines, Army and Royal Air Force personnel of all
ranks. A most revealing and authentic study based on interviews carried out by
the author over a two year period. These accounts vividly illuminate some of the
timeless characteristics of warfare: the loneliness, the camaraderie, the suffering,
the inspiration, the horror, and, 'above all, courage'.

820   **Iron Britannia.**
Anthony Barnett.   London: Allison & Busby, 1982. 160p.
A critical investigation of British attitudes towards the Falkland Islands crisis
with suggestions for a just settlement of the conflict between Great Britain and
Argentina.

821   **The Chile connection.**
Duncan Campbell.   *New Statesman*, vol. 109, no. 2810 (1985),
p. 8-10. map.
This article claims that within a week of the outbreak of the Falkland Islands war
in April 1982 Britain had reached a series of 'understandings' with General
Pinochet, President of Chile, whereby, in exchange for military aircraft and other
supplies, together with United Kingdom support at the United Nations, Chile
would afford Britain the use of Punta Arenas, an air base in southern Chile, for
Royal Air Force spy planes and the infiltration of Special Air Service (SAS) forces
into Argentina.

822   **Another story; women and the Falklands war.**
Jean Carr.   London: Hamish Hamilton, 1984. 162p.
The author, a journalist with the *Sunday Mirror*, investigates the effect of the
Falklands war on the wives of servicemen through a series of interviews. She
reveals the seeming indifference of government towards war widows and their
families.

823   **Latin America and the Falklands conflict.**
Gordon Connell-Smith.   In: *Yearbook of world affairs 1984.*
London: Stevens, for The London Institute of World Affairs,
1984, p. 73-88.
The main object of this paper is to examine how far the Latin American republics
were united on the issue of the Falklands invasion of 1982, and the extent to
which their relations with the United States and the United Kingdom appear to
have been damaged by the war.

824　**Falklands task force portfolio, part 1 and 2.**
Edited by Mike Critchley.　Liskeard, England: Maritime Books,
[1982]. 2 vols.
A photographic record of the British campaign in the Falklands in 1982.

825　**The RAF contribution to the Falklands campaign.**
Sir John Curtiss.　*Naval Review*, vol. 71, no. 1 (1983), p. 24-32.
A review of the role played by the Royal Air Force during the campaign of 1982.

826　**One man's Falklands.**
Tam Dalyell.　London: Cecil Woolf, 1982. 144p.
A strongly critical account of British policy towards the Falkland Islands by a
British Member of Parliament publicly opposed to any military solution of the
conflict with Argentina over sovereignty.

827　**Thatcher's torpedo; the sinking of the 'Belgrano'.**
Tam Dalyell.　London: Cecil Woolf, 1983. 80p.
The Argentine battleship *General Belgrano* was torpedoed by a British submarine
on 2 May 1982 with the loss of several hundred lives. This, claims Tam Dalyell,
effectively scuppered a Peruvian peace initiative. In this polemic the author
charges the British Prime Minister, Margaret Thatcher, with deliberately giving the
order to sink the vessel and thus ensuring the continuation of the war. The author
supports his case by means of some 300 parliamentary questions.

828　**The Falklands conflict.**
Christopher Dobson, John Miller, Ronald Payne.　London:
Hodder & Stoughton, 1982. 213p. maps. (Coronet Books).
A popular account of the Argentine invasion, the British counter-attack, the naval
and military gains and losses and the diplomatic initiatives. The authors are all
professional journalists. No sources are listed.

829　**Naval lessons from the South Atlantic.**
Martin Douglas.　*Jane's Defence Weekly*, (7 April 1984),
p. 519-23.
A review of the lessons learned from the Falkland Islands naval campaign of 1982,
Operation Corporate, the first full-scale naval conflict since 1945. These lessons
may well have a bearing on future limited wars in which NATO powers could be
involved.

830　**HMS *Coventry* in the Falklands conflict – a personal story.**
David Hart Dyke.　*Naval Review*, vol. 71, no. 1 (1983), p. 9-13.
A narrative covering the author's period of command of *Coventry* during the
Falklands conflict, 1982.

831   **The Falklands War.**
Paul Eddy, Magnus Linklater, Peter Gillman.   London: Andre
Deutsch, 1982. 274p. maps.
An investigation by the *Sunday Times* (London) 'Insight' team into the causes
and consequences of the war based on British, Argentine and other sources.

832   **Air war South Atlantic.**
Jeffrey Ethell, Alfred Price.   London: Sidgwick & Jackson,
1983. 260p. maps.
A full history of the air operations which took place during the Falklands conflict
of 1982 based on interviews with Argentine and British pilots from the various
combat units involved. As well as enabling the reader to gain a clear idea of
modern air tactics and weaponry, the book contains a detailed analysis of the
losses suffered on both sides.

833   **The sinking of the Belgrano.**
Arthur Favshon, Desmond Rice.   Sevenoaks, England: New
English Library, 1984. 238p. maps. bibliog. (New English Library
paperback edition).
Was the torpedoing of the Argentine cruiser *Belgrano* by the British nuclear submarine HMS *Conqueror* deliberately sanctioned by the British government in
order to scupper impending peace talks? The publication of this book in March
1984 (by Secker & Warburg in hardback), coupled with a subsequent British
Broadcasting Corporation 'Panorama' investigation, brought to light important
new evidence. Drawing on sources both public and private, and from both
Argentine and British sides, the authors, who are profesional journalists, have
produced a detailed account of the facts. They conclude that the sinking of the
Belgrano was deliberate and part of the cynical politico-military machinations
which typified both sides in the war.

834   **Operation Corporate – the Falkland Islands campaign.**
G. W. Field.   *Royal Engineers Journal*, vol. 96, no. 4 (Dec. 1982),
p. 230-43. map.
An account of Royal Engineers operations during, and immediately after, the
Falklands campaign of 1982 by the Commanding Officer of the 36 Engineers
Regiment. 'Operation Corporate' was the official code name for the British
military reoccupation of the Falkland Islands.

835   **Eyewitness Falklands; a personal account of the Falklands
campaign.**
Robert Fox.   London: Methuen, 1982. 337p. maps.
The author was assigned by BBC radio to cover the land campaign of the Falklands
war.

836 **Bridgehead revisited: the literature of the Falklands.**
Lawrence Freedman. *International Affairs*, vol. 59, no. 3
(summer 1983), p. 448-52. bibliog.

A survey of the published material currently available in Britain for a serious
study of the Falklands War, April-June 1982. The author concludes that while
there is a rich and varied literature on the British side much more needs to be
made available from Argentina.

837 **The fleet, the Falklands and the future.**
David Greenwood. In: *Yearbook of world affairs 1984*. London:
Stevens, for The London Institute of World Affairs, 1984,
p. 59-71.

An analysis, by the Director of the Centre for Defence Studies, University of
Aberdeen, of the effect which the successful outcome of the Falklands campaign
may have had on both the 1981 review of the United Kingdom's defence
programme and budget, and the White Paper *The United Kingdom: the way
forward* (Cmnd. 8288, 1981) which foreshadowed a reduction in the size of the
surface fleet.

838 **'I counted them all out and I counted them all back': the battle
for the Falklands.**
Brian Hanrahan, Robert Fox. London: British Broadcasting
Corporation, 1982. 139p. map.

A record of the authors' field dispatches broadcast by the BBC during the war of
April-June 1982.

839 **Gotcha! the media, the government and the Falklands crisis.**
Robert Harris. London: Faber & Faber, 1983. 158p.

An account of the war that went on in the background between the British press
and government over the handling of information about events in the South
Atlantic campaign.

840 **The Battle of the Falklands.**
Max Hastings, Simon Jenkins. London: Michael Joseph, 1983.
372p. maps.

Max Hastings provides an 'on the spot' report of the Falklands campaign and
Simon Jenkins, political editor of *The Economist*, traces the political and
diplomatic manoeuvres in London and Washington. Appendixes include a
chronology of events and details of the British naval task force.

841 **Hostilities in the Falkland Islands Dependencies March-June 1982.**
Robert K. Headland. *Polar Record*, vol. 21, no. 135, (1983),
p. 549-58. maps.
The author of this article personally witnessed some of the events described. He
chronicles the events immediately responsible for precipitating the Anglo-
Argentine dispute and the military activities which led to the occupation and
subsequent recovery of King Edward Point, the administrative centre of South
Georgia.

842 **America and the Falklands; case study in the behaviour of an ally.**
Sir Nicholas Henderson. *Economist*, vol. 290, no. 7315 (12 Nov.
1983), p. 49-60.
The author was British ambassador in Washington during the Falklands War of
1982. Here he gives his account of American diplomacy during that time. Due
credit is given to General Alexander Haig who perceived how close a bearing the
crisis had on the future of the Atlantic Alliance. The article shows that American
support for Britain was not something that could be taken for granted.

843 **Falklands/Malvinas; whose crisis.**
Martin Honeywell, Jenny Pearce. London: Latin American
Bureau, 1982. 135p. map.
The purpose of this book is to question the assumptions underlying Britain's
military actions in the Falkland Islands in 1982, and to challenge the pro-war
concensus then prevailing. The authors focus specifically: on the islands' declining
internal economy; on the conflicting British and Argentine claims to sovereignty;
on the historical relationship between the two countries; and on the military
dictatorship in Argentina since 1976 which received backing from Britain. An
appendix reviews the coverage of the war by the British press and discusses
public opinion in the country. Other appendixes relate to the Falklands
population, trade, and more especially to British trade with, and foreign investment in, Argentina.

844 **The Falklands war; a visual diary by Linda Kitson.**
Linda Kitson. London: Mitchell Beazley in association with
the Imperial War Museum, 1982. 112p. map.
Linda Kitson, the first official war artist to accompany front-line British troops,
landed on East Falkland in May 1982 and followed the army from San Carlos to
Darwin and Goose Green, Fitzroy, Bluff Cove and finally Stanley itself. The
sketches here reproduced with her diary describe the aftermath of battle. They
have the immediacy and intimacy of an eyewitness account without the inter-
position of the camera lens.

845   The Falklands affair: a review of the literature.
Walter Little. *Political Studies*, vol. 32, no. 2 (June 1984),
p. 297-310.

A valuable summary of the issues involved in the events leading up to the outbreak of war in the Falkland Islands, both from the British and Argentine viewpoints, with reference to some of the key publications in both English and Spanish.

846   Don't cry for me, sergeant-major.
Robert McGowan, Jeremy Hands. London: Futura, Macdonald,
1983. 317p. maps.

An 'on-the-spot', down-to-earth and sometimes hilarious account of the Falkland Islands campaign by two journalists who accompanied the South Atlantic task force.

847   The great white whale goes to war.
J. L. Muxworthy. [London] : Peninsular & Oriental Steam
Navigation Co., 1982. 191p. maps.

Considers the role of the ship SS *Canberra* in the Falklands conflict of 1982.

848   The other Falkland campaign.
Edgar O'Ballance. *Military Review*, vol. 63, no. 1 (1983), p. 9-16.

An examination of the reporting of the Falklands war by the British and Argentine media. The former, though heavily censored, attempted to be factual in spite of government restrictions but the latter was continuously exaggerated.

849   The Falklands crisis in the United Nations, 31 March-14 June 1982.
Anthony Parsons. *International Affairs*, vol. 59, no. 2 (spring
1983), p. 169-78.

An account from the inside of the United Nations Security Council's handling of the Anglo-Argentine crisis over the Falkland Islands in 1982 by the United Kingdom's then Permanent Representative, Sir Anthony Parsons. Sir Anthony concludes that 'the reputation of Britain in the United Nations has been greatly enhanced by our handling of the Falklands crisis'.

850   Weapons of the Falklands conflict.
Bryan Perrett. Poole, England: Blandford Press, 1982. 152p.

The author analyses the results achieved by both British and Argentine weapons during the conflict of 1982.

South Atlantic Islands. Falkland Islands. Falklands War (1982).
British unofficial sources

851 **Sea combat off the Falklands.**
Antony Preston. London: Willow Books, 1982. 140p. maps.
An analysis of the naval and air battles of the Falklands war of 1982. Appendixes
include a chronology of the campaign, a list of Royal Navy and Royal Marine
casualties in ships at sea, and recognition sketches of merchant ships comman-
deered for the Task Force. Sources are not attributed.

852 **P & O in the Falklands; a pictorial record, 5 April-25 September
1982.**
Compiled by Stephen Rabson. London: Peninsular & Oriental
Steam Navigation Co., 1982. 86p.
A photographic record of the role of P & O's ships in the Falklands campaign,
1982.

853 **74 days; an islander's diary of the Falklands occupation.**
John Smith. London: Century, 1984. 255p.
The first account of the Argentine invasion and occupation of the Falkland
Islands to be written from the inside looking out. The author, a resident of the
islands for twenty-five years, here describes, in a day-by-day account, the impact
of the invasion on the small island community. There are insights into the
character of the Argentine military and the way of life of the local people in
their dramatically changed circumstances. Finally the author provides a vivid
description of the events leading to the recapture of the capital town, Stanley,
by the British in June 1982. An appendix contains extracts from the hitherto
unpublished *Argentine Gazette*, a journal distributed among the occupation force.

854 **Sea change; the battle for the Falklands and the future of
Britain's navy.**
Keith Speed. Bath, England: Ashgrove Press, 1982. 194p.
An examination of shifts in British, American, NATO and Soviet maritime power
during the previous fifteen years, with an assessment of the British navy's perfor-
mance during the Falklands campaign. The author was formerly Parliamentary
Under Secretary of State for Defence for the Royal Navy.

855 **A message from the Falklands; the life and gallant death of David
Tinker, Lieut. R.N. from his letters and poems.**
Compiled by Hugh Tinker. Harmondsworth, England: Penguin
Books, 1983. 214p.
David Tinker, a British naval officer, was killed when his ship, HMS *Glamorgan*,
was hit during an Exocet attack. His letters home, collected by his father and
published here, cover his early career and his experiences in the Falklands campaign.
They are a moving record of a tragically short life ending in the pain and horror of
war.

856 **Authors take sides on the Falklands; two questions on the Falklands conflict answered by more than a hundred mainly British authors.**
Edited by Cecil Woolf, Jean Moorcroft Wilson. London: Cecil Woolf Publishers, 1982. 144p.

This book is the result of two questions addressed to authors in Britain and other English-speaking countries: 1, Are you for or against our government's response to the Argentinian annexation of the Falkland Islands? and 2, How, in your opinion, should the dispute in the South Atlantic be resolved? The answers of about 100 authors are here recorded and they represent a wide range of attitudes.

Argentinian sources

857 **Guerra aérea en las Malvinas.** (Air warfare in the Malvinas.)
Benigno Héctor Andrada. Buenos Aires: Emecé Editores, 1983. 239p. map.

An account of Argentinian air operations during the Falkland Islands campaign of 1982.

858 **Argentinian claims to the Malvinas under international law.**
Alfredo Bruno Bologna. *Millennium: Journal of International Studies*, vol. 12, no. 1 (spring 1983), p. 39-48.

The author, an Argentinian professor of international politics, argues Argentina's case for sovereignty over the Falkland Islands (Malvinas) on the basis of 'uti possidetis juris' as inheritors of the former Viceroyalty of La Plata, and the rights of sovereignty which a coastal state exercises over its continental shelf.

859 **Los chicos de la guerra; the boys of the war.**
Daniel Kon. Sevenoaks, England: New English Library, 1983. 188p.

A translation of the Spanish language edition first published in Argentina in 1982 by Editorial Galerna. In a series of interviews given to the author a number of young Argentine conscripts describe their experiences during the Falklands campaign and articulate their feelings about war in general.

860 **Malvinas: testimonio de su governador.** (Malvinas; the evidence of their governor.)
Carlos M. Túrolo (hijo). Buenos Aires: Editorial Sudamericana, 1983. 337p.

An account of the Falklands War as experienced by the Argentine military governor of the islands, Brigadier General Mario Benjamín Menéndez, and narrated to the author in the course of interviews extending over 100 hours.

Other sources

861 **The Falklands/Malvinas conflict; a spur to arms build ups.**
Jozef Goldblat, Victor Millan. Stockholm: Stockholm International Peace Research Institute, 1983. 63p. bibliog.

This booklet contains a concise report of events in the South Atlantic from 2 April to 14 June 1982 interwoven with a description of the abortive diplomatic efforts to stop the war. Its main purpose is to describe the consequences of the war both for arms build-ups in the two protagonist countries as well as for the state of security in the whole Latin American bloc. There is a very full bibliography of United Nations, British and Argentine official papers, books and articles.

862 **The unobvious lessons of the Falklands war.**
Stansfield Turner. *United States Naval Institute Proceedings*, vol. 109, no. 4, (Apr. 1983), p. 50-57.

The author, a retired admiral (US Navy), concludes that the key lesson to be learned from the war is the need for the USA to avoid the mistakes that carried Britain unwittingly into an unneeded war. This means developing a deeper understanding of what motivates other nations with whom one is involved, and maintaining one's naval strength.

Contemporary relations between Great Britain and Argentina, Sovereignty issues

863 **The Falklands crisis; the rights and wrongs.**
Peter Calvert. London: Frances Pinter (Publishers), 1982. 183p. maps.

About one quarter of this book is taken up with an explanation of why Argentina lays claim to the Falkland Islands; namely that nationalist aspirations help to distract public attention from trouble at home. There is a useful discussion of the reality behind claims to sovereignty at the present time but much of the book is merely a summary history of modern Argentina. Source references are provided in the chapter notes.

864 **El futuro de las Malvinas.** (The future of the Malvinas.)
Bonifacio del Carril. Buenos Aires: Emecé Editores, 1982. 83p.

A review of some pre-1982 British publications which appear to favour a compromise agreement between Great Britain and Argentina concerning the future government of the Falkland Islands. Also includes reflections on the postwar situation.

865 **El mar y los intereses argentinos.** (The sea and Argentina's interests.)
Mario Raul Chingotto. Buenos Aires: Ediciones Renglón, 1982. 197p. maps.

A textbook which relates Argentina's naval power to her maritime interests in the South Atlantic and Antarctic waters. It also deals with problems of national sovereignty in Antarctica, the Falkland Islands and its dependencies, and the Beagle Channel. A concluding chapter reviews civil and governmental sectors supporting the exploitation of Argentina's marine resources.

866 **The Malvinas, the South Georgias and the South Sandwich Islands.**
Laurio H. Destefani. Buenos Aires: Edipress SA, 1982. 143p. maps. bibliog.

A geographical, historical and legal justification of Argentina's claims to sovereignty over the Falkland Islands (Malvinas), South Georgia and the South Sandwich Islands. The volume includes chronological lists of Argentine and British governors of the Falkland Islands.

867 **The disputed islands; the Falkland crisis: a history & background.**
London: HM Stationery Office, 1982. 36p. map.

This booklet, the author of which is not stated, briefly outlines the geography and history of the Falkland Islands and their method of government. There is also a brief description of the two dependencies, South Georgia and the South Sandwich Islands. Britain's dispute with Argentina over sovereignty is outlined as is her view of the Argentine invasion of the islands in 1982.

868 **Las Malvinas, una causa nacional.** (The Malvinas, a national cause.)
Haroldo Foulkes. Buenos Aires: Ediciones Corregidor, 1982. 166p.

A journalist's account of a visit to Port Stanley, Falkland Islands, in 1976 where he discusses with Lord Shackleton and others Anglo-Argentine relations, problems of sovereignty, and also expresses his hopes for the future.

869 **Antarctica and the South Atlantic; discovery, development and dispute.**
Robert Fox. London: British Broadcasting Corporation, 1985. 336p. maps. bibliog.

The author, a BBC radio producer and reporter, covered the Falkland Islands campaign of 1982, and also wrote *Eyewitness Falklands; a personal account of the Falklands campaign* (q.v.). Early in 1984 he travelled in the South Atlantic and the Southern Ocean aboard the Royal Navy's patrol vessel *Endurance* and visited Antarctica as well as the Falkland Islands and their two dependencies, South Georgia and the South Sandwich Islands. In this book Robert Fox reviews the political situation resulting from the continuing diplomatic instability between Britain and Argentina, and considers the future of the Falkland Islands and their chances of economic development.

South Atlantic Islands. Contemporary relations between Great Britain and Argentina. Sovereignty issues

870 **The struggle for the Falkland Islands: a study in legal and diplomatic history.**
Julius Goebel. New Haven, Connecticut; London: Yale University Press, 1982. 482p.
A reprint of this fundamental study of the early history of the Falkland Islands from their discovery to their occupation by the British in 1833. It discusses the legal status of the territory and explores the origins of the disputes that have arisen between Argentina and Great Britain (with whose claims the author does not sympathise).

871 **The Falklands, the law and the war.**
Leslie C. Green. In: *Yearbook of world affairs 1984.* London: Stevens, for the London Institute of World Affairs, 1984. p. 89-119.
An historical review of the legal aspects underlying the dispute between the United Kingdom and Argentina over claims to the Falkland Islands.

872 **Malvinas: clave geopolítica.** (Malvinas: geopolitical key.)
Pablo José Herandez, Horacio Chitarroni. Buenos Aires: Ediciones Casteneda, 1982. 2nd ed. 133p.
A discussion of the geopolitical significance of the Falkland Islands to the South Atlantic region from Argentina's point of view.

873 **Title to the Falklands-Malvinas under international law.**
Jeffrey D. Myhre. *Millennium: Journal of International Studies,* vol. 12, no. 1 (spring 1983), p. 25-48. bibliog.
A discussion of who has the title to the Falkland Islands under international law – Great Britain or Argentina? The author concludes that the legal question of sovereignty is 'more complex and less clear cut than either President Galtieri or Prime Minister Thatcher ever acknowledged'.

874 **The Falkland Islands dispute in international law and politics: a documentary sourcebook.**
Raphael Perl, with an historic chronology and bibliography by Everette E. Larson. London: Oceana Publications, 1983. 722p. map. bibliog.
An introductory chapter reviews the modes of acquisition and loss of territorial sovereignty under customary international law, and considers Argentine, British and United States policy on sovereignty over the Falkland Islands. Sovereignty rights are analysed with recent historical precedents and an historical chronology is also provided. In addition the work contains reproductions of fifty-two documents ranging from the papal bull of Alexander VI (1493), to the United Nations General Assembly Resolution (4 November 1982).

875 **What future for the Falklands?**
Colin Phipps. London: Fabian Society, 1977. 16p. (Fabian Tract, no. 450).

In November 1975 the author, along with Sir John Gilmour, comprised a Commonwealth Parliament Association delegation on a three-week visit to the Falkland Islands and Argentina. This pamphlet, which analyses the political situation at that time, is based on wide-ranging discussions with senior Argentine officials, with Falkland Islanders and with the British ambassador in Buenos Aires.

El mar y la Antártida en la geopolitica Argentina. (The sea and Antarctica in Argentine politics.)
See item no. 263.

The politics of South Atlantic security; a survey of proposals for a South Atlantic treaty organization.
See item no. 272.

The future of British sea power.
See item no. 293.

Periodicals

876 **The Falkland Islands Gazette.**
Stanley, Falkland Islands: Government Printing Office, 1891- irregular.

The official record of all Falkland Islands Government business including, for example, official appointments, ordinances, bills and regulations.

877 **The Falkland Islands Journal.**
Stanley, Falkland Islands: Government Printer. 1967- . annual

This journal is chiefly devoted to historical articles based on local archives.

878 **Falkland Islands Newsletter.**
London: Falkland Islands Research and Development Association, 1976- . irregular.

The association was formed in 1976 to assist in the implementation of Lord Shackleton's Report of that year entitled *Economic survey of the Falkland Islands* (q.v.) and to act as a representative for the people of the Falkland Islands in London.

South Atlantic Islands. Falkland Islands Dependencies. South Georgia and the South Sandwich Islands

879 **Polar Record.**
Cambridge, England: Scott Polar Research Institute, 1931- .
3 times per year.
This journal regularly features contributions of general interest relating to the Falkland Islands, South Georgia and the South Sandwich Islands, including, for example, short field notes and book reviews.

Falkland Islands Dependencies, South Georgia and the South Sandwich Islands

880 **The Antarctic pilot; comprising the coasts of Antarctica and all the islands southward of the usual route of vessels.**
Great Britain. Hydrographer of the Navy, 1974. 4th ed. 336p. maps. bibliog. (N.P.9).
Provides sailing directions and valuable general information which is updated by periodic supplements. Chapter 3 covers South Georgia and the South Sandwich Islands.

881 **British Antarctic Survey Bulletin.**
Cambridge, England: British Antarctic Survey. 1963- . irregular.
This series contains the shorter scientific papers covering the Survey's work in South Georgia, the South Sandwich Islands and British Antarctic Territory.

882 **British Antarctic Survey Scientific Reports.**
London: British Antarctic Survey, 1963-73; Cambridge, England, British Antarctic Survey, 1973- .
A continuation of a series of specialised monographs first published under the title *Falkland Islands and Dependencies Scientific Reports* (London: HM Stationery Office, 1953-62) and dealing with the work of the Survey on South Georgia, the South Sandwich Islands and in British Antarctic Territory.

883 **Gazetteer of the Falkland Islands Dependencies (South Georgia and the South Sandwich Islands).**
Great Britain. Foreign and Commonwealth Office. London: HM Stationery Office, 1977. 9p.
This listing includes 763 place-names accepted for use in British official publications. They are arranged alphabetically with latitudes and longitudes. The first supplement was published in 1979.

884 **Report of the interdepartmental committee on research and development in the dependencies of the Falkland Islands with appendices, maps &c.**
London: HM Stationery Office, 1920. 164p. map. bibliog.
This is a key document for any study of the development of the whaling and other industries of the Falkland Islands Dependencies. The committee consisted of representatives from the Board of Agriculture and Fisheries, the Colonial Office, the British Museum (Natural History), the Department of Scientific and Industrial Research and the Admiralty. The report, which is a comprehensive and detailed document, recommended, *inter alia*, that the food for whales, i.e., fish and plankton, should be carefully investigated and that a complete hydrographic survey of the dependencies should be made. It asserted that the costs involved in making such investigations should be charged to revenues derived from taxes on the whaling industry itself. It was this report which gave rise to subsequent 'Discovery Investigations' in the Southern and South Atlantic oceans, see the *Discovery Reports* (q.v.).

South Georgia

General

885 **Antarctic housewife.**
Nan Brown. London: Hutchinson, 1971. 190p.
The author's account of a two-and-a-half years' residence on South Georgia where her husband was in charge of the radio station, 1955-57.

886 **South Georgia; a bibliography.**
Robert Headland. Cambridge, England: British Antarctic Survey, 1982. 180p. (British Antarctic Survey Data, no. 7).
A definitive work in this field, computer-set and likely to be updated periodically. It includes references to other bibliographies as well as serial publications.

887 **South Georgia, the British Empire's sub-Antarctic outpost.**
Leonard Harrison Matthews. Bristol: John Wright; London: Simpkin Marshall, 1931. 163p. maps. bibliog.
A reliable general account of such subjects as the island's climate, topography, flora and fauna, and whales, followed by a history of its discovery and exploration. The final chapters are devoted to the 20th-century whaling industry and the island's future prospects.

History

888 **Voyages to South Georgia, 1795-1820.**
A. G. E. Jones. *British Antarctic Survey Bulletin*, no. 32 (Feb. 1973), p. 15-22, maps. bibliog.
An account of British and American sealing vessels visiting South Georgia in the years after Captain James Cook's discovery of the island in 1775. It includes statistics of British seal skin imports from the 'South Seas' for 1777-84.

889 **South; the story of Shackleton's last expedition 1914-1917.**
Sir Ernest Shackleton. London: Heinemann, 1919. 368p. map.
The official narrative of Shackleton's British Imperial Transantarctic Expedition of 1914-17. It has been included here for its enthralling account of the voyage of the small boat *James Caird* from Elephant Island to South Georgia and the hazardous traverse by Shackleton, Frank Worsley and Tom Crean across the island's icy mountains to seek help from the whalers at Husvik for the rescue of the main party. A more personal account will be found in Worsley's *Shackleton's boat journey* (q.v.).

890 **The first South Georgia leases: Compañia Argentina de Pesca and the South Georgia Exploring Company Limited.**
D. W. H. Walton. *Polar Record*, vol. 21, no. 132 (1982), p. 231-40. map. bibliog.
The Compañia Argentina de Pesca was founded by the Norwegian Captain C. A. Larsen with Argentinian capital in 1904 and was the first land-based whaling company to operate in the sub-Antarctic from its base at Grytviken, South Georgia. The rival claims of the South Georgia Exploring Company compelled the British government to agree on lease terms and by 1908 the whaling stations were brought under the legal government of the Falkland Islands.

891 **Shackleton's boat journey.**
F. A. Worsley, introduction and notes by Duncan Carse. London: The Folio Society, 1974. 147p. maps.
A gripping account of Sir Ernest Shackleton's heroic boat journey from Elephant Island to South Georgia in the *James Caird* in 1915 and the subsequent trek across the mountains of South Georgia to seek the help of the whaling station in the relief of the main party. Frank Worsley, who accompanied Sir Ernest on this journey, was master of the expedition ship *Endurance* and kept a detailed log throughout these events. Duncan Carse has himself retraced Shackleton's route.

Nature and wildlife

892 **The fur seal of South Georgia.**
W. Nigel Bonner. *British Antarctic Survey Scientific Reports*, no. 56 (1968), 81p. bibliog.

A description of the early sealing industry and the biology of the fur seal (*Arctocephalus tropicalis gazella*) in South Georgia. The author concludes that the residual Antarctic fur seal stocks are undergoing a phase of expansion.

893 **The vascular flora of South Georgia.**
Stanley W. Greene. British Antarctic Survey Scientific Reports, no. 45 (1964), 58p. bibliog.

An historical and biological introduction with a detailed bibliography, and a check-list of fifty-one species. A total of twenty-four native and five naturalized species are described.

894 **The island of South Georgia.**
Robert Headland. Cambridge, England: Cambridge University Press, 1984. 293p. maps. bibliog.

The most comprehensive and up-to-date book in print covering the natural history of the island, its exploration and the Argentine invasion of 1982. The author has considerable personal experience of the island.

895 **The elephant seal industry at South Georgia.**
Richard Maitland Laws. *Polar Record*, vol. 6, no. 46 (July 1953), p. 747-54. map. bibliog.

A description of the history, methods and controls of modern sealing with tabulated statistics of commercial sealing on South Georgia, 1910-52.

896 **The history of the introduced reindeer of South Georgia.**
N. Leader Williams. *Deer*, vol. 4, no. 5 (Feb. 1978), p. 256-61.

The article includes a general description of, and a note on, the biology of the reindeer.

897 **The birds of South Georgia.**
L. Harrison Matthews. Cambridge, England: Cambridge University Press, 1929. (Discovery Reports, vol. 1, p. 561-92).

A summary of existing ornithological knowledge of the island including observations made during the 'Discovery' investigations of 1925-27.

South Atlantic Islands. South Georgia. Expeditions

898 Wandering albatross; adventures among the albatrosses and petrels in the Southern Ocean.
Leonard Harrison Matthews. London: Macgibbon & Kee with Reinhardt & Evans, 1951. 134p. map.

The author spent the years 1924-27 on South Georgia as a member of the 'Discovery' investigations studying birds, whales and seals.

899 Bird island in Antarctic waters.
David F. Parmelee. Minneapolis, Minnesota: University of Minnesota Press, 1980. 140p. maps. bibliog.

A field biologist's experiences among the birds and seals of South Georgia and Bird Island on visits in 1974 and 1976 as a guest of the British Antarctic Survey.

900 The current status of birds on South Georgia.
P. A. Prince, M. R. Payne. *British Antarctic Survey Bulletin*, no. 48 (June 1979), p. 103-18. bibliog.

A review of the status of all recorded birds in the island with an extensive bibliography.

901 Antarctic isle; wild life in South Georgia.
Niall Rankin. London: Collins, 1951. 383p. maps. bibliog.

The author spent the period November 1946-April 1947 studying the breeding habits of penguins and other birds. The book not only covers birds, however, and there are chapters on seals and whales.

Expeditions

902 Combined Services Expedition to South Georgia, 1964-65.
Malcolm K. Burley. *Polar Record*, vol. 13, no. 82 (Jan. 1966), p. 70-71. bibliog.

A summary report by the leader of an expedition which retraced Shackleton's trek of 1915, surveyed Royd Bay and made the first ascent of Mount Paget.

903 The German station of the first International Polar Year, 1882-83, at South Georgia, Falkland Islands Dependencies.
Robert K. Headland. *Polar Record*, vol. 21, no. 132 (1982), p. 287-301, maps. bibliog.

A description of the German scientific expedition to South Georgia, 1882-83, under the leadership of Dr. K. Schrader, and its station at Moltke Harbour, Royal Bay. A systematic survey of the ruins of the site was made in 1982.

904 Glacier island; the official account of the British South Georgia
     expedition 1954-55.
     George Sutton. London: Chatto & Windus, 1957. 224p. maps.
The leader's account of a mountaineering expedition to South Georgia.

South Sandwich Islands

905 Observations in the South Sandwich Islands, 1962.
     Martin Wyatt Holdgate. *Polar Record*, vol. 11, no. 73 (Jan.
     1963), p. 394-405. bibliog.
An account of the islands' topography, volcanic activity and terrestrial biology.
Appended is a chronological list of known visits to the islands before 1962.
The author visited the group in 1961 and 1962.

906 **The South Sandwich Islands.**
     S. Kemp, A. L. Nelson. Cambridge, England: Cambridge
     University Press, 1931. (Discovery Reports, vol. 3, p. 133-98,
     maps).
This is still the best historical and general description of these islands. It also
contains a report on rock specimens from Thule Island by G. W. Tyrrell.

907 **An expedition to the South Sandwich Islands.**
     C. J. C. Wynne-Edwards. *Geographical Magazine*, vol. 37,
     no. 10 (Feb. 1965), p. 766-77, map.
A report of a visit by a British Antarctic Survey scientific and survey expedition
to the group in 1964.

Bouvet Island (Bouvetøya)

908 **Historical and geological notes on Bouvetøya.**
     P. E. Baker. *British Antarctic Survey Bulletin*, no. 13 (1967),
     p. 71-84. maps.
An outline of the geology of the island and the results of a survey of the west
coast in 1964.

909 **Lonely Bouvet Island.**
     Edward Dickinson. *Geographical Magazine*, vol. 40, no. 4
     (Aug. 1967), p. 292-98.
A popular history and description of Bouvetøya.

910 **New Map of Bouvetøya.**
Sigurd G. Helle. *Norsk Polarinstitutt Skrifter*, no. 175 (1981),
p. 7-9. map.

Discusses the mapping of the island accomplished in 1978-79 by a Norwegian
Antarctic research expedition.

911 **Bouvetøya, South Atlantic Ocean; results from the Norwegian**
Antarctic Research Expeditions 1976/77 and 1978/79.
Norsk Polarinstitutt. *Norsk Polarinstitutt Skrifter*, no. 175
(1981), 130p. maps.

This work contains reports on hydrography, seismology, geology, glaciology,
meteorology and biology. Also included is a new map of the island on a scale of
1:20,000.

912 **De Lozier Bouvet and mercantilist expansion in the Pacific in**
1740.
O. H. K. Spate. In: *Merchants and scholars; essays in the history*
of exploration and trade. Edited by John Parker. Minneapolis,
Minnesota: University of Minnesota Press, 1965, p. 223-37.

On New Year's day 1739 the French explorer De Lozier Bouvet, with the ships
Aigle and *Marie*, discovered and named a prominent and icy headland, Cape
Circumcision, part of what was later named Bouvet Island. This voyage did much
to free this part of the South Atlantic from the mythical southern continent of
the armchair geographers 'Terra Australis'.

913 **Mystery island of the South Atlantic.**
E. R. Yarham. *Contemporary Review*, vol. 212, no. 1229
(June 1968), p. 307-11.

A popular general account of Bouvetøya and its history.

Index

The index is a single alphabetical sequence of authors (personal and corporate), titles of publications and subjects. Index entries refer both to the main items and to other works mentioned in the notes to each item. Title entries are in italics. Numeration refers to the items as numbered.

Atlantic Ocean, South *see* South
    Atlantic
Atlantic Pilot 453
*Atlantic; a preliminary account of the
    general results of the exploring
    voyage of H.M.S. 'Challenger'
    during the year 1873 and the
    early part of the year 1876.
    Vol. 1, 2* 44
Atlantic Quarterly 253
Atlantic rendez vous 239
Atlantic salmon 341
Atlantic salmon; its future 340
Atlantic slave trade and black Africa
    139
*Atlantic slave trade and British
    abolition* 132
Atlantic slave trade; a census 133
Atlantic telegraph 163, 200-201,
    204-205
Atlantic telegraph (1865) 205
Atlantide (vessel) 53
*Atlantide – report. Nos. 1-12. Scientific
    results of the Danish expedition
    to the coasts of tropical west
    Africa 1945-1946.* 53
Atlantis (continent) 7, 610, 614-618,
    630
Atlantis (vessel) 52, 251
Atlantis: from legend to discovery
    615
*Atlas of continental displacement, 200
    million years ago to the present*
    428
Atlas of maritime history 19
Atlas of the living resources of the seas
    322
Atlases *see* Maps and atlases
Atmosphere *see* Weather and climate
*Atmosphere and ocean; our fluid
    environments* 474
Augusta (vessel) 238
Aulry, O. 731
Australia 605
*Authors take sides on the Falklands;
    two questions on the Falklands
    conflict . . .* 856
*Aviation; an historical survey from its
    origins to the end of World War II*
    191
Aviation history 83, 184-199, 832

Azores 676-680
    agriculture 674
    birds 676
    economic history 666
    flora and fauna 631, 669, 676
    geography 665, 669, 671
    geology 667, 669
    guide books 667-668, 671, 673
    history 24-25
    life and customs 675
    pilots 495, 507
    scientific expeditions 53
    small boat voyages 583
    tourism 667-668, 671, 673
    trade 258, 569, 665
    travellers' accounts 39, 590, 601
    weather and climate 472
    whaling 677-680
Azores Plateau 405
Azpiri, J. L. M. 781

B

Babcock, W. H. 610
Babington Smith, C. 186
Back to Tristan 748
Backhouse, K. M. 551
Baffin, William 114
Bagrow, L. 12
Bahamas 258, 590
Baine, John
    journal 650
Baird, D. E. 757
Baker, F. E. 755
Baker, J. N. L. 13
Baker, P. E. 908
Baleia! the whalers of the Azores
    680
Ballard, R. D. 405
Balloon flights 187, 189, 193-194
Balloons
    Double Eagle 194
    Double Eagle II 194
    Rosie O'Grady 189
    Zanussi 189
Baltic Sea 123, 126, 363, 560
Bannerman, D. A. 676, 681, 687, 700
Bannerman, W. M. 676, 681, 687
Barbados 350-351, 590
Barlow, N. 42
Barnes, R. 800

Barnett, A. 820
Barratt, R. 153
Barros, J. 558
Barton, H. 582
Bathymetry 408, 433
Battle of the Atlantic 19, 30, 215-216, 227, 231, 233-237, 244-247, 249
Battle of the Atlantic 227, 234
Battle of the Atlantic September 1939- May 1943 236
Battle of the Falkland Islands (1914) 217-218, 221-226, 806
Battle of the Falklands 840
Battle of the Falkland Islands before and after 226
Battle of the River Plate 242
Bay of Biscay 123
Bay of Fundy 491
Bayliss, A. H. 716
Beagle (vessel) 41-43
Beagle Channel 263, 865
Beaglehole, J. C. 39
Beauchêne Island 777
  wildlife reserve 777
Beaverbrook, Max Aitken, 1st baron 228
Becher, A. B. 502
Beck, P. J. 801
Before Jutland; Admiral von Spee's last voyage. Coronel & the battle of the Falklands 225
Belgium 117
Belgrano (vessel)
  sinking of (2 May 1982) 818, 827, 833
Benners, Isaac
  journal 650
Bennett, G. 217
Berlitz, C. 611-612
Bermuda 258, 470-471, 583, 587, 601
Bermuda Triangle 611-613
Bermuda Triangle 611
Bertram, C. 254-255
Betzler, J. E. 251
Bibliografía de las Islas Malvinas, obras, mapas y documentos 768
Bibliographies 410
  Canary Islands 703
  charts 504
  communications 308
  exploration and discovery 13, 23, 58-59, 76, 103, 118

Falkland Islands 308, 766, 768, 788, 864
Falklands War (1982) 836, 845, 861
Faroe Islands 649
fiction 624
fish 519
fishing and fisheries 326, 332
geology, submarine 410, 435
Heezen, B. C. 411
islands 669
law of the sea 303, 308, 312
maps and atlases 788
maritime publications 627
migration 151
naval history 207
naval strategy 292
North Atlantic Treaty Organization (NATO) 265
oceanography 303, 369
pinnipedia (seals, sea lions and walruses) 556
pollution 303
Quinn, D. 103
St. Helena 738
scientific expeditions 32, 34, 37
seals 556
South Georgia 885
trade 119
whales 348
whaling 348, 356
World War I 219, 223
World War II 230
Bibliothèque Nationale, Paris 457
Biographies
  Columbus, Christopher 618
  Cunard, Sir Samuel 164
  Hakluyt, Richard 112
  Henry of Portugal, Prince (Henry the Navigator) 87
  Johnson, Amy 186
  Lindbergh, Charles 195
  Marconi, Guglielmo 202
  Tinker, David 855
  naval officers 210
Biography of the sea; the story of the world ocean, its animal populations and its influence on human history 509
Biology 3, 53, 56, 333, 377-378, 391, 509-557
Biology, Marine *see* Fauna
Biology and ecology in the Canary Islands 701

207

Bramwell, M. 484
Brander, J. 760
Brandt, Willy 290
Braynard, F. O. 156
Brazil 81-82, 116, 149, 251, 272,
    492, 592
Brazil (island) 610
Bree, M. 604
Brendan (vessel) 603
Brendan voyage 603
Brent, P. 57
Brewington, D. 343-344
Brewington, M. V. 343-344
Briggs, P. 413
Brinnin, J. M. 157
Britain
    annexation of Rockall (1955) 664
    colonies 105-107, 110-112, 161
    economic history 118, 129, 131,
        138, 152, 217
    emigration to North America 145
    exploration and discovery 16, 26,
        72, 101-114
    foreign relations 262, 296, 298
    foreign relations with Argentina
        816, 820, 821
    foreign relations with Latin America
        814, 823
    House of Commons 812
    House of Commons. Defence
        Committee 814-815, 817
    House of Commons. Foreign Affairs
        Committee 816, 818
    Interdepartmental committee on
        research and development in the
        dependencies of the Falkland
        Islands 884
    migration 143, 145, 146-147,
        149-150
    Ministry of Defence 814, 817
    slave trade 137, 161
    trade 127
    whaling 345, 357
*Britain and the Falklands crisis;
    a documentary record* 811
Britain and the western seaways 104
*Britain's imperial air-routes 1918 to
    1939; the story of Britain's
    overseas airlines* 192
Britannia (vessel) 167
British and North America Royal Mail
    Steam Packet Co. *see* Cunard
    Line
British Antarctic Survey Bulletin 881

*British Antarctic Survey Scientific
    Reports* 882
British Antarctic Territory 881
British Broadcasting Corporation 833,
    835, 838, 869
British Commonwealth 712
British Dependent Territories 712
British Empire 102, 128
British Guiana 593
British Museum 62
British Museum (Natural History) 53
British nuclear defence option 298
British Ornithologists' Union –
    expedition to Ascension Island
    (1957-59) 741-742
British West Africa 122
British Overseas Trade Board 665
*British transport; an economic survey
    from the seventeenth century to
    the twentieth* 162
Broadcasting
    BBC 833, 835, 838, 869
    St. Helena 722
*Broadcasting (sound) on the island of
    St. Helena* 722
Brochado, C. 83
Brønner, H. 659
Brooks, J. 574
Brooks, V. Wyck 100
Brookes, M. 732
Brown, Sir Arthur Whitten 185, 191
Brown, N. 885
Brown, R. 158
Brown, S. G. 345
Bruemmer, F. 358, 553
Brunel, Sir Marc Isambard 793
Bruun, A. F. 54
Bryan, W. B. 420
Buckley, W. F., Jr. 583
Building the Atlantic world 291
Bullard, Sir E. 412
Burke, K. C. 413
Burley, M. K. 902
Burton, R. 545
Business of tourism 577
Buxton, C. 773, 780
Buxton, M. 764
    diary 764
Bylot, Robert 114
Byron, John 783-784
    journal 783
    letters 784
*Byron's journal of his circumnavigation
    1764-1766* 783

209

213

216

Fernandez-Armesto, F. 704
Fernando de Noronha
  travellers' accounts 40-41, 350-351,
    713
  weather and climate 471, 596
Fiction
  bibliography 624
Fiction and fantasy 361, 610-625, 659
Field, G. W. 834
Field, H. M. 201
Fifty famous liners 156
Fighting chance 600
*First images of America; the impact of
  the New World on the old* 92
Fish 316, 319, 321-342, 511, 519-521,
    657, 711, 774
  bibliography 519
  cod 125
  Falkland Islands 774
  North Atlantic 519-520
  St. Paul's Rocks 711
  salmon 323, 328, 331, 337, 340-341,
    657
  stocks 315, 317-320, 322, 325,
    329-330, 518
  textbooks 521
  tuna 306
Fish farming 335
Fish recipes 321
Fisher, J. 524, 664
Fisher, Admiral John Arbuthnot 223
*Fisheries conflicts in the North
  Atlantic: problems of management
  and jursidiction* 336
Fisheries ecology 335
Fisheries resources of the ocean 325
*Fisheries resources of the sea and their
  management* 319
Fishery Committee for the Eastern
  Central Atlantic 306
Fishes of the Atlantic coast of Canada
  520
Fishes of the world 521
Fishing and fisheries 32, 54, 125,
    293, 300-302, 306, 309, 315-317,
    322, 325, 327, 330, 342, 367,
    381, 572
  bibliographies 326, 332
  cod 125
  climatic influence 320
  conservation 317-319
  economic resources 125
  Falkland Islands 766, 769
  Faroe Islands 656-657

herring 125
  Indian Ocean 54
  legal aspects 300-302, 307, 309, 313
  North Atlantic 54, 144, 306, 317,
    319-320, 334-336, 338-339
  organizations 306
  Pacific Ocean 54
  periodicals 328, 332, 342
  salmon 331, 341, 657
  South Atlantic 333
  statistics 342, 656
  sword fisheries 324
  technology 319
  tuna 306
Flanagan, D. 371
Flat Island Book (manuscript) 660
Fleming, R. H. 391
Fletcher, Francis 109
Flora
  Azores 631, 669
  Boutevøya 911
  Canary Islands 669, 690-691,
    701
  Cape Verde Islands 669, 681
  Falkland Islands 778-779, 782
  Faroe Islands 645-646
  Madeira 669
  maps and atlases 484-485
  North Atlantic 516
  Rockall 664
  St. Helena 631, 718, 721
  St. Paul's Rocks 710
  South Georgia 893-894
  South Sandwich Islands 905
  Tristan da Cunha 755-758
Flora of Iceland and the Faeroes 646
*Focke-Wulf Condor; scourge of the
  Atlantic* 240
Focus on the Falkland Islands 772
Fodor's Portugal 1985 667
Fodor's Spain 692
Foerster, J. W. 444
Folger, Timothy 457
Folklore *see* Literature
Food and Agriculture Organization
  322, 342
Fordham, A. 788
Foreign and Commonwealth Office,
  Great Britain 883
Foreign Affairs Committee, House of
  Commons 816, 818
Foreign relations 253-298, 380
  Argentina 272, 281, 843, 863, 865
  German Federal Republic 262

Hartley, K. 267
Hartshorne, D. 268
Harvard University Library 453
Harvey, J. G. 474
Hasler, H. G. 584
Hastenrath, S. 475
Hastings, MacDonald 165
Hastings, Max 840
Hattersley-Smith, G. 790
Haviland, H. F., Jr. 297
Hawaii 470
Haward, P. 588
Hawker, Harry 185
Hawkins, Sir John 135
Hay, W. W. 438, 442
Hayes, D. E. 439
Hayter, J. 668
Headland, R. 894, 903
Healey, P. J. 556
Heathrow-Chicago 579
Heezen, B. C. 406-407, 410, 418,
  513
  bibliography 410
Heighway, A. J. 316
Heirtzler, J. R. 419-421
Hekinian, R. 422
Helle, S. G. 910
Hellinger, S. 433
Henderson, Sir Nicholas 269, 842
Henry VII, King 108
Henry of Portugal, Prince (Henry
  the Navigator) 81, 86-87, 682
  biography 87
Henshall, J. D. 674
Herandez, P. J. 872
Herjulfsson, Bjarne 79
Herring fishery 125
Hey-day of the great Atlantic liners
  153
Heyerdahl, Thor 63, 589
Hibbert, E. 734
Hickling, G. 554
Hickman, M. E. 576
Hickman, R. H. 576
Hickman's international air traveller
  576
*High latitude crossing; the Viking
  route to America* 588
Higham, R. 192
Hillier, S. 27
Hill-Norton, Sir P. 209, 270
Hindenburg (airship) 187-188
*Hints to exporters: Portugal, Madeira
  and the Azores* 665

Hiscock, E. C. 590
*Historia completa de las Malvinas.
  Tomos I-III* 781
*Historia de la conquista de la siete
  islas de Canaria* 705
Historia general de las Islas Canarias
  708
*Historical and descriptive account of
  Iceland, Greenland and the Faroe
  Islands...* 638
History 2, 7, 11, 13, 15, 19, 20-23,
  25-26, 28-30, 70, 289
  17th century navigation & commerce
  666
  Africa 16, 124
  airships 187-188
  Atlantic, Battle of (World War II)
  19, 30, 215-216, 227, 231,
  233-237, 244-245, 247, 249
  Atlantic telegraph 201, 205
  Atlantis 614-618
  aviation 83, 184-199, 832
  Azores 24-25
  Bouvetøya 912-913
  British annexation of Rockall (1955)
  664
  British shipping industry (17c-18c)
  161
  Canary Islands 16, 24-25, 29, 682,
  702-708
  Cape Verde Islands 16, 24-25, 29,
  110, 682
  cartography 12, 15, 18, 29, 78, 108,
  452, 454, 457, 788
  communications 9, 308, 565
  convoys 216, 223, 230, 234,
  247-249
  Cunard Line 164, 168
  cultural 104
  Dutch voyages 115-117
  economic 7, 24, 76, 84, 118-142,
  152, 214, 666
  English voyages 72, 101-114
  evolution of the anti-submarine
  aircraft (1912-80) 243
  exploration 2, 7, 11, 13, 15, 17,
  19-26, 28-30, 57, 61-62, 65-68,
  70-74, 76-78, 80-117, 289, 589,
  601, 603, 783-784, 792
  Falkland Islands 768, 781-798, 803,
  806, 866-867, 870, 877
  Falkland Islands Company 787
  Falkland Islands Dependencies 786,
  877, 894

223

Isolationism 257
Israel, J. I. 117

J

Jackass penguins 776
Jackson, H. M. 275
Jamaica 258
James Caird (vessel) 889, 891
James Monroe (vessel) 157
Jameson, W. 526
Jane, C. 98
Japan 573
  foreign relations 814
Jellicoe, Admiral John Rushworth 233
Jenkins, S. 840
Jensen, Ad. S. 644
Jester (vessel) 584, 597
Joensen, R. 655
Johnsen, A. O. 356
Johnson, Amy
  biography 186
Johnson, M. W. 391
Johnson, R. 769
Johnson, Samuel 791
Johnston, D. M. 558
Jolly, W. P. 202
Jones, A. G. E. 888
Jones, E. B. 305
Jones, G. 65-66
Journal of Christopher Columbus 98
Journal of the Marine Biological Association of the United Kingdom 514
Journal of researches into the natural history and geology of the countries visited during the voyage round the world of H.M.S. 'Beagle' under the command of Captain Fitz Roy R.N. 41
Journals *see* Diaries and journals
Journals of Captain James Cook on his voyages of discovery. The voyage of the 'Resolution' and 'Adventure' 1772-1775
Journals of the Stanley expedition to the Faroe Islands and Iceland in 1789. Vols. 1-3 650

K

Kallsberg, Einar 641
Kampp, A. H. 656
Kaplan, L. S. 276
Karlsefne, Thorfinn 79
Kay, F. G. 7
Kelly, J. E. 18
Kemble, J. 735
Kemp, P. 8
Kemp, P. K. 231
Kemp, S. 906
Kemps directory 1982-83 vol. 3, international information 569
Kendal Whaling Museum paintings 343
Kendal Whaling Museum prints 344
Kendrick, T. D. 67
Kennedy, Ludovic 232, 621
Kennett, J. P. 423-424
Kensington runestone 74
Kent (vessel) 218
Kent, Sir P. 363
Kent University, Center for NATO Studies, conference (1980) 276
Kilronan 600
King, C. A. M. 377-378
King, Dafydd 62
King, Derek 591
King Edward Point 841
King, J. E. 541
King penguins 776
Kinne, O. 515
Kinsky, F. C. 525
Kintner, W. R. 291
Kirkpatrick, F. A. 89
Kitson, L. 844
Kittinger, J. W. Jr. 193
Kober, S. 277
Koers, A. W. 306
Kon, D. 859
Korngold, R. 736
Kremlin and the peace offensive 280
Kretschmer, Otto 245
Kunkel, G. 701

L

238

241

242

whaling 347, 350-353, 357
Southern oceans and the security of the free world; new studies in global strategy 295
Sovereignty
  British and Argentine claims to Falkland Islands 313, 769, 781, 786, 794, 801, 816, 826, 843, 858, 863-875
Spafford, R. N. 806
Spain
  economic history 118, 120, 126, 129
  history 104, 117
Spanish conquistadores 89
Spanish seaborne empire 90
Spanish voyages 11, 21, 25, 27, 88-10 88-100
Spärck, R. 54, 644
Sparks, J. 533
Spate, O. H. K. 912
Spee, Admiral Maximilian Johannes Maria Hubert, Graf von 225
Speed, K. 854
Spencer-Cooper, H. 226
Sperm whales 345
Spiess, G. 604
Spink, R. 54
Spitzbergen 363
Spowart, N. B. 697
Spratt, H. P. 174
Spring, Howard 238
Spry, W. J. J. 46
Stackpole, E. A. 354
Staff, F. 175
Stamp, Sir D. 565
Stanley, Falkland Islands 802, 844, 853
Stanley, John Thomas, 1st Baron Stanley of Alderley 650
Starbuck, A. 355
Statistics
  fishing and fisheries 342, 656
  trade 654
Steam conquers the Atlantic 177
Steamers, Paddle 174
Stehli, G. 427
Stein, R. 365
Stemman, R. 616
Stevens, C. 290
Stevens, R. H. 229
Stewart, S. 579
Stocks of whales 548

Stokes, T. 534-535
Stommel, H. 446, 459
Stone, P. B. 367
Stonehouse, B. 536, 741-742, 769
Storm passage 599
Story of the Atlantic telegraph 201
Stowe, K. 390
Straits of Magellan 41
Strange, I. J. 770-771
Strange voyage of Donald Crowhurst 607
Strategy, military 253-298, 377, 829
Strategy, naval 207-216, 224, 231, 289, 292-293, 310, 377, 829, 837, 854, 862, 865
Strausz-Hupé, R. 291
Strickland, H. 34
Stroud, J. 198
Struggle for the Falkland Islands; a study in legal and diplomatic history 870
Studies in British overseas trade 1870-1914 128
Study of the sea; the development of marine research under the auspices of the International Council for the Exploration of the Sea 393
Subject bibliography of the First World War: books in English 1914-1978 219
Subject bibliography of the Second World War: books in English 1939-1974 230
Submarine cables 163, 200-201, 204-205, 382
Submarine command; a pictorial history 211
Submarine geology 435
Submarines 181, 209, 211, 220
  Falklands War (1982) 833
  World War I 181, 223
  World War II 227, 229-230, 233-35, 237, 239-241, 243, 245-246, 249, 251-252, 623
Sullivan, D. 176
Sullivan, J. N. 622
Sullivan, L., Jr. 285
Sullivan, W. 55, 437
Sunday Times 831
Survival: South Atlantic 773
Sutton, G. 904
Svabo, J. C. 653

244

United States and Africa; a history
136
United States and six Atlantic outposts;
the military and economic
considerations 258
United States. Atlantic Council 564
University of Aberdeen, Center for
Defence Studies 837 .
University of Calcutta Law Faculty
307
University of Cambridge
Underwater Exploration Group
Expedition 710-711
Upland Goose; journal of the Falkland
Islands Philatelic Study Group
807
Ure, J. 87
Uri, P. 573
Uruguay 492
US Atlantic Fleet 236
US Board on Geographic Names 411,
508
US Commission on Fish and Fisheries
355
US Naval Oceanographic Office
395-396, 441, 448-450, 468
US Navy 236-237, 481-482
World War II 236-237
U.S. Navy marine climatic atlas of the
world. Vol. I North Atlantic
Ocean... 481
U.S. Navy marine climatic atlas of the
world. Vol. IV South Atlantic
Ocean... 482
USA
economic history 152
Falklands War (1982) 814, 842
foreign relations 257-258, 262, 266,
268, 274-275, 286-287, 290, 296,
814, 842
migration 143-152
military & commercial interests in
North Atlantic 258
naval history 215
oceanographic institutions 33
slave trade 136-137
whaling 346, 354
USSR
foreign relations 261, 280, 282, 285,
293, 295, 298
naval strategy 213, 255

V

Vallentin, E. F. 778
Vallentin, R. 782
Vamplew, W. 357
van Andel, T. 397, 442
van Loon, H. 483
Van Zandt, E. 616
Vanderbilt, C. 327
Vascular flora of South Georgia 893
Vaux, W. S. W. 109
Venables, B. 680
Venezuela 494
Verrier, J. Le 702
Vespucci, Amerigo 93-95
letters 94
Vessels see Ships and boats
Victory at sea 1939-1945 231
Vigneras, L. A. 98
Viking Expansion westwards 68
Viking saga 57
Viking voyages 57, 61-62, 65-66, 68,
71-72, 79-80, 581, 588
Vikings 62
Vikings and their origins 80
Villiers, A. 30, 608
Vincent, P. 769
Vinland see America, North,
Pre-Columbian voyages
Vinland map and the Tartar relation
78
Vinland sagas; the Norse discovery of
America. Graedlinga saga and
Erik's saga 69
Vinland voyage 581
Virginia (colony) 20, 111
Virginia voyages from Hakluyt 111
Von der Porten, E. P. 252
Vorsey, Jr., L. De 452-454
Voyage of discovery 366
Voyage of the 'Challenger' 47
Voyage of the 'Girl Pat' 593
Voyage of the iceberg; the story of the
iceberg that sank the 'Titanic'
158
Voyage to Atlantis 614
Voyages 5, 14
Dutch 115-117
English 16, 26, 72, 101-114, 608
Portuguese 29, 81-87
Pre-Colombian 11, 57-80, 581

Map of the Atlantic Ocean

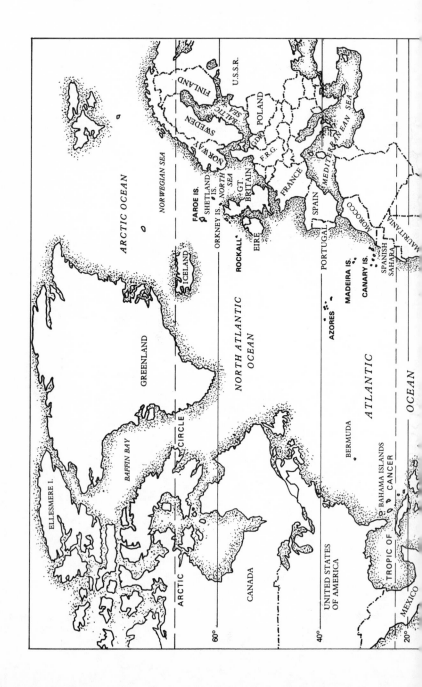

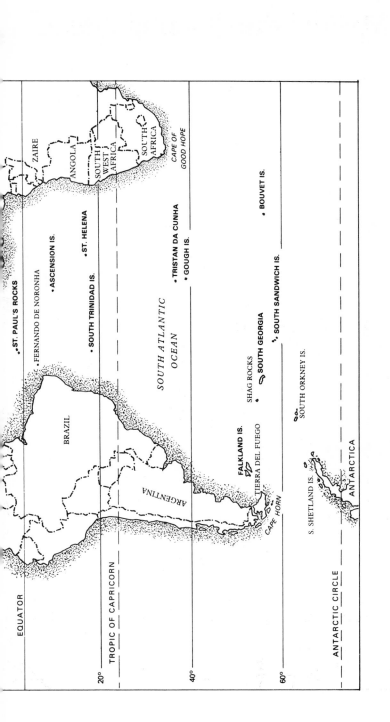